The Eight Immortals' Revolving Sword of Pure Yang

by

Dr. Baolin Wu

with

Michael McBride & Vincent Wu

Illustrations by
Oliver Benson

Three Pines Press
P. O. Box 609
Dunedin, FL 34697
www.threepinespress.com

© 2011 by Dr. Baolin Wu

All rights reserved. No part of this book
may be reproduced in any form or by any means,
electronic or mechanical, including photocopying, recording,
or by any information storage and retrieval system,
without permission in writing from the publisher.

9 8 7 6 5 4 3 2 1

Printed in the United States of America
This edition is printed on acid-free paper that meets
the American National Standard Institute Z39. 48 Standard.
Distributed in the United States by Three Pines Press.

Cover Art: Painting of Penglai Isle by Oliver Benson. Used by permission.

Library of Congress Cataloging-in-Publication Data

Wu, Baolin.
 Eight Immortals' revolving sword of pure yang / by Baolin Wu with Michael McBride & Vincent Wu.
     p. cm. -- (Dao today)
 ISBN 978-1-931483-19-3 (alk. paper)
 1. Swordplay--China. I. McBride, Michael. II. Wu, Vincent. III. Title.
 GV1149.5.C6W83 2011
 796.860951--dc22
                                2011009699

Contents

Editor's Foreword

Preliminaries

Master Wu   1
    Called to the Dao—The Magical Sword—The Cultural Revolution— In the U.S

Understanding the Sword   10
    Yin and Yang—The Dragon Sword—Prehistory—Daoist Sword Making—Practical Application

The Wider Context   23
    Acupuncture—The Five Phases—Daoist Exercise—The *Book of Changes*—The Eight Immortals

Protagonists

Li Tieguai, the Earliest Immortal   37
    The Creation—Culture Heroes—Looks Don't Matter—*Ling*, the Spiritual Core—The Virtue of Patience—Master Wu's Lesson

Zhongli Han, Subduer of the White Tiger   51
    The Dream of Fire—The Power of Dreams—Fortune-telling—The White Cloud Story—Conversion—The Tiger—Femininity

Lü Dongbin, the Supreme Swordsman   63
    Sexual Practice—Controversy—The Yellow Millet Dream—Being Tested—Further Trials—The Coin-Throwing Contest—The Stone Bridge—Wondrous Feats—The Emperor's Formula—Martial Training—Fighting Experience—Challenges

Zhang Guolao, the Old Sorcerer   86
    The Donkey Mystery—Immortal Teachings—Sexual Addiction—At Court—Imperial Ties

Lan Caihe of the Lotus Flower   97
    Connecting to Dao—Repaying Debts—Lotus Rising—The Healing Formula—Cultural Impact—Three Kinds of Emperors

Han Xiangzi, the Gentleman   110
    Flowers and Music—Clearing Vision with Feng Shui—The Post-lifting Contest—Fate and Destiny—Proper *Qi*—Destiny and Self

Cao Guojiu—Full or Empty, or Both?   121
    Making Amends—Life Events—*Youxin Wuxin*—Further Lessons

He Xiangu, the Lady Immortal   131
    Pure Heart—The Rains—Womanly Wiles—Punished for Doing Good—Immortal Transformation

Practice

Basic Set-up   145
    Equipment—Mindset—Warm-up—Breathing—Environment—Timing—The Elixir Fields—Movement—Practice Key—Anatomy of the Sword

Instructions   153

About the Authors   218

Editor's Foreword

The Eight Immortals' Revolving Sword is the second book in the new series "Dao Today." It presents an esoteric sword practice, based on teachings of the White Cloud Monastery, together with a general overview of Daoist worldview and a new and inspiring record of the lives and deeds of the Eight Immortals, masters of many Daoist techniques that have shaped Chinese popular religion over the last millennium.

The book is unique in that it combines concrete practice instructions with in-depth explanations and historical-legendary accounts of important Daoist figures. It also offers, for the first time in a Western language, a thorough account of the Daoist mindset as activated in the contemporary world. What exactly is the Daoist understanding of destiny? What role do the martial arts play in Daoist cultivation? How does the *Yijing* figure in the larger scheme of things? What is the relation between Daoism, healing, and Chinese medicine? What is the Daoist take on sex? On dreams? On money? On magic? These and many other questions are answered in Dr. Wu's account of the Eight Immortals, playfully embedded in wondrous tales and sharpened by records of personal experiences in China today.

In addition to being a sword master and an ordained Daoist, Dr. Wu is also a learned physician, trained in Western science and biomedicine, and today a resident of the United States. Thus thoroughly connected to and versed in modern culture, he does not limit himself to speaking in traditional terms, metaphors, and clichés, but adds an analytical level of interpretation to the account that is unheard of to date. What becomes clear as we read his work is that the worldview of Daoism, as it evolves to play a larger role in the 21st century, integrates new visions yet again—only this time, unlike in the past when it absorbed Buddhist and medical concepts, it adopts concepts and principles of the scientific discourse. The world according to Dao, shaped by all kinds of influences—traditional and modern—comes alive in this fascinating work.

—Livia Kohn

Dr. Baolin Wu

Preliminaries

Master Wu

In 1990, the Daoist master Wu Baolin entered the United States, accompanied by a mysterious companion: an item held in secrecy for centuries, something considered a genuine wonder of the world. A thousand-year-old sword dating back to the Tang dynasty, fully charged with actuated human potential. Along with the sword, Master Wu brought with him the mysteries and techniques of a spiritual practice steeped in Daoism (Taoism), the indigenous higher religion of China. A mystical system of shamanic heritage aimed at combining Heaven, Earth, and Humanity into one.

In 1999, Master Wu decided to reveal the knowledge of the sword's existence to the outside world. He then taught a small circle of students the inner records of the White Cloud Temple (Baiyun guan) in Beijing with the intent to compile a volume on the basis of his lectures. In the preceding years, he had already taught the secret internal sword practice connected to several disciples. His teacher had given him compelling instructions that, after formally beginning to teach this method, he must write a book and only then advance more teachings. This book fulfills these instructions. It intends to present the teachings in the original style of the oral tradition, reflecting the mindset and worldview of Daoism as well as its role in the natural universe: the teachings are circular, ideas are touched and built upon in layers, left open in the end, so people can come to their own understanding through personal experience and, most importantly, through practice. It also hopes to share a compelling part of its history, folklore, and technique, it becoming an open invitation to glimpse inside the halls, chambers, and libraries of a Chinese history less known.

The primary depository for Daoist knowledge for the last thousand years is the northern school of Complete Reality (Complete Perfection; Quanzhen), with headquarters at the White Cloud Temple and also of the Dragon Gate lineage (Longmen pai), established under the Yuan dynasty (13th c.). The monastery trains disciples in three main subjects of study: 1) Esoteric Healing Exercises (Qigong), 2) Martial Arts (Gongfa), and 3) the *Yijing* (Book of Changes). Among the many forms of martial arts taught, there is also a sword form in 108 movements called Eight Immortals' Revolving Sword (Baxian zhuanjian). It is highly valued, second only to

Laozi's Nine Palaces Microcosmic Orbit Q*i*gong and Five Centers Facing Heaven Q*i*gong, solar and lunar sets respectively.

This sword sequence initially consisted of eight martial postures related to each of the eight immortals, i.e., 64 moves. Not all of them originate in actual sword practice but also include other weapons, systems, and tools borrowed and modified to allow the use of the sword. For example, the crippled immortal Li Tieguai used an iron cane to walk and defend himself. Han Xiangzi carried a magical bamboo flute which he played skillfully and employed to remedy energetic imbalances of the earth as outlined in theory of Feng Shui. The lady immortal He Xiangu trained in martial arts with a fan—considered part of the sword family and thus easier to convert. Beyond the original 64 movements, 44 further moves go back to the only sword purist of the group, Lü Dongbin—making the total 108 with Lü's contribution at the center.

While still in its embryonic stages, the Eight Immortals sword outline was handed over to Lü Dongbin's finest student, Wang Chongyang (1113-1170), the founder of the Complete Reality school. He structured and organized the entire set, partially responsible for converting the diverse techniques into sword practice. In doing so, he also added various encrypted, esoteric diagrams and configurations, hoping to open passages into the spiritual realms of esoteric meditation to make sword intention easier to exercise. Although he studied briefly with the seven other immortals to learn their array of martial arts, he studied primarily with Lü Dongbin and became the master of a strict sword regimen.

In 1167, after completing the task of blending the Eight Immortals sword practice in a cave for two years, Wang Chongyang, on the 9th day of the 9th lunar month, took an oath to popularize and teach this practice throughout the world. Because of his sincere devotion and capacity, Lü Dongbin gave him his blessings. The day of the vows has since become a Daoist holiday called Double Yang, symbolizing pure heaven and also Wang's Daoist name. It is still celebrated in honor of Lü Dongbin, Wang Chongyang, and the sun as the source of pure heavenly potency.

Since these beginnings, the Longmen branch has produced one or seven major disciples. Among the seven, only one can be chosen to serve as leader of the next generation and be responsible for the transmission and enforcement of the spiritual teachings. The inaugural ceremony of transmission involves the passing on of a rare sword—the symbol of an uninterrupted succession through the ages. It is bestowed upon one carefully chosen initiate who serves as its official guardian.

In terms of relics and possessions, the sword that Master Wu brought to the U.S. is of vast significance for the White Cloud Temple and its lineage. Said to have belonged to the immortal Lü Dongbin himself, its scabbard shows the names Lü Dongbin, Wang Chongyang, and Qiu Chuji

(1148-1227), the Baiyun guan founder. It is called the Sword of Pure Yang, and its present guardian is Master Wu.

Called to the Dao

In 1958, when Wu Baolin was four years old, a grave illness threatened his life. The diagnosis was an advanced case of "white water," a noxious disease of the blood which had almost run its course, so that Little Wu had only two weeks to live. Despite hailing from one of China's most prominent medical families going back seven generations and despite using all available medical resources in Beijing, his affliction was incurable. Early one morning, out of desperation, his mother left him outside the front gate of the White Cloud Temple hoping that the monks of the temple would work one of their well-known miracles.

At sunrise, the monks found Little Wu outside the southern gate. Taking notice of his high fever and weakened constitution, they promptly reported his condition to the head abbot, Master Du Xinling. He evaluated the situation and responded to the boy's symptoms and treated him with acupuncture, medicinal herbs, and external qigong, using his own internal power to eliminate the negative properties from Wu's bloodstream while replenishing the boy's vital life-force (*qi*) and stabilize his fragile state.

In addition to these treatments, Master Du also submerged the youngster in a barrel of dry herbs specifically known for the cleansing and rejuvenation of blood. This treatment over several weeks allowed Little Wu's pores to breathe in the essence of the herbs' healing power. Master Du encouraged him to rest, saying, "Sleep Wuweizi, sleep." *Wuwei* means "nonaction" and is one of the key qualities of the Daoist sage. The term eventually became Master Wu's Daoist name. In addition, Master Du frequently swept the blade of an old weathered sword along Little Wu's body, thereby to eliminate malevolence from the child's aura. Over two months, this treatment succeeded in delivering Master Wu from the imminent danger of death.

A year later, Wu Baolin had recovered completely. Blessed with a new lease on life, he was discharged from the monastery and sent home to his parents. It had never been a mystery whose boy he was. The Wu family rejoiced in the wonder of his survival and homecoming and continued to show their appreciation to the monastery with regular, generous donations.

However, after a short time at home, Little Wu suffered a frightening relapse. His parents ushered him back to the monastery as fast as they could, then witnessed the strangest thing: the moment they entered the temple gates, his fever broke and he reverted back to normal. Still, the abbot suggested that the child stay for a few days of observation and rest to be sure he was medically sound. This sequence repeated several more times, Little

Wu getting sick at home and healthy in the monastery. Eventually the masters realized that this was a sign from heaven and that he was destined to become a Daoist monk. He was duly entered into the monastic ranks and began the specialized training which had saved his life.

Immersed in his monastic upbringing, Wuweizi's childhood was soon filled with miraculous events and amazing Daoist stories. From an early age, he learned the martial arts, beginning his training with the Eight Immortals' Revolving Sword, a favorite practice of his teacher. Every night he would practice in the open courtyard next to his cell, repeating the age-old sword movements to strengthen his body and boost his immune system. He also marveled at the legendary tales of the Eight Immortals, matching each set of movements, thus supplementing and expanding his understanding of the martial tradition.

The Magical Sword

One day, Master Du Xinling took Little Wu to an old stone tablet in a corner of the monastery grounds. Its inscription contained a long poem about the legendary relationship between Lü Dongbin and his magical sword. It reads:

    I, the Immortal Lü Dongbin carve this stone tablet with my magical sword.
    I have practiced and cultivated between mountains and rivers for 49 years.
    In all those years the sword has never left my sight.
    When I slept, the sword was my pillow

When I walked, the sword watched my back.
We shared every meal together and
When I used the lavatory,
The sword never touched the ground.
We are inseparable.

The text then describes the sword's power to fly:
Simply state a name, an address,
Or present an article belonging to an evil doer—
And off the sword will fly banishing them forever.
After severing the assailant's head,
It will shape change a green dragon and
Return carrying the cut-off head in its mouth.

The inscription furthermore explains that Lü Dongbin's mind, body, and spirit are melded into the body of the sword: they form a single entity. After 49 years of intense practice, the immortal faced the portal of transfiguration. On the day of Mid-Autumn Festival, the 15th of the 8th month, he fused his every cell into his sword's molecular structure. Some say, he flew up into the heavens riding a dragon; others claim he became the sword itself.

Having shown this extraordinary stele to Young Wu, Master Du told him his own story. At that time he was the ancestral descendant of the Dragon Gate lineage and the last abbot of the White Cloud Temple to be appointed before the Cultural Revolution (1966-76). A master of high merit at the Purple Cloud Temple (Zixia gong) on Mount Wudang, he received this appointment after a stringent selection process in the 1930s from the Daoist Association at the time. His promotion to abbot forced him to leave the southern headquarters of the Complete Reality school, where he had lived most of his life. His main task was to reestablish the missing components of energetic cultivation which had been gradually diluted in the north. He thus became the leading authority of the wondrous sword of Immortal Lü, commanding an amazing level of intimate knowledge of the sword's power. He then shared an important event with Master Wu:

In 1945, Fengtai village on the western outskirts of Beijing was threatened by two gigantic serpents disporting an insatiable appetite for destruction. The pythons consumed humans and destroyed structures on a steady rampage. The locals called in the military, but their weapons had little or no impact on the predators. Government efforts could do little except contain the creatures inside the city limits. When the news reached the White Cloud Temple, droves of people flooded the gates to send prayers for relief.

The precious sword of Lü Dongbin was placed on the shrine of Qiu Chuji, guarded by sixteen monks, active in daily rotation. Master Du came before it, writing out and then reading a talismanic prayer that entreated the sword to alleviate the emergency. This activated the sword's powers, and people were allowed to pray in its presence. Without any other outside influence visible, each prayer led to the spontaneous twirl of the sword and scabbard. Monks kept count of every rotation and noted 365 over a three-day period.

On the evening of the third day, a majestic rainstorm moved over the monastery. A tremendous force of electricity exploded, rending the skies with thunder, lightning, and a heavy downpour. An intense bolt of lightning struck, reaching into Qiu's shrine and touching the sword. The guardian monks turned in alarm, frightened by the sudden intrusion of light: they saw the precious sword unsheathe from its scabbard and soar into the night air. This occurred at 7 p.m.

The monks immediately reported this to their superiors who ordered them to stand fast and hold their position. Nine hours later, at 4 a.m., a swift wind moved through the shrine, followed by the clashing metallic sound of the sword sheathing itself back into its scabbard. On the ground were scattered traces of blood. Later that morning, news came from Fengtai village that the two giant serpents had been slaughtered mysteriously in the darkest hours of the night: the sword had killed the monsters. The story made it into the Beijing newspapers; it is just one of many actual events Master Du experienced during his possession of the immortal sword.

The Cultural Revolution

In the 1960s, Master Wu Baolin had his own encounter with the extraordinary sword. He was in his teens when the Cultural Revolution led to the persecution of religion; it was called antiquated and superstitious thinking, a mind poison no longer needed by modern society. Many Daoists and Buddhists were imprisoned or executed, often after being taken to the south for sentencing. Much a target, Master Du fled the monastery to avoid detainment by the authorities. Leaving Lü Dongbin's sword in the care of Master Wu as his youngest and most unassuming student, he plotted his escape route and set a time and place to meet. The young acolyte would travel west from Beijing to Shanxi and there redeliver the sword to his teacher—using all means necessary.

At the appointed departure time, Master Wu disguised himself, then wrapped the sword and fastened it at a vertical angle along his spine. He had to pass through many checkpoints, manned by Red Guards who had sectioned off the country and only opened after presenting authorized passes and proper identification. Wu traveled smoothly until he came to the last checkpoint, where he was denied entry into Shanxi, his papers not being valid for this province but only allowing him free movements in his birth district. Nervous and uneasy, he stood immobilized at the barrier, the words of his teacher echoing in his mind: "using all means necessary."

Master Wu made his decision. Without receiving permission, he took a deep breath and darted through the checkpoint, sprinting past the guards as fast as he could. As far as he remembers, there were no verbal warnings; only the sound of guns being fired and bullets whizzing through the air near his head. He thought he would drop dead any moment. The guards continued to shoot their rifles with the intent to kill him, firing several rounds at his fleeting silhouette. Then, however, Lü Dongbin's sword began to shift. It literally jumped several inches out of its scabbard, jolting his body and shielding the back of his head. The flying bullets ricocheted off the blade, pinging into another orbit. He never looked back, hearing only the sound of his breathing until the sword pushed its way back down into the scabbard, resealing itself at the hilt.

Later Master Du achieved the highest level of perfection in Daoist *qi* cultivation, earning him the title "Elder of Purple Radiance" (Ziyang daozhang). He achieved the high age of 116 years before undergoing immortal transformation--at high noon and in front of over 200 witnesses, including government officials. His entire being dissolved into a red nimbus of smoke and light, then flew up, straight as an arrow, directly to the ninth level of the sun. A delicate sweet, delightful scent filled the area for many hours. So perfect was his exodus that not a single hair, fingernail, or other organic remnant remained. This level of transformation into a rainbow body has only happened seven times in all of Daoist history.

On the eve of his transformation, Master Du first privately, then also in public, bestowed onto Master Wu—his disciple for over twenty years—the celestial seat of the Dragon Gate lineage. He had thoroughly trained him in the Daoist arts, pouring many ancient secrets into him, like from one teapot into another. Master Wu thus became the 17th generation Dragon Gate lineage holder. This appointment was sealed with his reception of the magical sword, now his to look after.

In the U.S.

After immigrating to the United States in 1990, Master Wu encountered many more manifestations of the sword's potency. One time, a blackbird perched on a telephone pole near his home in Southern California, crowing loudly. In Chinese culture, the crow is likened to a soldier and usually perceived as an ill omen; just seeing or hearing it is considered bad fortune. Master Wu politely asked the bird to move on. It did so, but only for a brief time before returning to the same place.

He had always had a strong curiosity, which on occasion led him into trouble. That day he wondered what effect the sword would have on the bird. He decided to remove it from the red silk cloth in which it was stored, walked outside with it in hand and pointed its tip directly at the obnoxious crow. He only meant to scare the bird; instead, he watched it fall to its death! It happened so fast that he could not retract the sword in time. Once again he realized that the sword was not a simple object to wave around freely.

His teacher warned him many times of the sword's powers and potential dangers. Once he told him that for miles around it there would be no signs of insects. Of course, Master Wu had to experience this for himself. He got the chance when ants infested his kitchen. To avoid killing the colony, he brought the sword out and set it in the center of the house. Soon thereafter, the ants dispersed, never to return.

For a time the sword was stored in a safety deposit box in the U.S. and withdrawn only once a year, during the Mid-Autumn Festival. Master Wu would then pay his respects to Immortal Lü and his teacher, Master Du, following a thousand-year tradition and honoring the most auspicious period for the White Cloud Temple. He also made offerings to the sword itself, providing ripe fruit and high-quality moon cakes, and took it on a moonlight drive. Riding in the back seat, the sword would absorb the essence of the moon's magnetic energy to restore its spirit. Once, while doing this, Master Wu turned around to look at the sword, sensing an overwhelming sadness. Its *qi* conveyed unhappiness, and it began to crack, its blade covered with a heavy black tarnish. In the face of this rapid deterioration, Master Wu spoke to it, assuring it that he would soon return it to its rightful home. At these words, the sword perked up and once again began to shine. It was this emotional exchange that prompted Master Wu to return the sword to China.

Seeing the precious sword under normal circumstances, it is not much to look: at first glance it looks old and dingy. Some may consider it worthless, but its blade is still so sharp it can split a hair. It weighs 600 grams and has the tendency to become heavier when stowed for a long time. The scabbard originally had thirteen jewels, but some have been lost over the centuries. In addition, when appropriately honored, the sword has an ethereal body and radiates a glow. In complete darkness, it becomes pure white light as if it were the moon itself. Based on his own experience, Master Wu believes that the precious sword is Lü Dongbin himself, immortalized.

In a conversation with two antique collectors from Taiwan, Master Wu casually mentioned having the precious sword in his possession. They were intrigued by the possibility of owning such a rare and historic artifact. Sight unseen, they offered him 35 million dollars, but Master Wu replied: "Maybe I will let you look at it for that." They all had a good laugh. However, to him this was no joke.

Understanding the Sword

What is the driving force behind such acts of potency and immortal accomplishment? That answer is *qi*, the central force of the universe and material power of Dao. *Qi* is the formless form and path of eternal Dao, the vital energy connecting all existence to the source of creation, the essential substance that makes all beings come to life. *Qi* is an all-pervading biomagnetic force coursing through the atmosphere and all that exists; it is responsible for nourishing and animating the infinite multitude of living entities, present both high and low, as well as in past, present and future. *Qi* is the life breath of the universe, allowing it to expand and contract as a single organism without bounds. Words cannot begin to define it: its manifestations are ever changing, never subject to the limits of time and space. Realizing its subtle vibrations and their purposeful differences is the internalization of the way of nature.

Living beings receive the unique powers of *qi* and its perceptible sensations through their five senses and the mind. It manifests in the wave of a mother's love or the sound and vibration of exquisite music. It is in the special taste and smell of a favorite food, in the warmth of the sun's rays. It is the sensuous touch of a gentle breeze on the skin, the brief morning rain that turns the day a vibrant green. It can also be an unimaginable dream that takes place a galaxy away. While it is present, there is life; without it, there is death. "No *qi*, no life." For this reason, Daoists in many ways pursue the conservation and enhancement of *qi*.

Human beings are imbued with three heavenly forms of *qi* from birth: primordial essence (*jing*), a crude energy stored in the sexual glands; primordial energy (*yuanqi*), accumulated in the lower elixir field (*dantian*) in the abdomen beneath the naval, and primordial spirit (*shen*), the most refined form of *qi* that resides in the heart. They are called the Three Treasures of the body, matching the prenatal *qi* inherent in all beings. According to Daoist teachings, the three must be carefully safeguarded and unified through cultivation. Thus one can not only achieve longevity but can also begin to realize the plethora of ancestral information stored deep within. Without working with these resources, a human being has enough raw fuel to live for approximately 120 years. Their preservation and cultivation, on the other hand, greatly enhance the person's intellectual and creative development by igniting dormant sectors of the brain along with supporting spiritual evolution. They make it possible to avoid disease and degeneration, escape the pitfalls of the aging process, and keep the immune system in sound condition. Still as long as people are alive, even the most basic actions of eating, walking, reading, breathing, having sex, and sleeping to some extent burn off the original fuel provided by the Three Treasures of the body. This reality posed some questions to ancient longevity seekers: "What other sources of *qi* can we access and how can we best use them?" Their queries led them to certain discoveries.

Outside the body, in the heavens and on earth are timeless reservoirs of *qi* which never age or lose their rhythm. They are the sun, moon, and stars (the Three Treasures of the heavens), as well as fire, water, and wind (the Three Treasures of the earth). Life in the greater universe is thus connected to a major living body maintained by the incessant processing of *qi* on all levels. Human beings, animals, plants, and minerals—everything that exists on land and in the oceans—can be classified in many different categories; however, in the end they are all part of a massive, interlocking continuum, reliably linked by *qi* in its many different forms.

In addition to being active participants in this system, Daoists also conducted observational experiments, hoping to discover the most powerful forms of *qi*. They ascertained that without ingesting *qi* from food, a person could sustain life for about a month, without water the survival rate was still about two weeks, but without breathing it was a matter of minutes. Thus they determined that breathing was both indispensable and the most readily accessible type of *qi*. It was life's essence at its purest. In addition, breathing is a major common denominator shared by all life forms living both in and out of water, thus marking them as sharing a similar energetic nature. Daoists thus came to value accessing *qi* through breathing as more important than eating, drinking, or sleeping—yet without excluding these activities entirely. Based on this realization, they focused their exercises on breathing, developing techniques in conjunction with biodynamics.

Among monks of the White Cloud Temple, the average life expectancy over the last millennium has been 110 years. Longevity is a primary goal of Daoist cultivation, enhanced by capturing and borrowing *qi* from the treasures of heaven and earth with the help of specialized breathing techniques accompanied by precise movements and visualizations. All of these form part of the Eight Immortals' Revolving Sword and many other Daoist qigong practices. The combined activities guide the *qi* through the body's passageways and refines it in designated areas of the internal landscape where it is then stored. The body acts as a refinery in this process, replenishing and energizing itself down to its most cellular intricacies—similar to the photosynthesis process of plant life. As a result primordial energy is preserved and alchemically refined to reinforce and grow the immortal embryo, the accumulation of spirit energy developed internally and thus supporting an increased health, vitality, and longevity.

Yin and Yang

The Dao gives birth to the One;
The One gives birth to the Two;
The Two give birth to the Three;
The Three give birth to the myriad things.
All things carry yin and embrace yang;
All things mix these forces to create harmony."
—*Daode jing* 41

The symbol of the Great Ultimate (Taiji) shows how the two forces are interlinked in Daoist thought. The Great Ultimate is the One: born of mysterious Dao, the mother of all things. It is the core representation of the Daoist universe, showing the two complementary forces, yin in black and yang in white. When every kind of light in the universe combines, the result is pure white; when every color in the universe is mixed together, the result is deep black. Together they show the coming to and going out of life as each reaches its zenith and the other begins. Their peak transformation points continue to revolve: night into day, day into night. Daoist practice, thought, and cosmology accord with their cyclic processes of infinite change.

As "the One gives birth to the Two," yin and yang split, forming the principal structure and function of creation in the manifest physical world. Their interplay coexists like the positive and negative currents of the earth's magnetic field—not unlike those found in an ordinary battery. They are also reproductive energies—the masculine and feminine aspects of nature joining to perpetuate existence in daily communion. The formation of a child growing in the womb is thus a complete turning of the Great Ultimate. All organisms contain the vital forces of yin and yang, no matter their size or shape. Yet, however much they are contingent upon one another, the two have extremely different qualities.

The Chinese character for *yin* 陰 literally means "cloudy day" or "shady side of the mountain." Yin thus has the attributes of emptiness, water, night, cold, dark, feminine, inside, even numbers, passive, horizontal, and the moon—to name a few. Yin thus stands for the earthly aspects of nature. The character for *yang* 陽 means "clear day" or "the sunny side of the mountain." Yang thus corresponds to fullness, fire, day, hot, bright, male, outside, odd numbers, aggressive, verticality, and the sun. It thus includes the various heavenly aspects of nature.

When yin and yang are perfectly balanced, there is harmony and abundance between heaven and earth. Although located on converse sides of the spectrum, each aspect of yin and yang contains the opposite pole: motion in rest and rest in motion.

How they contain their counterparts is evident in natural communication. For example, examining a flowing river, the water belongs to yin with its cool, soft, descending nature. This is its structure. The energy or *qi*, on the other hand, which powers and moves the water belongs to yang. This is its function. Or take a cigarette lighter: the flammable fluid and container are its yin structure; the ignited flame is its yang function. These examples illustrate the nature of the sophisticated labyrinth of existence, where yin and yang act together to form a magnetic energy grid through which *qi* relays everywhere.

All matter is contained within this fibrous construct: all things are invariably stimulated and driven by the vast interrelationship of yin and yang. This magnetic field is part of the space-time continuum; Daoist believe that all higher vibrations of consciousness found in nature can travel through the grid and into limitless space, much like the Chinese silk as a conductor of *qi*. Yet only after levels of perception have shifted can the human spirit partake experientially in this energetic network.

An example of passage through this fiber network is when the sun's rays shine on the pale moon. The reflection of yang energy bounces off the yin structure and transfers to rule the ebb and flow of the tides, in effect also influencing human nature as much as the human body itself consists to a large degree of water. Discovering these various cosmic and energetic connections led to the emergence of yin-yang cosmology with Daoism. Research based on these principles led to profound realizations pertaining to the true inner nature and position of humanity in the greater universe.

The Yin-Yang school saw the human being as the complex microcosm of the universe, a replica of heaven and earth, geographically and energetically enclosed in a human body. Humans consist to about 80 percent of water; the same ratio as the oceans covering the planet. The average temperature of the human body is 98.6 degrees Fahrenheit; the same warmth prevails on an average summer day. Body hair is a reflection of the trees and grass; the shoulders are like mountains; the arteries and veins match rivers and streams on earth. People are clearly connected to yin and yang. Studying and understanding the equilibrium of these forces as it operates in the macrocosm, Daoists developed profound insights into human nature and potential. They developed a philosophy of following the way of nature and worked to merge humanity and cosmos into one.

As "all things carry yin and embrace yang," so human beings embody both forces but are predominantly yang as reflected by the infinite measure of the heavens. Generally, yang is alive and yin is dead. Because of this understanding, Daoists always move toward enhancing yang-*qi* either through direct absorption or through transforming yin. They thus practice yang without negating yin.

The Dragon Sword

The dragon in China is a sign of great power and a symbol of celestial achievement. Dragons are almost always associated with the heavens and traditionally embroidered on the robes of emperors. Straight swords are thought as kindred spirits of dragons both in resemblance and nature. The centerline on the sword's blade is called the "dragon's spine," while the tassel is its tail. Although the sword is generally considered a yin device because of its steel structure, in the hands of a skillful practitioner yang energy is conducted through the dragon's spine to the tip of the blade or top of the head. This flow or pulse of *qi* converts the sword into a yang implement and an integral part of the player. Practicing sword cultivation is thus a form of transmuting yin into yang by virtue of the human spirit. This is done with mind intent (*yinian*)—the dragon's, so called because Daoists consider human beings to be dragons, i.e., the descendants of heaven.

A text ascribed to Laozi contains a discourse on swordplay in terms of yin-yang dragon's path. It highlights the parallels between sword practice and a dragon's activities, both mirroring natural interaction. It first explains how water is the dragon's prime essential. Depending on water for survival, the dragon must spend long periods of time hibernating in the stillness of water and shorter periods flying. Because of this time difference, water is called the dragon's home or the yin palace. A sword dwells inside its scabbard most of the time: the scabbard is the sword's home and its yin habitat.

Next, the dragon takes flight, rising out of the water and into the skies, thereby generating wind, clouds, and rain. Daoists see this in serpent-like coils of fog dancing amidst mountain peaks, ocean sprays of air, and an early morning mists rising from a still lake. The waters transform as the dragon makes its way upward with the rising sun. Scientifically speaking, this simply reflects the evaporation process; however, in ancient legends dragons were gods in charge of rain, thunder, and lightning. In practice, it means the sword is unsheathed and flows into action, stirring the forces of nature: going from yin to yang, from stillness to movement.

During cultivation, the sword blade collects a fusion of natural yin and yang forces in the form of numinous *qi*, the spirit of nature that resides in all living things. Likewise, the dragon steadily gathers atmospheric moisture, wind, and *qi*, forming storm clouds and crystalline raindrops. Then precipitation begins: the dragon descends back to the pools on earth while in the body blood streams to rest as the practitioner meditates in stillness. This is a move from yang to yin: the sword returns to the scabbard. It is yet another turning of the Great Ultimate.

The symbol is often read as the image of two fish swimming in opposite directions or following each other in a circular pattern. This is true to an extent, but a more accurate interpretation lies in its whirling center line: Daoists see it as a dragon flying between heaven and earth. However, supporting the interpretation of two fish, Laozi notes that new thoughts are created as part of this same yin and yang function. The sword text uses the analogy of a body of still water containing a fish. Both water and fish are yin. Once the fish begins to swim, it takes on the function of yang, the spark that develops new images and ideas in the mind's eye. Fish, moreover, have a direct link to the brain; the imagery of fish and their movement forms part of some yin-based *qi* exercises, used to enhance brain functions and enhance healing. Based on the early work, it is thus no coincidence that fish is widely accepted as brain food.

The text associated with Laozi goes even further and applies theories of sword and scabbard on a geographical scale, noticing a constant, natural flux, followed by self-regulating checks and balances, patterns of high and low, in and out. There is first the world's highest and longest mountain range, the Himalayas in the northern regions of Tibet and Nepal. It can be seen as a collection of snow-covered swords pointing up to the heavens: such is the high. Further south, near the birthplace of Chinese culture in Henan, are the Yellow and Yangtze rivers: they represent the low. If the Himalayas were inverted and placed in the two massive rivers, they would—based on the principles of yin and yang—make a perfect fit, like hand in glove or sword in scabbard. This match is made on the vertical plane, north reflecting south. After coming to the United States, Master Wu visited the Grand Canyon and put theory to the test. After careful calculations, he concluded that Mount Tai in China matched the Arizona canyon perfectly. This match is made on the horizontal plane, east reflecting west.

This allows a deeper understanding of yin and yang, not easy to define. It is sometimes difficult to differentiate the how and why of yin and yang. For example, a mountain is considered yin since it is part of the earth; but because it vertically projects toward the heavens, it is also yang. Another example is looking at a set of double doors: when they are closed, they are as one and yang, since one is a yang number, despite the fact that "closed" belongs to yin. When the doors are open, however, they are two, an even number which is clearly yin. However, "open" is classified as yang and this again overrides yin.

In the study of the interaction of yin and yang in the Great Ultimate, perceiving transformation is key. The definition of true yin and true yang is a multilayered and convoluted subject. Realistically, there is no absolute yin or yang. Thus Laozi explains the applications and extensions of sword practice.

Prehistory

Spiritual sword cultivation has played an essential role in Chinese civilization throughout history. Many are the practitioners who rose every day with the sun and danced along the moon, cleansing their swords and spirits in their beams. The history books are full of legends and fables of righteous heroes, wizards and warriors rescuing people, towns, and even kingdoms from the jaws of calamity with sheer willpower and a sword. This close, poetic relationship is ancient indeed.

The sword arose with the beginnings of humanity; with the first *homo erectus*, the sword was born in essence. Walking upright, humans came to perceive a new vantage point of the world and opened to new discoveries. In the Paleolithic, they first invented tools and pottery; they struck mountain stones to spark fires. Continuing to use these stones, they eventually learned to chip and flake them into sharp edged objects. They thus molded these "bones of the earth" into the first swords and knives. In due course, they began to hunt and explored the world, expanding their horizons.

Primitive men soon determined that lighter and longer tools could be made more easily from the bones of wild animals, bones that closely resembled the original shape and size of the straight sword. They quickly became superior hunting weapons, allowing the hunters to keep a longer distance from the dangerous action and affording a greater margin of safety, thus helping survival. There is thus an inseparable association between the sword and human bones. Even today, when measuring the appropriate length of a sword to suit an individual, the size is matched to the distance from the top of the iliac crest or naval to the heel on the ground.

The bone sword became a reliable and vital weapon as clans diverged and planet's population increased. Tribal and territorial rivalries unfolded, and the first concepts of the classical martial arts evolved. Skillful and strategic fighting maneuvers developed and became critical to the formidable new challenges. Those who outlasted their enemies in battle contributed to the rapid growth of knowledge of combat and military strategy; they soon formed a structured ranking system. This stage of human development lasted for quite some time.

The next major revolution occurred with the advent of the Bronze Age, forging a permanence of unbreakable spirit inside him. Economic systems of trade materialized, including a new currency that involved gold, silver, and bronze ingots. The production of cast iron tools created instruments of greater duration; iron cookware allowed for more elaborate cuisines. All this soon led to the true art of sword making.

Daoist Sword Making

Ever since the Bronze Age, the forging of raw ore into steel has been an alchemical art form. The expandable and malleable complexities of heated metal at the time opened infinite options that thrust the sword into a new dimension. Techniques of shaping and empowerment made possible by the innovative forging processes left the weapon limited only by a sword maker's imagination and his knowledge of nature. Many factors and considerations have become essential since then.

First of all, the grade of iron chosen is based not only on the maturity of the ore but also on its *qi* level. High levels of *qi* in the metal suggest that the element is alive and thriving. These levels are measured by distinct physical qualities such as color, aura, and the richness of the surrounding environment where it is found. Those more evolved have even higher standards for choosing, standards that are based on intuitive readings, i.e., direct communications with the numinous *qi* of the object.

Similarly, after the completion of a sword, special tests measure its sound frequency and tone quality. A single finger nail is used to flick the dragon's spine approximately five inches above the guard. This gives off a distinctive tone, depending on the overall virtue of the sword. The more refined and alive the blade, the longer it sings and resonates; the less the quality, the shorter the resonance. A poor sword might have a dead-pan sound effect or no sound at all. Another way of testing is to forcefully draw the sword from the scabbard in an overhead position. The friction of the sword's sharp edge against the inside of the scabbard, when spirited, sounds like a chime. During these examinations the blade is never touched: any skin contact might tarnish or disturb the numinous *qi* in the sword.

Another integral aspect in sword making is the source and quality of the water. Any time a sword is tempered, hammered, and shaped—before it goes into and as soon as it comes out of the furnace—it is immediately immersed in water. To create a feature piece demands the purest waters, high in both mineral content and *qi*. The water, in which the glowing red hot iron is plunged, both absorbs its essence and stores itself into the steel. The greater the water's *qi* content, the more splendid the sword's outcome. Traditionally water from the Yellow and Yangtze Rivers were believed to hold the wisdom and powers of the ancient heavenly dragons and were thus sought after in sword-making. Perhaps the most famous sword-smiths in China are those of the Dragon Spring Sword Company (Longquan Jian). The name comes from the spring near the Shaolin Temple where they get their water, which contains an unusual amount of a magnesia carbon mixture known to give swords high integrity and durability.

Other sources of water from legendary mountain springs and magic wells are equally recognized for their sword-making prowess: they include the Seven Star Spring in the Song mountain range. However, water alone is not the first choice regardless of its origin. Better than water, and believed to be most effective, is urine, used whenever available. The best urine is that of young boys before they age of nine, since they are thought to embody pure heavenly yang energy. Although a yin product, their urine is sterile and contains a particularly pure numinous *qi* not found anywhere else. Beyond this, the only other type of urine acceptable in Daoist sword-making is that of a white stallion. To this day, the Dragon Spring Sword Company still applies this in a select number of projects. The belief is that the urine from either a young boy or a white stallion infuses a protective talisman against evil inside the sword's body. Lü Dongbin's magical sword contains the former.

As regards timing, a powerful sword needs at least nine days of working and shaping. Anything created in less time is considered immature and only worthy of being called a knife. In addition to the fundamental nine days, sword-making also works with formulas lasting 18, 49, 81, or 365 days—the latter applied to Lü Dongbin's sword. The exact periods are calculated on the basis of the *Yijing*, the numbers also significant in cultivation and qigong practice, marking special levels of spiritual enlightenment.

Daoist swords, moreover, are prepared for highly specific tasks. The White Cloud Temple used to have huge ovens, 12 feet high and 6 feet wide, designed to infuse various natural properties and special functions into individual swords. Each oven had 9, 18, 49, or 81 slots which also matched the time allotment for smoldering. A 9-slot oven holding 9 swords would smolder them for 9 days; one with 18 slots held 18 swords for 18 days, and so on. Special wood, stones, or herbs thought to cure sickness and banish evil were added to the burning mix, so they could permeate the swords in their porous stage. Afterward, depending on the infusing phases chosen, the swords could be used for healing, exorcism, battle, cleansing of misfortunes, expulsion of ghosts, and other spiritual or magical tasks.

Practical Application

One technique in particular entails the careful guiding and contouring an empowered sword around a person's body: it eliminates undesirable energy parasites that cling to the ethereal body. The continuous outline of the patient's body is repeated as many times as s/he has years so that, for example, a patient of the age of 35 will need 35 revolutions for the sword healing to be effective. While this application has good results, the active practice of the entire sequence of the Eight Immortals' Revolving Sword will also potently eliminate disease.

At the White Cloud Temple, there was once the case involving a paralyzed man who he had mysteriously lost the use of his legs after "falling off a horse"—the metaphorical way of describing injuries sustained during sexual activity—and was quite unable to walk or move his legs. Having heard of Master Du's uncanny healing powers, he sought a consultation with him. After a brief examination, Master Du suggested that he observe the Daoist monks practice the Eight Immortals' Revolving Sword every day for six months. The man expected to receive some herbal medication, acupuncture, and massage, commonly used in Chinese medicine. Although somewhat confused, he followed the abbot's prescription and attended the practice sessions. After six months, whatever had caused his paralysis left his body and he regained full use of his legs. This is an example of how sword play and the potent talismans imbued in the metal can affect the surrounding environment.

Once a sword has been prepared in this way, the question still arises: is it already fully "cooked"? Not yet. In addition to the various methods described, the sword still has to undergo further empowerment, "cooking" it to activate its spirit by infusing a special *qi*. This *qi* has to come from one of two sources: the first and most potent is human blood. Since the sword is seen as an archetypal symbol of human existence, to nourish it with blood actively transforms its nature and makes it into a living and breathing entity, giving it a life of its own.

A good illustration appears in the story about "The Female and Male Sword" from the Warring States period (480-221 BCE). At this time, efforts to unite China under one government were often spoiled by ruthless and treacherous warlords, seeking power to glorify themselves. Only through the mysterious martial underworld called "Rivers and Lakes" (*jianghu*), a secret society of itinerant wanderers made up of fighting monks and warriors—so the common belief—could true power be manifested and aligned. In this society the sword was the superior weapon, necessitating highest proficiency, and skilled, innovative sword makers were immensely important.

As time went on, the conflicts were coming to a turning point, and an expert sword maker was commissioned to produce a sword of the highest caliber in the hope to shift the tide against vigorous rebel forces who had gained great momentum. Under great duress, the sword maker proceeded to create something truly exceptional. He gathered superb ingredients and forged them inside the blade, however, despite his careful engineering and concentrated efforts, he intuitively knew that his almost finished work lacked the necessary vigor and superiority. He mentioned this to his only assistant, his daughter, who had been trained in the ways of sword making since childhood. Fully aware and sympathetic to both her country and her father's dilemma, she sacrificed herself and leaped herself into the caldron, magnanimously fusing her blood, spirit, and *qi* with the sword. Later on, the sword was wielded by a male warrior, hence its name "The Female and Male Sword." It came to play a crucial role in controlling rebel forces and ending the period of the Warring States.

Unlike in this story usually a sword is "cooked" after it has been forged and fully dressed. If done with blood, this commonly occurs in battle by capturing the enemy's spirit on the blade. Anytime a sword is stained by human blood—which is not completely wiped off—it continues to accrue numinous *qi*, thus adding a special aptitude to the weapon.

The second major method to "cook" a sword is with salivary gland secretions from snakes. Various snakes of all shapes, sizes, and colors, harmless and venomous, from anywhere and everywhere in the world are collected and placed inside a special vault. The sword to be "cooked" is removed from the scabbard and placed among the snakes. The hope is that they coil around it, licking the steel repeatedly with their tongues, so they discharge their saliva and lethal bodily fluids. The blade is honed so sharply that when the snakes coil around it, they suffer lacerations all over their bodies and mouths. Strangely enough however, the snakes do not bleed. After either 49 or 81 days, the sword is removed: a cold, chilling light emanates from the blade, which indicates that the sword is done and has attained the lightning force of the serpents.

Another way of empowering is by creative images etched, carved, attached, and cast all over the handle, guard, pommel, blade, and scabbard. Throughout Chinese history, swords were beautifully decorated with fine jewels and artistic renderings: depending on its nature and its owner's personality and inclinations, creatures such as longevity deer, immortal cranes, majestic lions, ferocious tigers, or heavenly dragons and phoenixes added to the sword's potency and performance. The symbols also made the sword into a signature item of social status, indicating military rank, scholarly achievement, swordsman skill, family position, social alliances, martial fraternities, provincial origin, and more.

Thus, within the government, for example, every official level had its own sword designs. An ambassador's scabbard was adorned with eight jewels; a governor's displayed seven. The purpose was to unmistakably identify the officers and be able to address them correctly. A sword placed at the door of their living quarters helped visitors and servants to positively identify the occupant's rank. Fans were often substituted when attending social functions to avoid the sometimes cumbersome feeling of carrying a sword. However, the fans still visibly displayed the individual's rank.

Along the same lines, the emperor's sword was ornamented with nine dragons and nine jewels, the symbols of heaven. When the emperor could not attend a political affair, the prime minister would come on his behalf, bringing the nine-dragon sword along as a sign of the emperor's presence. Dragons generally only appeared on swords and scabbards of people with heavenly skill. Two dragons, one on either side of the scabbard or blade, showed greatest sword mastery.

Swords might also be used in courting: if a man placed his sword outside the door of a young maiden's home, he meant to propose marriage. Based on the sword's ornamentation, her family could ascertain the suitor's identity, clarifying his social rank, financial security, and family's future. Carrying a sword however, was not always about rank, recognition or even sword play.

Thus Confucius never practiced the sword or sought social rank and acceptance, yet he believed so strongly in its power to ward off evil that he constantly carried one at his side. Why? Swords are thought to carry righteous energy or proper *qi* (*zhengqi*), a particularly light and healthy level of energetic vibration, an aura that resists danger. The same belief also causes people to hang a sword on the wall of their house, thereby to ward off calamities and disease—not unlike Christian believers placing a cross on their wall or wearing it around their neck. If despite these actions, misfortune and disease enter a person, moreover, miniature swords in the form of acupuncture needles are called into battle.

The Wider Context

Acupuncture

Acupuncture is the primary healing practice in China and many East Asian cultures. It involves the insertion of ultra-fine, sterilized needles of different sizes and lengths into specific points on the body. These points are located along energy meridians which course on vertical and sometimes horizontal planes. When opened, they activate the energetic system, thus creating a shift or movement of *qi* which stimulates healing. Based on theories of yin and yang, this activation flushes stagnant *qi* out of the body and nourishes the desired areas with fresh energy, coincidentally rejuvenating connected internal organs. This boost and adjustment increase the strength and effectiveness of the immune and nervous systems. Acupuncture is thus a sort of microsurgery approach to medicine without the invasive tactics of full surgical techniques. It supports the body's natural healing mechanisms.

The first acupuncture needles came from bone splinters and were thus related to the sword early on. Initially used for puncturing painful spots to relieve pressure, their system developed through trial and error, and a body of healing knowledge began to grow. Nowadays, acupuncture needles are simple and disposable for sanitary reasons. But in the past they were designed and crafted much like swords, often using precious metals and stones such as gold and jade. These refined materials were thought to carry higher frequencies of *qi*, facilitating quicker and better quality healing.

Master Wu once saw the application of a special set of old acupuncture needles. Cast of pure gold and dating back to the Tang dynasty, their handles had coiled dragons designed around them. No matter whether used for mild or grave illnesses, they had positive, immediate, and sustainable results. Like a good sword, they had accumulated large quantities of proper *qi*, lending greater efforts to the battle against disease.

Another large exponent of proper *qi* is bamboo trees. In one Chinese region only acupuncture needles made from bamboo are used. The different types, sizes, and ages of bamboo needles all create unique healing effects. In fact, there are entire systems of medicine and diet that depend mainly on bamboo: from the roots to the leaves and everything in-between, all its parts are applied to the healing agenda and everyday lifestyle. Bamboo needles are categorized as wood swords. Wooden swords make up a large portion of the weaponry in the White Cloud Temple. An entire wall in the monastery was once dedicated to keeping rows of various types and sizes of tree branches, including bamboo. Every entity in the world, according to Daoism, has a creative and controlling power. The vibrations vary from tree to tree and may remove or control other forces. To activate them, the monks would regularly tap their bodies with the different types of wood to maintain good health and protection. The proverb accordingly says: "A hundred different types of trees can cure a hundred diseases."

Perhaps the most famous and important wood used in the White Cloud Temple and Daoism in general is peach. The peach tree is believed to possess unique magical powers, including the ability to control hungry ghosts and demons. Besides hanging a branch over the door, which is effective in its own right, people use peach wood to carve sword; they are best suited for practicing talismanic sword forms. The Eight Immortals' Revolving Sword set, when practiced with a peach wood sword, can clear a physical structure, a large area, and even an entire region of malevolent entities—depending on the practitioner's internal skill level.

Practicing sword play, either with wood or steel, ultimately means merging the self with the macrocosm. It can treat the external world in the same way an acupuncture needle treats the internal body: by aiding nature to strike its own balance and overcome challenges and disease. Internally, practitioners clear their own microcosm by releasing proper *qi*, allowing it to push outward and sever negative thinking patterns and predispositions. They in effect lift the veil that clouds momentary glimpses of the enlightened mind of Dao, peacefully quieting and emptying the heart, and achieving a deep concentration where heart and sword are one.

Daoists also place much faith in a sword's combined effort to command the surrounding phases of nature. In his youth, Master Wu recalls, a big affair occurred at the White Cloud Temple. Master Du had received an extraordinary gift in the form of a uniquely empowered sword from the Dalai Lama, and a ceremonious procession was arranged. The possession of this particular sword is believed to contain the balancing power of ruling over both China and Tibet beyond politics; it is a balancing beam between the two countries. In the inner world of religion, this sword can only be bestowed on the most purified and highly developed individual in the land. Master Du was the most acclaimed monk of his time, reaching unprecedented heights only few have known in the last two millennia.

Daoists have placed great emphasis on the sword as an instrument of self-cultivation; working with it far beyond merely heating, pounding, shaping, and practicing. Instead, they reach to the creating and controlling cycles of nature, classified as the five phases (*wuxing*).

The Five Phases

The five phases are wood, fire, earth, metal, and water: everyday materials from which the things of the world are made. Produced from yin and yang, their physical presence connects one to another and they form a transformational paradigm which controls, creates, and organically continues the cyclical changes of life. All perceptible phenomena, known as the ten thousand things of the colorful world, match the five phases either while thriving or diminishing. The regulation and balance of yin and yang inside each phase enable, moreover, perpetuates their driving functions and purpose to persist.

The five phases were first recognized under the Western Zhou dynasty (1122-479 BCE) when people observed nature and realized that their existence depended upon them, and then formed appropriate theories on their uses and changes. The *Shujing* (Book of History) records: "Food depends on water and fire, while production relies on metal and wood. Earth gives rise to everything. They are instruments of the people." This also applies to human physiology, being a microcosm of the universe. True wisdom and knowledge can thus be extracted from the interaction of the five components.

The generating aspect of the five phases as shown below begins with wood which matches the east and the rising sun. Circular and clockwise, wood gives rise to fire in the south. Fire in turn replenishes earth located in the center of the four directions. Earth beneath its soil creates metal in the west. Metal transforms into water in the north, and water returns to nourishing wood in the east, thus completing the generating cycle. This pattern is a form of continuous nourishment, reaching from mother to son and again from mother to son.

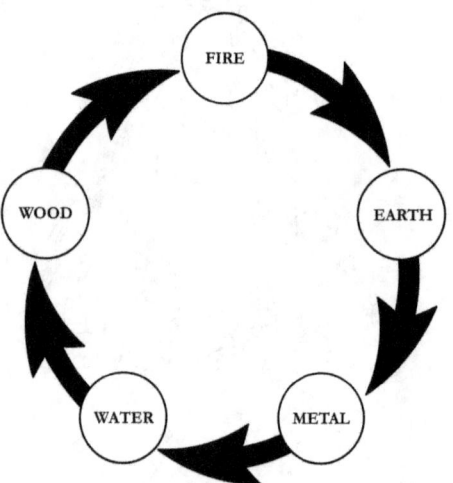

The controlling cycle, as shown next, also begins with wood. Instead of moving in a circular pattern, it moves in lines to reach the countering phases and looks like a five-pointed star. In this system, starting once again in the east, wood controls earth in the center, breaking the soil with its roots and drawing in its essential nutrients. Earth controls the northern water with its ability to absorb large quantities of liquid into its porous grounds. Water flows toward fire in the south to extinguish the flames. Fire, containing immense heat, liquefies metal in the west. The controlling cycle completes itself with metal, like an ax, chopping through wood. Although sometimes referred to as "destructive" when in excess, the controlling cycle serves as a positive counterbalance to the affirmative generating cycle and thus helps to maintain overall stability.

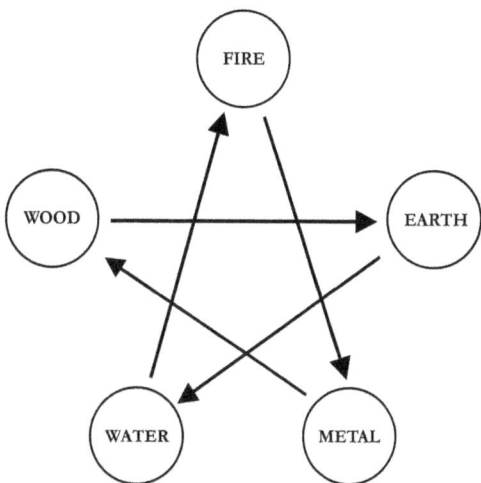

Theoretical system of the five phases, developed over many centuries, has extended into every facet of Chinese culture. Acupuncture, herbal medicine, military strategy, nutrition, and Feng Shui all make ample use of it. In fact, Beijing was chosen as the new capital of China by the Daoist master Liu Bowen largely because the ground in its area naturally contained soil of five different colors, which reflected the five phases.

In addition, the five phases have several subcategories that directly affect the human condition. In the heavens, they manifest as the five planets: Jupiter, Mars, Saturn, Venus, and Mercury. On earth, they appear as the seasons: spring, summer, Indian summer, fall, and winter. In human vision they are the five colors: green, red, yellow, white, and black. In the taste of food they appear as: sour, bitter, sweet, spicy, and salty. In music, they are the five tones. In addition, there are five mystical animals: green dragon, vermilion bird, yellow ox or bird, white tiger, and black tortoise. They reside as constellations in the stars and also inhabit the five inner organs of the human body: liver, heart, spleen, lungs, and kidneys. According to Chinese philosophy, the organs are the internal palaces of the five phases. Daoist exercise, then, serves to cleanse and harmonize these organs, profoundly affecting our living environments.

Over the centuries Daoist masters have widely experimented with the environmental and internal reversal of the five phases, leading to the conviction that their potent manipulation can enhance longevity and emotional balance as well as lead to the arising and fall of powerful dynasties. Many times dynastic collapse was aided or prevented through the military application of the five phases. Still, before the political dimension, Daoists prefer to use the phases in their cultivation practice to promote health and happiness.

Daoist Exercise

Daoist exercise is based on the workings of nature as expressed in yin and yang and helps to harmonize the five phases in the body. Over hundreds of years of observation and study, they found that sword play could cleanse the body of impurities and evil influences while simultaneously enhancing creativity and longevity. Impurities and negative forces, either physical or psychological, get stored in the five organs as negative emotion: anger (liver), hate (heart), worry (spleen), depression (lungs), and fear (kidneys). The body's organs, according to Traditional Chinese Medicine, naturally circulate *qi* either of yin or yang quality in the generative cycle of the five phases. This is ideal. However, toxins accumulate and form blockages in the organs' channels. They obstruct the flow of *qi* and, if left untreated, reverse its direction into the controlling cycle, thus creating a yin- yang imbalance which eventually brings about disease.

Daoist sword play was designed to guide the *qi* of the body and the *qi* of nature simultaneously along the routes they were intended to travel, following the direction of the solar system which only revolves in one direction. This intent balances the two polarities of inner and outer, enhances communication between self and atmosphere, and balances yin and yang energies in both dimensions. Also, the movements of the Eight Immortals' Revolving Sword, both symbolically and physically, cut away old patterns of thought and external energies which may have attached themselves during life's experiences. Being liberated from such weight, along with the resurgence of uninhibited *qi*-flow, makes a major difference in health, career, and emotional stability. It also serves to unclog the mind, allowing it to perceive the deeper layers and developing a more accurate appreciation of the natural rhythms and pulses. To reach these levels of spiritual growth, the five phases of the body must be properly activated and, like crystals, charged with a radiant brightness.

The Daoist exercise formula first considers how best to begin nourishing the organs. A tree is only as strong and healthy as its roots, and the roots of the human body are the kidneys. Daoist cultivation thus always begins with strengthening them, in contrast to Buddhist practice which focuses on the heart in its quest for enlightenment. Daoists prefer to begin with longevity and let enlightenment follow. Sword practice works wonders for the kidneys; it is much superior to other form of martial arts, whether with weapon or unarmed (lit. "fist;" *quan*). Although the latter helps to build and maintain a strong body, it rarely has as much internal benefit.

As Daoists strive to follow nature, and all things grow from the ground up, they place great emphasis on the growth and maintenance of the kidneys. The kidneys nourish the bones and enhance their density, which supports the production of fresh blood cells, thus keeping the body invigorated. They also support and maintain the brain. As long as the kidneys are not neglected, heart and mind remain in full alertness far into old age.

Healthy kidneys, moreover, strongly contribute and support the health of the liver (water generates wood). The liver in turn filters and cleanses toxins from the bloodstream and, when healthy, assists in maintaining a restful disposition and calming emotional turmoil (wood generates fire). Plus, the liver being the storehouse of the spirit soul, its healthy *qi* ensures high levels of concentration and spiritual growth. Along another line, the accompanying transformative organ of the liver is the gallbladder, perhaps the greatest benefactor of sword practice. Its energy is in charge of decision making and its stagnation leads to confusion and uncertainty that disrupt the thinking mind. This in turn leads to a lack of creativity, intense frustration, and even psychological disorders.

The story of the calligrapher Cong Zhengshi illustrates this. As a young man, he showed great promise and, after years of steady practice and improvement, reached a high plateau. However, he then slowly began to lose his inspiration. Without the passionate drive of his early years, his brushstrokes started to lack vitality and energy, the essence of the art. His creative fire had become all but extinguished.

Then, one day, the young master went for a walk. On his trip he came across a woman practicing sword in an open clearing. Looking at her from the perspective of the calligrapher, he saw her as an artist painting the canvas of earth and sky using a sword as her brush. Enthralled and intrigued by the similarities between calligraphy and sword play, he followed up her practice to learn more. First he paid her the highest compliments for her skills. Flattered by his genuine interest, she offered to teach him her style. He accepted and soon after he started sword cultivation, the blockages restraining his creativity were released and new thoughts and ideas began to emerge, blossoming into some of his finest calligraphy yet. Continuing to fuel his brush with his sword practice, Cong Zhengzhi in due course became one of the most praised and admired artists of his time and, indeed, in Chinese history.

How, then, does the sword method build up people's energy and direct it toward righteousness and the positive opportunities of life? How does it illuminate the path and bring about clarity of mind, so that we can make positive choices for our destiny?

The sword acts like a lightning rod or a steeple, attracting and conducting electromagnetic forces of the greater universe and charging the body's cells and internal organs with it. Because of this, we say it contains a life-force of its own and is an independent entity filled with spirit. Those who practice say: "Sometimes the sword follows you; sometimes you follow the sword."

In ancient times, many people practiced sword cultivation to achieve godlike powers and immortality. The sword was thought to be a medium, a conduit of the numinous *qi* of the universe to humanity as well as an energetic tool not unlike the magic wand of sorcerers. Sword cults flourished and people paid daily homage to sword deities known to wipe out plagues and epidemics beyond human control. Since people could not reach supernatural powers as easily with other weapons or unarmed practice, the sword was the most popular choice in the martial arts: "the king of weapons."

The Book of Changes

The *Yijing*, one of the deepest and most arcane books in all of China's history, to the present day works as a tool of divination and ritual, serving to gauge and maintain harmony between human beings and the universe. Legend has it that its symbols were discovered by the sage emperor Fu Xi. He was meditating on the bank of the Yellow River when he saw a tortoise surface from the water which had the symbols of the eight trigrams (*bagua*) inscribed in its shell—which also form the starting point and model of the Eight Immortals' Revolving Sword.

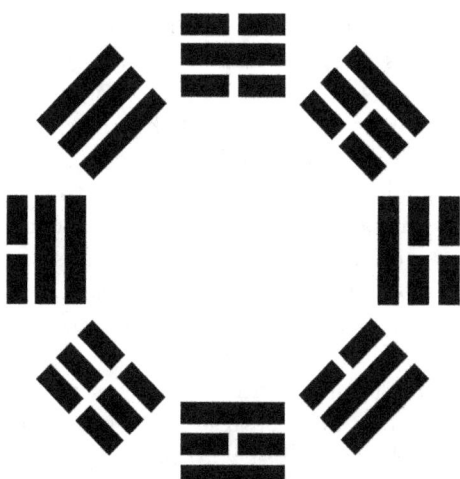

Solid and broken lines, symbolizing yang and yin, combined into trigrams, each face one of the eight directions. The exact arrangement was both a symbolic and numerical formula modeling the inner and outer workings of heaven and earth. Fu Xi further developed them into sets of two each, combining them into 64 hexagrams, which form the foundation of the book. Each hexagram represents an essential aspect of life's wisdom, reflecting growth, danger, or decay. In combination, they guide people in the direction of goodness by warning seekers about dangerous pitfalls and suggesting less attractive choices regardless of personal desire. It is said that "heaven has its opinion." The *Yijing* voices that opinion.

The sequence of 64 hexagrams came about in a most sublime way: imitating the flight patterns of birds. For Daoists, birds have a special relationship with nature and serve as the messengers of heaven. They can set the changes of the eight trigrams in motion in linear, polar, and circular configurations to reveal heaven's many secrets. For this reason, initiates of the Dragon Gate lineage do not cook or consume them.

The trigrams' foundation is the simple binary composition of one solid (yang) and one broken line (yin), patterns best known today as the root of modern computing. However, encoded in the binary symbols, and thus in the eight trigrams, are an infinite number of calculations. The mathematically advanced code of the *Yijing* can esoterically be configured to reveal the past, present, and future of the universe in any number of estimations with a high degree of accuracy. It contains a level of knowledge well beyond current technology and modern computer systems.

The Eight Immortals, inspired by Laozi, as a group follow the mathematical formulas and conventions of the *Yijing*. Over the centuries, each immortal was carefully classified, required to match a trigram relevant to his or her strengths, personality, skill, and physiological make-up. They each also used a particular form of qigong and martial arts to acquire a particular essence that was, moreover, associated with a trigram. Not only linked with one trigram, they also incorporated the texture of the other trigrams so that each of the eight could successfully crossover, adapt, and change positions with all others. By the same token, eight people practicing the sword in synchronized fashion, turning and changing the dial settings of the eight trigram pattern in a closed space, can mutate repeatedly to create any number of combinations. Eventually, the multiplicity of permutations forms a sphere: 64 on the way road to 10,000.

While the periphery of the circle is marked by the eight trigrams, the number nine, the highest number, rests in its center. To arrive at the escalating figures of the *Yijing* during sword practice, the number nine must be added in the center. In terms of the Eight Immortals, the ninth figure is Wang Chongyang, the disciple of Lü Dongbin and founder of the Complete Reality school. In terms of practice, the many movements within the circle form a dazzling spectacle, confusing to the untrained eye. In this manual, therefore, the practice is documented in a linear format to allow for a clear teaching of proper postures and footwork. Although highly beneficial in this framework, the highest levels of the Eight Immortals sword power can only be truly activated by practicing the movements in a circle. Only then will it become a dynamic trigram formation.

The trigram shape, when properly set, is the supreme battle configuration and one of the most efficacious symbols in all of Daoism, said to preclude all phases of evil magic from any direction, above or below. In Daoist cosmology, then, the Eight Immortals form an organic weapon that serves to maintain and protect the balance of nature and its six coexisting dimensions that occupy the same space as we humans do. The Eight Immortals' starting positions are accordingly:

Li Tieguai stands in the south at the Li (fire) trigram; his spontaneous, unpredictable personality perfectly fits this fiery yang trigram. Zhongli Han sits in the lofty northwest position atop the Qian (heaven) trigram. Lü Dongbin is wedded to the Kan (water) trigram in the north, reflecting his wisdom and adaptable leadership. The donkey riding immortal Zhang Guo-lao is found in the west at the Dui (lake) trigram, a suitable location for his quick, witty tongue. The forever young at heart Lan Caihe makes his home at the Gen (mountain) trigram in the northeast. The immortal Han Xiangzi is perfectly placed in the southeast at the Xun (wind) trigram, used for powering his flute. Cao Guojiu manages the Zhen (thunder) trigram in the northeast. And last but not least, the lady immortal He Xiangu perfectly matches the Kun (Earth) trigram in the southwest, the trigram of pure yin.

The Eight Immortals

The Eight Immortals have a long and complex legacy, pervading all aspects of Chinese culture and mythology and widely influential throughout the last thousand years. Their staying power is due to the fact that each of them has a unique skill (*gongfu*), that they form a colorful menagerie of masterful expressions, that they represent a vivid oral tradition of adventure, and that they made various contributions to humanity which are impossible to forget or ignore. The Daoist subjects they have mastered include herbal medicine, botany, military strategy, sexual cultivation, fortune-telling, and many more. Yet despite this variety of great talents, the one practice they all share is sword cultivation.

Their displays of magical feats, heroic chivalry, and human compassion connect people to the old days, to ancient lore and wondrous magic. For centuries, tales about them have captivated the hearts and minds of children and adults alike, quietly imbuing lessons of ethics and morality into human society. Told in works that are stored in libraries ranging from primary school to university level, their stories have molded countless generations and ignited fires in innumerable lives.

Both art and literature are full of them, documenting their continued influence in Chinese society. The most famous depiction captures them crossing the ocean, arriving at the mortal world from their home on the isles of Penglai, a legendary and mystical place that cannot be perceived with ordinary senses. Each immortal carries a specialized tool of his or her craft, prepared for unexpected challenges. For many people their image and tales show just how vast the ocean of life is and what unfathomable mysteries and dangers we may encounter as we pass through it. The Eight Immortals truly inspire the achievement and mastery of personal and life skills as a way to safely navigate the ocean of human existence.

Their stories are mere myths; some go back to a vivid oral tradition, others are documented in writing. The White Cloud Temple still owns hand-written compositions by five of them, some of which are very old indeed. Their various practices, moreover, have been handed down over generations and carefully guarded by practitioners. Thus the *gongfu* skills developed by the immortals and the stories of their personal experiences have stayed alive and continued to flourish, deeply rooted in the rich soil of Chinese culture. The wisdom contained in their tales continues to be remembered, celebrated, and practiced to this day as practitioners are committed to serve the people and the nation.

Protagonists

Li Tieguai, the Earliest Immortal

Li Tieguai, as documented in the White Cloud Temple's research on the order of the Eight Immortals, occupies the first position among them because he is the oldest member of the group and supposedly was the only one to study directly with Laozi or Lord Lao, the highest deity of the Daoist pantheon.

Born during the Sui dynasty (581-618) under the name Li Xuan, Tieguai is described in literary works as a jovial character and shown in art with a large, robust frame and full, round belly. The records also mention his previous incarnations on earth, suggesting that also he lived as a mythological figure in ancient China long before he was born to fulfill his quest for immortality.

Reincarnation is a central topic in both Daoism and Buddhism, with particular details worked out by the Tibetan or Lama school with its advanced astrological sciences. Within the Chinese tradition, mathematical calculations and cosmological tables based on the *Yijing* make it possible to track souls with precision, pinpointing both past and future incarnations. This science charts stars and their movements in a celestial network of gates and pathways fueled by karma. It applies birth records, including those of the subject's immediate family, and enters them into formulaic equations to reveal different karmic aspects of an individual's spiritual journey through the universe.

If some information is not available for processing, other methods beyond the scope of scientific calculations yet allow a proper understanding of the specifics. These methods include esoteric investigations conducted by highly cultivated individuals, who have internalized the processes of the *Yijing* through sword practice and qigong cultivation. They have acquired special fortune-telling abilities and thus have access to unique knowledge. One of their abilities is due to polishing the diamond mind, a multifaceted mirror at the center of the brain which reflects narrative images of *qi*. If any subject matter is presented for survey, their *qi* registers the same information as that acquired by numerological calculations—probably with even greater accuracy and in more vivid detail.

If the subject is not present, any objects belonging to that person or even a photograph can also be used as a link to their *qi* track: past, present or future. Using both methods simultaneously is the most reliable approach but only few masters, including Master Wu, who possess this skill. "If you can walk out of the White Cloud Temple, you are said to have a diamond in your pocket." This refers to the ability of being able to see more than 500 years into past and future.

Stories about Li Tieguai similarly indicate that his numinous *qi* had been circulating in the universe for several thousand years, making many stops in worlds beyond our own before descending to the planet once again during the Sui. The first link in his chain of lives occurred under the earliest emperors of Chinese civilization, whom he served as a rain maker with supernatural powers. These stories which go back to the beginnings of time seem to be just mythic tales, but in fact they contain distant memories of the past and provide a better understanding of the unique roots of esoteric Daoism, its rituals and artifacts. The oldest such tale is creation myth centering on Pan Gu, which is more imaginative than modern accounts but less commonly acceptable than today's "big bang" theory. Still, from the Daoistic point of view, it provides the template for the rainbow body, the ultimate achievement in *qi* cultivation.

The Creation

Once upon a time, long before distinctions existed, all matter was merged in a single chaotic mass. Inside this dark egg-shaped mass, an incomprehensible presence hibernated for 18,000 years. At the end of this deep sleep, the great Pan Gu awoke. He drew a sword from the inside and severed the egg-shaped mass in half, thus creating heaven and earth. The light, pure essence floated up, while the dark, dense energies sank down. Thus we say: "Pan Gu separated heaven and earth; was the beginning of the world."

Next, Pan Gu stood up straight with his hands over his head, thrusting the heavens above and holding the earth below under his feet. He grew at a rate of ten feet per day, undergoing nine continuous transformations. Each day, the heavens expanded and the earth thickened. This went on for another 18,000 years, then cohesiveness suspended the new universe, allowing Pan Gu to let go his stance. His cultivation concluded, his body began to transform into a rainbow, merging with the new universe.

His left eye became the sun, and his right eye the moon. His breath was the wind, and his voice was the thunder. His blood vessels laid down the rivers and pathways, while his bones formed mountains and rocks. His four limbs were the four cardinal directions, and his bone marrow transformed into jade and crystal. The hair on his head became the flickering stars. His skin and muscles founded fertile land for the flowers, trees, and grass. The fleas which inhabited his body migrated down to earth and became all the creatures we know today, including human beings.

Culture Heroes

Pan Gu was succeeded by the sage emperor Fu Xi, the first of three noble emperors known as the Three Sovereigns (Sanhuang). He was important and made many contributions, so people call him "great teacher" or "master" (*shi*). Fu Xi was responsible not only for discovering the eight trigrams but also for making fishing nets, breeding silkworms to produce clothing, and domesticating wild animals. He invented the stringed instrument and the five tones scale, which helped harmonize and heal the five organs. His calendar system aided farmers in maximizing the planting and harvesting of crops. He is also credited with organizing the hundred surnames and the rule that marriages can only take place between persons of different last names and after taking out a proper marriage license. He was an extraordinary figure: these great features of cultural progress could not have come from an ordinary person.

After him came the heavenly emperor Shennong, the "Divine Farmer," who is credited with setting up the first Chinese *materia medica*, later called the *Shennong bencao jing* (The Divine Farmers Pharmacopeia). The text's information was based on trial and error experimentation, done by the emperor himself. He observed, consumed, and documented the effectiveness that each herbal essence had on his physical, moral, and mental constitution. His *materia medica* lists 365 types of plants and minerals with their appropriate uses, including herbs suitable for religious and shamanic rituals. It was the first of its kind published in China.

Beyond these substances, Shennong examined thousands of others over many decades, including those from the animal kingdom. Much of his research remained inconclusive, but he documented it anyway so future generations of doctors and herbalist could develop it. In addition, he is also credited with first coming up with agriculture and forestry as well as with having invented plow-and-trough mechanism.

An old record contains the description of a "rain master" who lived for 300 years. Rain-producing deities in Chinese mythology are usually dragons, however, this rain god was half-goat and half-bird. He had horns on his head and the body and legs of goat, yet he also had six fully operational wings on his back, three on each side. These wings gave him the ability to travel over and around the universe at the speed of lightning. He supposedly was Li Tieguai in an earlier incarnation. The eccentricity of this earlier life apparently followed him through the ages and into his human form. However, in this lifetime he had a balding head, a distaste for shaving, and a temperamental mood as well as a tendency toward unpredictable antics—all contributing to his clown-like character.

His name Tieguai means "Iron Crutch;" he is also called the "Crippled Immortal." His unthreatening, handicapped routine combined with his stocky, heavyset, slow-moving appearance makes him seem harmless at first. This works in his favor as he can enter into service to those needing assistance. In fact, his beggar's husk hides the ferociousness of a tiger, and Li is an expert martial artist specializing in cane practice. He uses his iron crutch to sweep adversaries off their feet, moving cleverly and with lightning speed. He especially goes after fellows taking advantage of innocent people or trying to best a crippled, old beggar, setting an example for followers of cane practice within the martial arts. Beyond that, his true power lies in the medicine gourd he has hanging from his belt. It stores the magical elixir whose recipe he received directly from Laozi: it can heal serious illness and exorcize evil, pulling either out of their victims, as well as assist in various transformational purposes. How, then, did Li get to be so uniquely powerful?

Looks Don't Matter

Li Tieguai originally was an exceptionally handsome and attractive gentleman named Li Xuan who cultivated his spirit in a cave on West Mountain. He practiced the Daoist alchemical arts as well as qigong, martial arts, and divination according to the *Yijing*, rapidly excelling in these subjects and achieving a high proficiency. He soon became a fully qualified instructor of Dao, even at a young age selecting and guiding his students on the path to enlightenment.

Early one morning, as he was meditating inside his cave, Laozi appeared to him in a vision, extending an invitation to him. On a certain day, Li should leave his physical body behind and in his original spirit (*yuanshen*) and spirit soul (*hun*) fly to Mount Hua to receive more profound training in the infinite. Before disappearing, Laozi demonstrated the technique that Li should use to open the channels of spirit travel. Li was delighted; this opportunity was a dream come true.

He prepared his journey by taking a special diet and undergoing sword purification rites. He also drilled his senior disciple to safeguard Li's virtually vacant body from hungry ghosts and other predators lying in wait between the dimensions. They might well come, be seeking a new host while Li's original spirit was traversing in space. The guardian student had to oversee his master's body for seven days, continuously chanting scriptures and burning incense to maintain a solid protective shield. Under no circumstances was he to abandon his post until Li's original spirit had returned safely. However, should he not have returned after seven days, the disciple was to cremate his body at 1 p.m., thus allowing Li's transition to a higher level.

On the designated day, Li carried out the proper rites and set himself free. His disciple followed his instructions to the letter, staying awake and vigilant day and night for six days. On the sixth day, however, unexpected news reached the cave. The disciple's mother had suddenly grown deathly ill and her life was coming to an end. Weighing the situation, he decided to remain at his teacher's side, since this was his primary obligation. He would address his filial responsibilities on the seventh day, after Li had come back to his body.

Time passed. At 1 p.m. on the seventh day, when there was still no sign of his master, the disciple cremated the body in the firm belief that Li had been promoted to heavenly office. Then he rushed off to be with his dying mother. Meanwhile, Li was slowly floating back from his training session with Laozi, carrying a gourd-full of new medicine for healing the sick. He was running slightly behind schedule, but figured his reliable young novice wouldn't hastily burn his suspended body—completely unaware of the personal emergency that had arisen in the meantime. When he came flying into his cave, he was horrified to find just a pile of smoldering ashes where his mortal body had once sat. Circling the interior walls of the cave near his disintegrated remains there was only one thing left: his material soul (*po*), left behind to keep his body from decaying.

As his initial shock turned to anger, Li collected himself and flew out of the cave, desperately searching for an alternate body to house his soul. There was little time. He had to find a vessel for his spirit lest he be caught in the otherworld and forced to reincarnate through the six realms, beginning his training all over again. He would lose the work of a lifetime. Seeking high and low, he finally discovered the lifeless body of a beggar, lying face down in the snow. Without hesitating, he slipped into the corpse, reanimated it, and came to his feet. Much to his surprise, he didn't feel half bad.

Li Xuan was overwhelmed with a deep sense of gratitude for this new chance at life—until he tried to walk. He took two steps forward and felt off balance. Looking down at his new body, he found he now had one leg shorter than the other. He panicked, snatched up his medicine gourd, popped off the lid, and gazed into the liquid elixir to see his reflection. Staring back at him was a total stranger: an old man with a bald head and a scruffy beard. He had gone from young, handsome, and at ease to old, ugly, and dirty, and with a wildly flaring temper. Enough was enough. He pulled his energies in to escape this wretched body—and stopped short. Someone behind him was clapping and laughing loudly.

He turned around to see Laozi beaming at him with sparkling eyes and a comforting smile, himself cloaked in a majestic jade-colored robe, lightly ruffling in the breeze. Li was speechless in complete amazement. So much was happening, he couldn't take it all in, and his consciousness began slipping away. Laozi jolted him back to reality by dusting off his clothes and abrasively cleaning his face. "To practice Dao, you don't need an aesthetically pleasing body, just a keen mind. To attain immortality, beauty is of no consequence."

Li did not appreciate these pearls of wisdom. Ashamed and on the verge of tears, he covered his eyes with his hands so he wouldn't have to see himself any more. Laozi removed his hands from his face and forced him to look down into the medicine gourd. Li saw how his eyes were bulging out of their sockets, making his already disgusting looks even worse. How could he ever practice the martial arts again with a body like this? But Laozi handed him an iron crutch: "Don't worry, Iron Crutch Li! Your skills will be better than ever."

Ling, the Spiritual Core

A key concept in Daoism is *ling*, often rendered "numen" but best described as "soul force." The word indicates the supernatural or divine dimension of spirit and intelligence. *Lingqi* consists of cosmic particles that float freely throughout the universe, boundlessly permeating everything and allowing the person to experience an uninhibited, inseparable sense of self and reality. Formless and not tied to the body, *ling* or numinous particles remain unattached until they are assigned a destination in the physical world. Humans, animals, trees, plants, rocks, minerals, and all other life form contain a unique pattern of numinous *qi*, some more evolved than others. These patterns are much like highly sophisticated DNA strands that store generations of information and history, all the way back to the beginnings of time.

Each numinous particle can be broken-down into three sub-divisions called spirit (*shen*), spirit soul (*hun*), and material soul (*po*). In human beings, spirit resides in the heart, the spirit soul is stored in the liver, and the material or animal soul dwells in the lungs. Together they form the quintessence of nature. Originally, moreover, they are perfectly synchronized, arriving with the first breath or cry of a newborn baby.

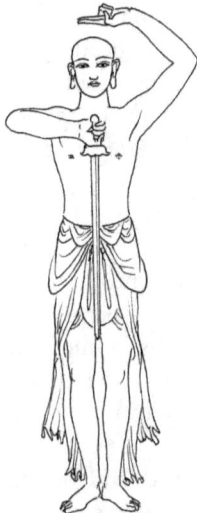

Ling energy begins the process of incarnation as a star in the sky. In the moment before birth the star separates into two halves: the numinous half descends at a fifteen-degree angle from the seven stars of the Dipper, moves toward the earth, then joins a new body like air sealed into a tight jar, and stays there until the body dies. The other half of the star is called the secret match (*miying*). Much like what people in the West call the "higher self," it remains in the celestial regions to help the numinous part in fulfilling its destiny. "As many stars as there are in the sky, there are human beings on earth," as the saying goes.

Master Wu heard this as a child and asked his teacher: "Why does it look as if there are far more stars in the skies then humans on earth?" Master Du pointed out that there are many levels of life in addition to this planet, in other solar systems, galaxies, and far-off dimensions. The greater universe is, after all, inundated with innumerable kinds of numinous beings.

For the immortality seeker and internal alchemist, numinous *qi* forms the base material. Its cultivation in the body requires ten months of consistent sword and/or qigong practice, leading to a reactivation of its natural patterns. In this first phase, the *ling* within begins to generate a new light-body called the original match or original spirit. Steadily persevering and continuously accumulating outer numinous *qi* from nature for support, the new spirit body comes to emerge into the senses. Esoterically, it grows in the image of a lotus flower, spreading its roots through the body's energy meridians. Along these paths are special points, gates through which it can exit to mingle with the outer world: Hundred Meeting (*Baihui*) at the top of the head; Gate of Life (*Mingmen*) between the kidneys opposite the navel; Labor Palace (*Laogong*) point in the center of the palms.

Going beyond these three, Daoist practitioners strive to open a total of 84,000 gates known as the Ghost Gates (*Guimen*), which are in fact the pores of the skin. When they are unobstructed, the original spirit's inner light can access the macrocosm and serve as the vehicle for cosmic *ling* to mingle with other numinous forces in nature. When the two worlds unite, a communication transpires that is both overt and lucid, providing wisdom and warnings. This is expressed in the saying: "Humanity and the universe combine into one." When the personal *ling* thus consciously reaches to the outer realms, one has secured enough force and maturity in the flowering of the lotus. An uncultivated or immature numinous spirit can also leave the body, but it is subject to danger: energy parasites and ghosts can attach themselves to it, absorbing the life force from weaker beings, delaying their spiritual progress, and causing sickness. It is thus very important to continuously reinforce energy practices. Only then one can undertake spirit excursions in one's *ling*—consciously undergoing and directing an experience that usually is limited to the dream state.

Why, then, does the original spirit leave the body at all? When cultivated, it develops an awareness of its intrinsic mission: to find its secret match, its other half that has stayed behind in the heavens. Once successfully reunified with it, the spirit achieves a deep alignment between the lower and higher self and reestablishes an open connection. Then the person is guided at all times by its original spirit, which has full knowledge of its proper destiny. This also enhances the intuitive qualities of the conscious and subconscious minds, rising up as an inner voice that can be clearly heard and fully trusted. Having access to this level of celestial perception expedites response dexterity in the presence of unanticipated occurrences. It becomes a priceless asset which permits what was once predestined and unshakable to be consciously directed and even changed by as much as fifty percent. It makes a huge difference between success and failure, fortune and misfortune, long life and early death. The rejoined stars' sense of certainty, moreover, provides a service to other numinous beings by setting up a solid beam of light from heaven to earth, a beacon that can safely release and guide lost souls back to themselves. As the Daoist saying goes: "There is a deity three feet above every head."

All these stages are only small rays of enlightenment that must be built upon further to achieve Dao. They alone do not release the aspirant from the wheel of life and death or allow ascent to immortality. True enlightenment occurs only when the jar is unsealed and the *ling* escapes freely into the vast ocean of cosmic energy without going through death first. There are no more separations or obstacles that might impede the ecstatic feelings that go beyond all measure of love. Otherwise, the only other alternative is to wait for death to unlock the *ling* from the body. The ling soul, however, that is set free by death must first cycle through the six realms of reincarnation, going through a place of karmic reckoning and experiencing yet another future still ruled by physical laws.

Theory of *ling* is only one of many jewels of cultivation hidden in this story about Li Tieguai. More jewels are found in another, from the oral tradition of the White Cloud Temple and thus insider information.

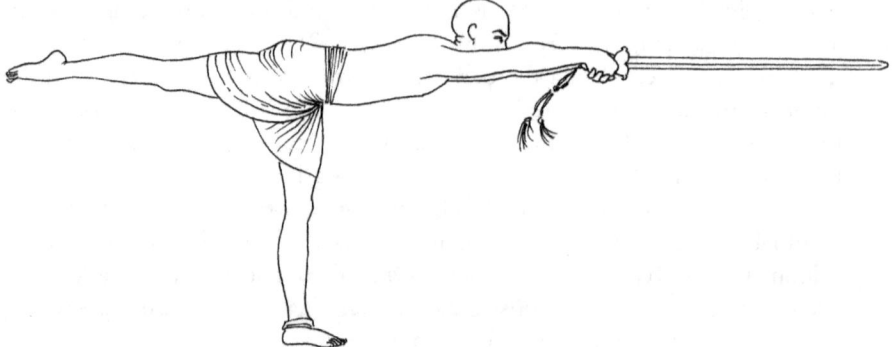

The Virtue of Patience

From childhood, Li Xuan was an enthusiastic and avid practitioner of the martial arts; he spent hours and hours every day in search of perfection. His diligence duly came to the attention of the officials in charge of annual tests geared to discover the top adepts of martial combat for military recruitment. Li was invited to join the competition of his generation and placed a respectable fifth in the finals. Even though this result was generally considered excellent—the equivalent of a state championship in his home province—he had long envisioned himself proudly wearing the national champion's uniform and large, special hat. His unfulfilled dream left him with an unquenchable thirst to grow and improve.

At this point he had exhausted all he could learn from the local masters, so he set out to find advanced edification. Traveling from village to village, asking everywhere for the true masters, he heard time and again: "In Shaanxi province, north of Xi'an city, lives a master by the name of Laozi. His martial skill is unsurpassed." Young Li was inspired by the unanimous referrals and sought directions to find this reputable sage. As it turned out, locating Laozi was not as difficult as he had imagined. Even at their first meeting, although few words were exchanged, Li Xuan had the feeling that the old master had been expecting him. Laozi remained seated and never stirred, then cut to the chase and asked Li to give a demonstration of his skill. Intimidated by the absence of formalities thus far, Li showed his technique, putting his whole heart and strong ambition into it. When he finished, he stood in a nervous sweat waiting for the Old One to decide his fate. Having seen his potential, Laozi accepted him as his student.

Li Xuan soon took notice of Laozi's unique approach to self-cultivation, striking an obvious contrast to his previous instructors. The Old Master was incessantly writing, reading, and speaking in philosophical maxims and riddles only he himself could understand. This left Li in a constant state of perplexity. The only physical training Laozi imposed on the novice was the art of breath control. "Just fill the belly," he would say. This was boring but, following a vow he took before becoming Laozi's disciple, Li never questioned the practices he was asked to undertake.

Eleven years went by, and never once did Li witness the prowess of Laozi's famed martial arts. His patience was wearing thin, and doubts began to arise in mind. He began to question the authenticity of the elderly sage. Had he been duped into servitude just to care for the old man's needs? Hindered by doubt in his commitment to Dao, Li's clever mind quietly plotted how to best unveil the true level of his teacher's martial arts.

Then, one day Laozi announced he would be taking a journey into the mountains to contemplate existence. He firmly ordered Li to remain behind and practice his breath control and meditation for however long he was away—an unspecified length of time. Laozi mounted his ox backwards so he could use the animal's wide hips as a table-top for reading, writing, and lecturing, having every bit of confidence that the beast would know the route to take. Li Xuan, on the other hand, saw this as his chance to satisfy his curiosity.

Somewhat familiar with the mountainous path Laozi had chosen, Li set out to ambush him at a bend in the road. He took a shortcut through the forest, running at full speed over rocks and tree roots in order to reach the planned point of attack before Laozi. When he arrived, he climbed up a towering tree, placed a black hood over his head, and waited patient—like a stealthy panther primed to pounce on its prey. Shortly thereafter, he caught sight of his quarry, the yellow ox methodically hoofing up the trail. He planned to leap down from the tree disguised as a bandit in order to force Laozi into combat as soon as the ox passed directly underneath him. When the critical moment arrived, Li explosively launched himself out of the tree, raising a blood-curdling war cry.

He hit the ground kicking and punching from all angles, but Laozi remained undisturbed, keeping his mind steady like a placid lake on a windy day, his eyes uncompromisingly glued to his workbook. He just casually waved his fly whisk, nonchalantly countering Li's ferocious foray of strokes, softly deflecting the blows, and leaving frustration as the only reciprocity for his efforts. Li Xuan flanked around to his left to gain the advantage of his teacher's blind side. Simultaneously the ox turned his head to take a look at all this commotion. As the beast swiveled to look left over his massive shoulder, his horn met Li's thigh, deeply gashing his flesh. His war cry suddenly became a loud wail of excruciating pain. Then the ox turned his head back forward to once more look at the trail. Doing so, it tore the large, piercing horn from Li's leg, sending him tumbling to the side of the road, gripping torn muscles.

In one smooth move, Laozi dropped from the animal to unmask his attacker. He pulled the hood off and to his dismay discovered his own disciple. He sighed in disbelief and asked: "Why did you do such a foolish thing?"

Grasping his injured leg, Li Xuan replied: "In eleven whole years I have followed you in hopes of learning the martial arts. In all that time I have never once witnessed even the slightest glimpse of your craft. Now, Master, I finally know what you mean when you speak of the subtle moves and mechanisms of the universe."

"You have paid a high price for this lesson. But, yes, I will teach you my martial arts once after you have recovered from this fiasco."

After several months Li Xuan got back to his feet, but did not emerge unscathed: he had developed a noticeable limp. In the meantime Laozi had cast him an iron crutch, thus the name Tieguai. As promised, Laozi proceeded to teach him the martial arts. He even specially designed a tailor-made system of offensive and defensive movements for Li. The iron crutch was the central focus of this practice and would be utilized like sword and cudgel combined in methods of hooking, prodding, sweeping, and crushing.

Li Tieguai finally reached the level of martial arts mastery he had always dreamed of, but only after he had become physically challenged. The experience forced him to look within and by doing so he realized certain truths about life's mysteries that go far beyond martial practice. Expanding his vision, he found true rewards serving those in need. After many years of helping his fellow man, Li Tieguai finally attained full enlightenment. On that day, he ascended to heaven by swinging his iron crutch, transforming it into a dragon, and riding it into the realm of immortals.

Master Wu's Lesson

Growing up, Wu Baolin was constantly challenged by his teacher concerning the contemplation, meaning, and purpose of existence and destiny. Master Du would place his young pupil in seemingly random and useless situations hoping that the child would extract meaning and perspective from his life. Once he challenged him to observe a colony of ants near a small brook outside the monastery. Master Du told Little Wu he would return at the end of the day and question him about any discoveries or revelations he might make. From morning to afternoon, Little Wu watched the army of ants marching hither and thither. When Master Du returned and asked him what he had gathered from the experience, Little Wu reported on the obvious behavior attributed to ants, such as a strong work ethic and enormous strength, and gave a detailed description of the various tasks they performed. Master Du just nodded and said they would do this again the next day.

Little Wu duly spent another day in the same location. Master Du again came and questioned him. Although inventive, Wu Baolin's answers were quite like those of the previous day. Master Du accordingly had him continue with the exercise for an entire week. Little Wu was less then thrilled by the news.

On the fifth day, all patience had deserted him, and Wu begged his teacher to explain the lesson to him. Without saying a word, Master Du picked up a long branch which had fallen from a nearby tree and gently laid it across the creek, bridging the two banks of the streaming water. As master and disciple watched, the ant colony filed into a line and marched first toward the branch, then across it until they all reached the other shore. Master Du faced his Daoist son: "In just the same way as we look down upon these countless ants and help them reach their destiny, so higher and more advanced beings above in the heavens look down on us and help us reach our destiny."

As things were thus placed in perspective with the laws of nature as the teacher, it became more and more apparent to Little Wu, who was a natural skeptic, that the various ideas of gods, alien creatures, and life beyond this world were quite appropriate and made sense. His lesson with the ants evoked a profound understanding and belief in Wu Baolin's heart, something that had not been there before. Daoist philosophy began to grow in his mind, giving fruition to seeds planted by his teacher years earlier. Every morning between 3 and 5 a.m., the monks chanted sacred scriptures in homage to saints and deities such as Laozi, Wang Chongyang, the Buddha, and the Eight Immortals. They prayed to men of antiquity who had risen to immortality for protection and guidance. All these figures had finally become real and acceptable to the boy, who found a new sense of purpose in the thought that human beings were only one of many species, not much different from the ants below his feet. He began to trust that the immortals in the heavens would take care of him and give him sanctuary.

Theory behind the ant lesson goes back to Laozi's concept of the Dao as being "so big there are no boundaries and so small there is no inside." When something is so small that there is no longer an inside, it has fallen into nonexistence or infinity. If you follow a single living cell inward, you find its nucleus. If you look deeper, you come to a molecule, then to an atom. Protons are next, then lepton particles—so minute that they have no strong interactions. Leptons and their counterparts, quarks, are the ultimate building blocks of matter. They have no inner components, or at least nothing that science can measure at present: they are "so small there is no inside." In other words, beyond these particles there is just empty space inside of matter.

Moving in the other direction, going outward instead of inward from where we stand, "so big there are no boundaries" takes us to the outer edges of reality: past clouds, stars, solar systems, galaxies, and black holes to where nothingness sleeps. Nothingness is like a womb containing all matter. Beyond this point is also infinity: outer space without measure. This empty darkness in Daoism is known as non-ultimate (*wuji*) or the void (*xu*): it gives birth to all life. Creation here begins with a miniscule spark that is again "so small there is no inside." Yin and yang at their greatest expansion and contraction, as noted earlier, simply become one another: there is a fine line between big and small. Laozi said: "The entire universe can be found in a single grain of rice." A human being is one form of that grain of rice, embodying every particle in the universe, big or small. Inner reflection and contemplation, moreover, using the alchemical process of Daoist esoteric exercise, expand the frontier of exploration within.

Zhongli Han, Subduer of the White Tiger

Zhongli Han, also known as Zhongli Quan, was born in Shanxi province during the early Han dynasty (206 BCE-220 CE). His given name was Quan, which means two things: balancing weight and weighing the relative importance of two things. It is this second meaning that would greatly affect his decision when he came to the major crossroads in his life: have a successful military career or become a Daoist recluse. His nickname Han goes back to his being born during the Han dynasty.

Artistic renderings tend to show him as holding a fan, an emblem that empowers him to wake the dead and control the seas. He usually has a long beard and protruding belly, indicating his wealthy lifestyle. Born into a warrior family, abundance was his birthright. His father was a dedicated official in the national army who excelled in the conquest of Turfan. Upon returning victorious from the battlefields, he was promoted into the military elite, setting the stage for his son's future greatness as a warrior—also presaged in a miraculous dream.

The Dream of Fire

Mrs. Zhongli, Han's mother-to-be, had been toiling for nine months with her pregnancy. One night she lay down to rest and went to sleep. Suddenly an extremely large man, all of nine feet tall, entered her room. His eyes gleamed, staring deeply into her innermost essence. A mysterious relay of electricity connected them. He told her telepathically that he was the incarnation of a great sage who lived at the same time as the Herb Master of antiquity (Shennong). Then an intense beam of light shot from the giant, overpowering the shadows in the room, bathing the entire space in a glow, and insulating it with a protective aura. As the light continued to intensify, a fire arose in the center of the room, softly illuminating everything with a warm orange glow.

As if hypnotized, Mrs. Zhongli found herself captivated by the sphere of dancing flames as they gradually formed between her and the stranger. All else seemed to disappear. Forged inside the flames, a newborn child emerged. The pregnant woman's gaze continued to be fixed on the fire's creation as she witnessed the luminosity in the room beginning to wane, converging on the child's small body. The ball of fire then began to gyrate and roll toward her, vanishing into her womb. Soon after, she awoke, full of strong visceral sensations and the realization of just how real this dream had been. Her recollection, however, was quickly interrupted by birth pangs and the arrival of the child. Such was Han's entry into the mortal world.

As Mrs. Zhongli examined her baby boy, she was struck by his curious resemblance to the child of fire and light in her dream. She further realized that her son was no ordinary infant, observing various strange characteristics he had of someone much older: his head was too large in relation to his body, his ears were extremely thick, his eyebrows were unusually long. He already looked like a three-year-old. For six days and nights he did not make any sounds, shed any tears, eat a single morsel of food, or swallow a drop of milk. On the seventh day, as he lay in his crib, he spoke: "I am an immortal from heaven!" he said, to the great astonishment of his parents. However, after this, he was like any other infant, dependent on his parents for care and sustenance.

His father had learned about his wife's vision and keenly observed the unusual features of his newborn son. Seriously concerned about his future, he made sure that Han was never alone and had both his older brothers watching over him like sentinel lions guarding an emperor. As he grew older, moreover, his father provided him with the finest education and martial arts training available. When the appropriate time came, he assured that Han would receive a commission as a military officer.

The Power of Dreams

The *Longmen jing* (Dragon Gate Classic) says: "If you do not dream, you are not alive." With these words Laozi raises the awareness of the internal landscape and its vision, whose manifest signs and confirmation serve to connect the *qi* of the mysterious Dao to that of dedicated adepts, giving them the option to play a significant part in shaping their fate and fortune.

In self-cultivation, dreaming is essential for monitoring spiritual progress and social issues, either personal or on a wider level. Visions and everyday events help create advantageous positioning. Foreknowledge and solid preparation provide both immediate and long-term direction for the completion of personal destiny. People usually see the abstract symbols and images subconsciously projected in dreams as isolated, distorted, and exaggerated mental events that have neither rhyme nor reason. The inner and outer worlds of dream and waking mirror one another, but cast altered reflections that are easily discarded for lack of proper understanding and decryption—a skill that comes with training.

Those born with a propensity for the mystical are the exception: they take their dreams seriously from the beginning. However, even they still require guidance and development. In the world governed by the conscious mind, people tend to ignore most apparently exceptional events or consider them random and irrelevant. They find it hard to make sense of these events, especially today when people live in a highly technological age populated by machines, whose education systems fail to nurture any form of intuition or innate instincts. From a Daoist perspective, giving due consideration to all sorts of minor, apparently inexplicable incidents and their karmic links is a dire necessity. It furnishes important pieces of a puzzle that can help construct a clear path to the realization of blessings, good fortune, and long life.

Any event is presaged by advance warnings. Reading them carefully gives us an opportunity to change our destiny or that of others. For example, before a rainstorm, dragonflies tend to fly low, while ants hustle into their hill or into an underground haven. Reading these signs can prevent us from being stranded in nasty weather and avoid potential pneumonia. Similarly, before an earthquake or other natural catastrophe, animals tend to rustle about, making howling, barking, shrieking, and other sounds and exhibiting various kinds of strange behavior. Their actions give us a window to prepare for the unexpected. There are many such indicators that all have their own level of accuracy. The key to working with them is the individual's level of cultivation: it either limits or enhances their foresight of upcoming situations.

As noted earlier, during the nine months of pregnancy, the yin-yang in the Great Ultimate turns about completely. Developing a child in a woman's body is the natural way of cultivating and unearthing the already planted sensory systems of detection. One benefit of going through this process involves the attunement of a "women's intuition," thereby instinctually safeguarding the offspring. Another type relates to longevity, in a form of reproduction training available solely to women.

Men upon entering fatherhood also have increased awareness; however, in women the emotional bonding through the umbilical cord never ceases even after it is cut at birth. It provides a perfect analogy to practicing Daoist exercise: the results of *qi* cultivation are just like it but not restricted by gender because Daoist procreation works on a spiritual level, using *qi* rather than flesh and blood.

Fortune-telling

On the eve of Zhongli Han's birth, his mother received a powerful message indicating the importance of her child in the world. Many Chinese legends similarly disclose elementary levels of fortune telling: regardless of whether the stories are fact or fiction, they convey important insights into the body of knowledge sages and followers of the Dao have collected over the ages. A case in point is the description of Han's physical attributes as an infant; they seem amusing at first, yet when closely examined give insight into his character.

Thus his thick ears show that the infant is blessed. Long ears at birth indicate longevity like a long river that finds the ocean. Round ears usually mean monetary fortune, either now or later—they match traditional bronze coins which were round with a square opening in the center. Soft ears are signs of a flexible, objective, and conforming personality; stiff ears show the opposite—a characteristic of many politicians.

By the same token, Han's long eyebrows pertain to an extended life expectancy; but more importantly, they divulge the extent of his wisdom. His large skull, on the other hand, shows his immense intellectual capacity. The fire and light by which his spirit is forged in the story, moreover, offers insight into his nature and personality as well as and his preferred occupation: a fiery constitution is essential to military leadership. A case in point is that the toughest soldiers in China tend to be from Sichuan province, a place of an excessively hot climate, the growth of hot chilies, and a very spicy cuisine. All these factors contribute to an invigorating, passionate, and competitive attitude which goes hand in hand with military demeanor.

Daoist fortune-telling, then, leans toward the reading of symbols with some intuitive support. It is based on philosophical naturalism, the rootstock of Daoist verification and decoding of the determinative act or agency in the patterns of cause and effect. Although less difficult then reading *qi*, it still necessitates deep study. Both techniques ideally are combined through spiritual cultivation.

To predict events Daoists further use all sorts of natural workings, gathering signs variously: by casual observation, dreaming, meditation, or concentrated exercise, in conscious or subconscious states. Their findings are recorded, in some cases spanning several centuries, while images are collated and quantified into numbers for calculation. From here they connect to the *Yijing*, which postulates that everything has its number. Thus they place information into *Yijing*-based mathematical tables, traditional search engines that can trace common and uncommon patterns of nature to their predictable outcomes, thereby to expose the accuracy of the gathered intelligence.

Negative predictions, moreover, are not set in stone, but there is always the chance that alterations can be made either under the careful direction of an accomplished *Yijing* master or by the individual himself—provided he or she has received proper training and reached a state of immediate cognition, like the hypersensitive instincts of animals. A heightened environmental awareness is a return to nature; this is advanced human technology, leading through what Laozi calls "the nine levels of dreaming."

The White Cloud Story

People familiar with the White Cloud Temple and its surroundings know that to borrow luck from the heavens, they must rub five stone monkeys found on the temple grounds before leaving its red gates. The first monkey is located on the outer wall of the temple, left of the southern gate. The second is just inside, carved on a stele at the foot of a stone bridge leading over a moat into the heart of the monastery.

At the doorway of the first island hall, moreover, is the sword guardian (Lingguan). Inside the hall, there were once two large panoramic frescos: Lü Dongbin and a green dragon plus Zhongli Han and a white tiger. The tiger was depicted blocking the entrance to a trail designed for human use yet completely inaccessible. The image showed Han's coming of age as a *bona fide* immortal, the scene placed near his last military victory.

The White Cloud Temple version of this life-altering story is close to the popular but it does not credit Li Tieguai as his teacher. Rather, it has him play a complex role in the radical shattering of Zhongli's brash military personality, preparing him for the reshaping into a Daoist immortal who in due course comes to meet the central sage himself: an incarnation of Laozi. The story is entitled "Zhongli Han Subdues the White Tiger to Become Immortal." It goes:

Raised as the pride of his family and military community, Han had come into his own. Solid nurturing had formed a strong, skillful, and intelligent young man. His father's plan was perfect and he was quickly becoming an expert military strategist. His innovations were of immense importance to the security of the Han dynasty, and he was one of few field strategists in Chinese history to masterfully implement the eight trigrams on the battlefield. This made his leadership invaluable, his combat techniques almost invincible. He accordingly rose swiftly through the ranks and he soon was one victory away from a seat on the emperor's core cabinet.

Xinjiang at the time was a neighboring country that resisted allegiance to the Han, but was close to being conquered. Fighting vigorously on their own against an overwhelming power had worn down their troops' morale and they were on the brink of exhaustion. Han scouts, informants, and double agents provided much needed information about their state. Zhongli, at the helm of superior servicemen and with the country's full support, promised a methodical dismantling of an already crippled Xinjiang military and assured that victory would be attained the next morning.

As both sides pitted themselves against each other, tensions escalated and large-scale assaults began. Flying high above the hostilities, resting on a billowing cloud, was the immortal Li Tieguai, taking notes about the situation below, curious to discover the outcome through his own reckoning. In the spirit of doing good deeds, he decided to try and save the lives of many Xinjiang citizens as well as Zhongli Han's future. Li noticed some unique attributes radiating from the young field commander, showing that Han had once been an immortal himself but due to some wrong-doings in the heavens had been exiled to the world of dust below. Li thought, "If Han is victorious today, he becomes a war hero like his father. He will become deeply confirmed in mortal life, so that regaining immortality becomes almost impossible."

Li Tieguai, with his bird's-eyes view, soon formulated a strategy to radically upset Han's battle scheme based on the eight trigrams. The immortal then descended to earth and altered his appearances, entering the Xinjiang military camp disguised as a wise old man and proposed to the desperate officers a feasible plan of counter attack. They accepted his suggestions and an unexpected wave of hope radiated to the Xinjiang militia, reaching also the field generals who carried out the final orders to redirect the oncoming power of Han forces. Before long, Xinjiang turned the tide, gaining a momentous advantage. Utterly unprepared, the Han troops were forced to retreat.

Conversion

Stupefied by these developments, Zhongli Han mounted his horse and retreated along with the rest of his soldiers but in the ensuing chaos was separated from his troops and rode into a dense forest. Strangely free, he realized that his life was collapsing around him. Aware of the large bounties placed on the heads of high ranking officers, he continued to ride, aiming toward high mountains in the distance as a safe hiding place. After several hours, he was exhausted and in disarray, his horse was close to collapse and urgently needed water. Looking up, Han realized that he had reached the entrance of the mountains and spotted a Buddhist monk by the roadside. Making eye contact, the monk waved him forward like an old friend and joined him.

As the path became more treacherous, Han dismounted and continued to follow the monk, climbing up a steep mountain trail into a world that insinuated change with every step. The singing of birds replaced the sound of war cries. Live, thriving trees replaced catapults and lookout towers constructed of bald dead logs.

For Han, this was the first time he had ever been away from home completely on his own. All his life he had been taught to conquer and kill, to do whatever necessary for victory, to follow the strict guidelines of government protocol. Then a Daoist enclave on a high mountain ridge came into view, and Han had a revelation: he felt a sense of security and homecoming as the strings of his past were being severed.

The monk helped him settle his horse in a make-shift stable, and then took him into the main chambers of the head Daoist. With the monk standing just outside the chamber door, the abbot addressed him warmly: "Greetings Zhongli Han. I am called Master Donghua." Tired to the point of delirium, Han vaguely wondered how the man knew his name. He was not familiar to him and he was sure that he had not spoken a word, ever since delivering his command of retreat on the front lines, not even with the monk. Master Donghua then ordered simple food and made simple if slightly uncanny conversation to let the tired soldier unwind.

However, Han could not relax fully. He still had flashbacks of his battle failure, going over the events time and again in his mind and trying to find where he had gone wrong. His musings were interrupted by Master Donghua who raised his voice to that of a professor taking command of his class and uttering the words that were to dissolve Han's misconceptions about life and earth. He said:

"Money, fame, and success are but fleeting illusions which disappear at any moment when you are not looking. Regardless of whether you won or lost today in the theater of war, an unforeseen order lies beneath the surface. There is a clear destiny in store for you and today it was to lose. There is no shame here. What happened was predetermined by the heavens; it has nothing to do with your personal aptitude. Just look back into history. Can you honestly say whose country this truly is? It belongs to the one who holds the power, yet this never lasts too long. Eventually rulers die, relinquishing what was never actually theirs. No country can ever be anyone's possession. Can't you see that?"

The Daoist thus reminded Han of a reality he had already seen in his own mind. Subconsciously, he had chosen the path leading away from the valley where his comrades fled. Swerving toward the mountains signified his departure from the mundane world. From a distance, he could clearly see that a country's power and fortune never lasted long and that his efforts on the battlefield were ultimately futile and meaningless. As the Daoist opened the window of his soul, Han was encouraged to abandon all ideas of fame and power in imperial service and instead step forward to the Dao, setting himself free. His ambitious nature began to dissipate as he began to awaken to Dao. Enveloped by this rare moment of complete reality, he respectfully entreated Master Donghua for guidance.

Han soon put his entire inquisitiveness and intellect toward his new path. He wanted to learn all the ways of maximizing *qi* to regain a healthy and lasting perspective. As he was ready to revise his life, the master gave him a detailed exposition on the path to immortality. "The key to attaining eternal life is refining your heart-mind into oneness by cultivation through meditation. It requires purging the heart-mind of irrelevant and random thoughts." Zhongli Han found this rather abstruse, so Donghua continued: "The heart-mind is the leader of the body, therefore it sits in the center. In order to rule your own destiny as the emperor rules his country, refining the heart-mind is essential and it is necessary to have a pure heart-mind free from distractions. There are no other secrets."

Han deeply thought about Donghua's advice and came to see that the Daoist had much more to offer than what was waiting for him back home. As far as his family was concerned, he was missing in action. Instead of returning home, he accordingly took up the path of enlightenment and became a student of the Dao.

Training began with breathing exercises for optimum health and to unravel all conditioned thinking patterns. As Han progressed, the Daoist also introduced him to sword play, which gave him the means to pierce through anything in his way: physically, spiritually, or psychologically. The sword technique he learned was the Green Dragon Sword, transmitted day and night until nothing was left to elucidate. Han's focus sharpened and his mind grew still; he came to experience the pure heart-mind. At this moment he turned to share his deep gratification but no one was there to receive it. He was alone. Master Donghua had vanished, never to return. But Han remained at the temple for several years.

The Tiger

After accomplishing much along the path, Han felt a growing desire to share his special knowledge and decided to leave the mountain. His first thoughts were to go back and teach his brothers who had watched over him as a child. He walked off the temple grounds and retraced his steps back to his hometown. As things became familiar, memories bounced off his motionless mind. His brothers almost did not recognize him, he was so different. Han wasted no time and offered his invitation. So impressed with their baby brother's reconditioned individuality, this was all the persuasion they needed. They all stepped on the road toward the mountains, looking forward to their new life.

Many days later the three brothers reached the foothills, where they were met by local villagers who alerted them of dangers ahead. Apparently a ferocious white tiger had maimed and killed a considerable number of people over the past week. The tiger's voracious appetite, they said, was fueled more from sport and gluttony than survival. It kept many mountain dwellers from returning home, fearing they would be next. The three brothers moved carefully forward, navigating their way in silence. They went deeper into the territory than others and soon saw the tiger just inside the mountain entryway, pacing back and forth as if deranged. Had his cubs been taken by humans? Had he lost a loved one to hunters? Was he an avenger seeking retribution? One could not be sure. But he needed to be dealt with immediately. If the locals waited for the tiger to leave of his own free will, he could return unannounced at anytime to terrorize and cause havoc.

Zhongli Han stepped forward into plain sight as his brothers grasped and reached for him, trying to pull him back to safety. Neither could stop him. The tiger caught wind of his advancement and flexed his sinews to test if Zhongli was serious. His Daoist-trained mind remained calm in the face of the tiger's boisterous growl; its sinister eyes could not intimidate him or rattle his spirit. He drew himself into a deep concentration and smoothly drew his sword to play out the Green Dragon Sword movements, blending the forces of heaven and earth. Priming itself for an attack, the tiger collected its force deep into its tail and prepared to pounce on its prey. The moment the tiger's *qi* uncoiled, Han ceased his fluctuation, focused his *qi*, and exploded into a bombastic yell, launching his sword to cut the maneater in two. This supernatural feat surprised even Han himself. It revealed the measure of his martial prowess: he was immortalized.

Femininity

In folk stories, a softer side of Han emerges, and he is the subject of many tales. Some tell of his descent from the heavens either as himself or dressed as a woman, yet always carrying a feathery fan and a peach of immortality. This feature matches the tendency among immortals of an altruistic nature. They often adopt different identities in various situations which called for either infiltration or gaining the favor and trust of others, all for the sake of people's safety and positive change in the world. The Eight Immortals each possess genuine gifts of power that help to heal human suffering; they often display mysterious skills as ice breakers to capture the onlookers' attention and curiosity.

Thus Li Tieguai appeared as a non-threatening, wise old man to infiltrate the Xinjiang military camp, then offered them a plan worthy of acceptance. His actions served both the best interest of Zhongli Han and the Xinjiang military without yet incapacitating the core functions of Han rule. The alternative would have more blood spilled and an inescapable military, non-spiritual future for Zhongli Han. Normally, choosing between the lesser of two evils is neither formidable nor inspiring, but Li Tieguai was able to save face on both sides by adopting resolutions that all parties could accept. Managing volatile situations such as this to everyone's benefit takes great foresight and capacity. In some instances it requires even taking on the appearance and heart of a woman. Li Tieguai's natural physiological characteristics make it difficult to assume this role, but Zhongli Han can do so quite readily.

Han's cross-dressing maneuvers made him a popular folk hero. The idea came to him from the experience that befriending people, especially women and children, required a delicate approach, something men often lacked. Being a stranger in town (as immortals, as travelers, often were) meant being suspicious; unfamiliar faces evoked a sense of insecurity, newcomers triggered defense mechanisms. Women, however new or strange, were often more easily accepted or at least met with less suspicion. After often being abused verbally, Zhongli Han thus began to tap into the more receptive side of his being.

But why would one go to such trouble? Why risk a heroic reputation just to get closer to people? The answer is that the effort is worth it as part of educating people in Daoism to keep it alive and spread it at the grassroots level of society: teaching the Way is a key objective of the Eight Immortals. It forms part of the continuing opening of people's hearts-minds. Generally, human beings at some point reach an age where they have personal thoughts based on information received from parents, schools, and the society as a whole. At this point, unless they are molded properly, the growth of their heart and mind can be stunted or closed. Submerged in folly, people disconnect from their original link with heaven. Releasing yin essence and impersonating women, immortals can radiate a softer, gentler, and nurturing energy, becoming able to attract the audience and transmit the Dao.

Most learning in the early stages of education, both at home and at school, is provided by female teachers. Daoists, too, have noted that women have a great impact on early schooling; they explain this with the natural qualities of yin-*qi* and with women's inherent patience. Feminine support usually provides an indispensable soil for children, allowing them to nourish their roots. Male sunlight is also crucial to strong rearing, but if children are overexposed to it at an early age they may easily be scorched. The immortals' good intentions to reach children at a time when they can still be influenced thus leads to actions of wisdom and compassion.

Another feminine figure in the Chinese pantheon, even more popular than Zhongli Han, is Guanyin or Guanshiyin, the bodhisattva of compassion. The name translates the Sanskrit Avalokitesvara, which means the one who "listens to the voices of the [suffering] world." A major figure in the ancient Buddhist pantheon, the deity arrived early in China and has been widely worshiped ever since. Contrary to popular belief, Guanyin is actually a man. Sometime during the Tang dynasty, religious artwork began to show him more and more as a woman, which has led to the popular consensus that Guanyin is a woman, the Goddess of Mercy. The metamorphosis is usually associated with the outreach, rescue, and support Guanyin provides, but the physical changes are attributed to specific practices, primarily the cultivation of yin-*qi*. Never imagining a man to be so kind and gentle, people began to draw parallels between Guanyin's spirit and motherly love. It is said, "Compared to a mother's love, all other loves are secondary," and many seeking conception pray before sculptures of Guanyin holding a baby.

Lü Dongbin, the Supreme Swordsman

Lü Dongbin was born in Shanxi province during the late Tang dynasty, the golden age of Chinese history. He is the most famous, important, and influential representative of the Eight Immortals. Being the core figure, the movements and configurations of the Eight Immortals' Revolving Sword tend to be connected mainly to him, and he is credited with creating the majority of the set, while the other immortals supplemented it. Celebrated historically as a supreme swordsman, Lü's legacy yet goes beyond the martial realm. Hailed as a Daoist saint, he was a poet and excellent writer, to whom extensive works on Daoist history and spiritual cultivation are attributed.

In addition, his interpretations of ancient texts helped spur the growth of Daoism in what came to be regarded as the renaissance of Chinese religion and culture under the Song. His scholarly efforts include works on poetry, herbalism, qigong, and martial arts. Several books expounding Daoisms systems for the attainment of health, longevity, and immortality are also credited to him. Completely versed in the teachings of Confucianism and Buddhism, he combined them with Daoism and formulated the foundational teachings of the Complete Reality school, whose followers honor him as one of six founding patriarchs.

Lü Dongbin's legendary reputation as a swordsman came from a strong foundation of specialized training. He directly inherited the most eminent secret Daoist sword practices, developed by highly saintly and perfected masters, including the likes of Laozi, Zhuangzi, and Sunzi—the latter best known as the author of the strategic military masterpiece, the *Sunzi bingfa* (Master Sun's Art of War). Absorbing the essence of the past, Lü created his own practice called the Dynamic Vast Sword, a technique to control inherent *qi* and generate enough natural force to expand and contract space, time, and matter. After its conception, the essence of this sword practice came to form the basis of the Eight Immortals' Revolving Sword.

Sexual Practice

Lü Dongbin is particularly honored for three great achievements—sword cultivation, internal alchemy, and literary works—but he is also the subject of controversy regarding sexual dual cultivation. His support of sexual practice as a means of spiritual advancement attracted the scrutiny and criticism from both Daoist and Buddhist circles, who considered celibacy as the only way to enlightenment or immortality. Conserving *jing*, the primordial essence within the body that appears as sexual fluids, had always been an important requirement for the alchemical process, leading both to self-preservation and increased supernatural power. Monks and many practitioners thus see sexual intercourse as imbued with physical and emotional attachments, presenting a dichotomy they find impossible to conquer. They follow the thought expressed in Laozi's words, "humanity and universe united in oneness." Oneness as a concept in practice requires a mind free from all desires, since Dao always seeks an empty vessel to dwell.

Lü Dongbin's brilliance, on the other hand, allowed him to separate himself psychologically from the lustful and dangerous aspects of sexual intercourse. He also created a new theoretical standpoint for his position, evolving the Daoist concept of following the "way of nature." His central theory, which serves as the basis for his acceptance of sexual practice, centers on the interaction of yin and yang as a means of producing increased yang energy. The order of creation as described in Daoist texts and in concordance with nature works by yin preceding yang, therefore, yang is born of yin. The beginning of all creation is called nothingness, emptiness, or the non-ultimate (*wuji*). This void belongs to yin. The first verse of Laozi's philosophical treatise, the *Daode jing*, states: "Nothingness is the name of the beginning of heaven and earth." Following this, Lü Dongbin formulated theory that absorbing yin-*qi* from the female to create and strengthen yang-*qi* in the male is in fact in accordance with the Daoist goal of returning to Pure Yang. It was not a highly popular understanding.

As Lü Dongbin continued his research, he closely examined Daoist and Buddhist scriptures and found some interesting information about the immortals of antiquity. Laozi, a sage of the highest decree, discouraged marriage and having children because of the inevitable distractions of raising and maintaining an expanding family. They would hinder focus and concentration and take up much time, making it nearly impossible to cultivate oneself. By the same token he did not support divorce for moral reasons. Still, he did not explicitly mention sex itself as being damaging to spiritual cultivation. Similarly, the great sage Confucius, his student, was married and still managed to attain the Dao of heaven. Sakyamuni Buddha, too, was married and fathered a child in his early manhood. Although he taught celibacy after enlightenment, his earlier sexual encounters quite possibly could have enhanced his *qi*, supplementing his quest for perfected wisdom. Lü Dongbin, looking at these sages, concluded that even the highest immortals might have benefited from sexual energetic exchanges. Then he went on to examine nature, which to Daoists is the ultimate, true teacher and soon demonstrated that only inside an empty vessel—the sacred space of a woman's uterus—could life come into existence. On this basis he formulated specific alchemical techniques and outlined methods to counter the risk of depletion.

Controversy

Lü Dongbin's ideas about sexual practice were misconstrued by religious administrators, who accused him of challenging Daoism to condone marriage and sexual intercourse. This was never his agenda. On the contrary, he retorted, attesting that in nature animals engaged in sexual intercourse without marriage so why shouldn't human beings? Standing firm, he maintained that sexual alchemy was a legitimate method for returning to the Dao. This led to Daoism becoming a political target for the representatives of other Chinese religions, who attacked its ethical standards and tried to discredit Lü while also hoping to gain political favor and increase their following. Although one of Daoism's highest initiates, he faced a barrage of critical opponents questioning his loyalty and character. He was labeled a lustful maverick.

Lü Dongbin was also censured for his love of fine rice wine. Not only consuming his favorite vintage when writing, he used rice wine instead of water to dilute his ink and dip his brush. After finishing his intense outpours of streams of consciousness, he would drink the ink-blackened wine from the inkstone, then grab his best friend, the Precious Sword, and express how he conceived life and Dao in physical movement. He thus manifested the balance of yin and yang, thought and body, duly leading on to a state of oneness. He apparently could do what others could not without being subjected to harm, exhibiting immunity to even the most hazardous habits that a monk could possibly have and gathering inspiration even from drunken revels.

Despite his many critics, Lü Dongbin was a rational, well mannered, and highly cultured individual with an unwavering determination. He continued to enhance his yang-qi with the regular practice of dual cultivation and eventually managed to make sexual alchemy into an acceptable part of Daoist cultivation. The development of his "100-day practice with 100 women" has been shrouded in secrecy for centuries, but is still practiced today and seen as a superior method. It requires a specialized qigong background using the Five Centers Facing Heaven as a starting point. The exercise trains the internal control mechanisms of the viscera, allowing adepts to redirect sexual fluids into a cycle of refinement rather than allowing them to disperse and flow out. Once the male has absorbed and ingested female essence, he refines it into yang-qi through fire-and-water alchemy, sword practice, and qigong.

Lü Dongbin was very good at separating his emotions from the practice. As a rule, because of emotional dangers, practitioners of dual cultivation must undergo years of preparation both mentally and physically, and originally the practice was reserved for practitioners in the middle and latter stages of life to replenish their waning life-force. It allowed those past their prime the opportunity to restore their vitality, making maturity the greatest asset of the practice. This was Lü's ultimate quest, since he himself did not join Daoism until middle age.

The Yellow Millet Dream

Lü Dongbin, then known as Lü Yan, was a fine scholar on his way to the country's capital to take part in the civil service exams for the Tang government. An accomplished scholar, fully versed in the Confucian classics, he hoped to pass the official examination. He had high aspirations of one day serving the emperor as leading advisor in the position of Heavenly Teacher.

On the way he stopped to rest at a roadside tavern in the town of Chang'an. Sitting at a table enjoying his tea, he noticed an older gentleman with an unusual lightness of being. He walked over to converse with him; they engaged in idle chit chat, then discussed poetry, a favorite passion of Lü Yan. The stranger was impressed with his zeal for the subtle nuances of verse and wrote a poem on one of the tavern's walls:

> Perched or reclined, holding my vessel of wine,
> My two eyes perceive not the imperial city
> But the celestial zones.
> One with heaven and earth, I remain nameless.
> Nonexistent I wander,
> In the mundane world alone.

Lü Yan immediately recognized the Daoist undertones of the stanza and asked the stranger if he was a Daoist. The stranger laughed out loud, as if this was completely absurd yet did not deny it. He soon invited Lü to his nearby room, where they continued to talk and Lü bared his soul, discussing his goals and dreams of government service. In reply, the stranger suggested that following the Dao might be an alternative worth considering. He outlined the heavy toll of government service, stressed the rules he would have to observe, and stressed the lack of freedom. However, he could not persuade Lü, who remained oblivious to the stranger's message and fixated only on taking the examination and his projected success. Adamant about his aim of personal advancement, he drove himself to the point of fatigue. Meanwhile, the stranger placed some yellow millet on the stove.

The heated discussions and the warmth of the fire made Lü drowsy and he soon fell into a deep sleep.

As the yellow millet cooked, Lü Yan began to dream vividly. His vision carried him to the imperial examinations where he scored highest. No longer a candidate, he received a good position as junior secretary. Opportunities opened before him, and with each passing year he continued to climb the administrative ladder, occupying many important posts. He also married twice, entering wealthy family circles with immense political influence. He raised several children, who all married successfully and prospered in their own right. Every aspect of his life blossomed.

He reached the pinnacle of his career when appointed to the rank of Heavenly Teacher, i.e., prime minister. The direct link to the emperor, he had great responsibilities and worked hard, keeping the office with all its power and privileges for over a decade. Then, he was accused of making an error in his calculations. Unbecoming of a Heavenly Teacher, he argued that the mistake was not his own but that he had been sabotaged. Without proof, his words fell on deaf ears; he was relieved of his duties, and found guilty of the crime. Things went downhill from there.

As his assets were confiscated, his family members were separated, exiled to remote places across China, never to be seen again. He was deeply shocked by the unimaginable turn of events. Exiled himself, with just the clothes on his back, he wandered about aimlessly in the dead of winter, banished from the empire he had so loyally served for over forty years. Starving, alone, and freezing, Lü Yan wept like a baby. His soul diminished by sorrow, he laid himself down ready to take his last breath—when he suddenly woke up and found himself back next to the stranger. At this precise moment, after a mere half hour later, the yellow millet was fully cooked. As they began their meal, the stranger spoke to the still numb Lü: "The yellow millet's cooked; your solitary dream and imminent danger have passed."

Amazed and convinced of the stranger's Daoist powers, Lü Yan stuttered his pledge to follow him into the Dao. The stranger said: "My name is Zhongli Han. I reside in the high Zhongnan mountains where I cultivate the way of heaven. Life is but a dream: full of ups and downs, joys and miseries. Now that you have experienced this for yourself, is it enough to be sincerely interested in the truth?"

Lü Yan lowered his eyes to think about this. When he looked up again, the immortal had disappeared. Lü's hesitation, however slight, had exposed his reservations, and Zhongli Han decided to step back and test his quality of mind.

Being Tested

Lü Yan's life had been radically altered. He avoided the road to the capital and headed toward the mountains, hoping to find a Daoist teacher as a guide. After several months of wandering, he managed to find someone willing to instruct him. The mountain dweller imparted seven magic sword movements to him which he practiced day and night for several years. As he made great strides in sword cultivation, his *qi* stabilized and his mind sharpened like that of a sword's blade. This in turn gave Zhongli Han a good reason to reappear. Still not totally convinced of Lü's commitment, he decided to subject him to a series of ten trials. The Daoist wizard craftily entered Lü's consciousness, creating various images and scenarios that were each designed to challenge Lu Yan's will, character, and better judgment.

The first challenge he experienced in this manner was that he saw himself returning home after a long day's work to find every member of his family dead from the plague. Undisturbed, he followed the natural course of events and prepared a traditional funeral for all his loved ones. During the funeral rites his kindred lay in their caskets calm and serene, then suddenly rose back to their feet. Seeing this, Lü realized that life was an illusion and death was the true awakening.

Next, he had a vision of being in a busy marketplace where he was scheduled to meet a local merchant to finalize a business deal. He soon discovered that the merchant was reneging on the previous terms of the agreement. Clearly understanding the deceitful ways of the world, Lü decided he wanted no part of it, turned around, and walked away—leaving his merchandise, money, and afflictions behind.

The third ordeal came from a beggar. One evening while celebrating the New Year, Lü heard a rap on the door. He opened it and found a poor wandering beggar asking for money to buy some food. Without hesitation, he reached into his pocket and handed the beggar an offering. Unsatisfied, the beggar stood in the door, requesting a larger sum. Lü apologized and gave him more gold. With a gleam in his eyes, the pauper turned around. He was laughing cheerfully as he walked away, having given Lü an opportunity to be unattached to material wealth.

In the blink of an eye, Lü next found himself a herdsman in the countryside, guiding a flock of sheep through a mountain pass. Suddenly he spotted a hungry tiger leaping from the heights, ferociously hungry eyes fixed on the helpless herd. Although totally unarmed, Lü Yan ran forward to stand between him and his sheep. This valiant effort caused the tiger to stop in its tracks and timidly retreat: he had been defeated by Lü's courage.

In the fifth trial he saw himself as a recluse in the quietude of the mountains. One evening a beautiful young woman came to his door in search of shelter from the cold night. Lü cordially invited her inside his cozy cottage. The attractive women soon became flirtatious, showing warmth and affection toward the hermit scholar and hoping to make love. He was flattered and intrigued, but politely refused the allurement and retired to his study.

Further Trials

Continuing the series of trials, Lü Yan next imagined himself coming home from work to find his humble abode ransacked, with nothing left to show for his hard work. Instead of getting angry and depressed, he grabbed his gardening tools to collect herbs and vegetables from the nearby forest for dinner. While digging, he unearthed several gold pieces, a great deal more valuable than his original belongings. Having realized, however, the trouble that comes from wealth, he buried the gold pieces again—even deeper so that no one would ever find them.

Gold continued to follow him. One day he purchased two bronze vessels and returned home to polish their surface, when he discovered that they were made of gold underneath the bronze plating. He promptly returned them to the merchant who had obviously made a mistake. The storekeeper was thankful for his honesty, refunded his money, and gave him two other vessels at no charge.

The eighth test put him in a situation involving a Daoist wizard. Lü Yan saw himself inside a closed chamber, standing before a table with several herbal concoctions. They all seemed perfectly fine, except for the one being offered to him. The Daoist handed him a cup with a watery liquid that reeked of deadly poisons. Surrendering completely to the Dao, Lü swallowed the liquid. Instead of killing him, it sent him into an airy and delightful state.

Next he had to contend with the forces of nature. He found himself guiding a boat down a river when a big storm rolled in. It caused massive swells, the rising waves threatening to capsize the vessel. Unable to manage the small ship any longer, he abandoned the helm and sat down quietly. He closed his eyes and focused his mind, imagining himself as the eye of the storm, and deeply accepted impermanence. Sometime later, he opened his eyes to find clear blue skies and calmly flowing currents.

His last test required the most serious sacrifice: his very life. Sitting peacefully in his house, Lü Yan found himself surrounded by a legion of ghastly ghosts and monstrous demons, wielding an array of ungodly weapons. The creatures threatened, poked, and prodded him in the attempt to disrupt his tranquil state. They were unsuccessful. Then a hellish lictor appeared, getting the demons to roll out a rack of torture. It had a captured soul tied to it, who had been condemned to eternal punishment. The prisoner addressed Lü: "I have a grievance! It is because of you that I am trapped here. You murdered me in a past life, so now I suffer this hell. You have to bail me out!" Lü Yan immediately agreed and offered his own life and soul in atonement for the crime he committed in a previous life. But just before he could leap into the abyss of hell, a loud clap sounded from above, followed by a voice commanding the mischievous phantoms to disperse. The whole scene dissolved into thin air.

Instead, there was Zhongli Han, laughing happily and congratulating him on his resounding success. "There is no doubt you will attain immortality with your strong ethics and genuine wisdom," he said. "In three thousand years, after completing your service on earth, you will recover the purity of heaven." Lü Yan wholeheartedly agreed to obey the orders of the Jade Emperor and to remain in the earthly realm until his mission was accomplished. This was all Zhongli Han needed to hear. Smiling with approval, he led him into the secret realm of esoteric knowledge and on the road to spiritual awakening.

To be initiated into the tightly sealed circles of Daoists and Buddhists, it is mandatory to pass a series of tests of the nature of one's heart and sincerity of one's pledges. As illustrated in Lü's ten ordeals, these trials may involve any number of angles and situations. The ancient knowledge of the sages cannot be easily shared, to avoid supernatural powers falling into the wrong hands. People are as changeable as the weather, and extreme testing serves to confirm their strong determination and solid inner strength. Having to drink poison or being asked to perform deeds that cost one's life are acts of trust. They prove beyond a shadow of a doubt that one has the commitment needed for attaining Dao. "Practice is not easy," as the saying goes.

Most historical records agree that Lü Dongbin learned from the masterful Zhongli Han. Daoist sources, too, accept that Han initiated Lü, but claim that he was not his main teacher, instead merely setting him on the path and teaching him introductory skills and the correct protocol of the Daoist order. He also introduced him to his major master, the Perfected Fire Dragon (Huolong zhenren), from whom he received his exclusive sword and alchemical training. According to the White Cloud Temple, there is another story which epitomizes the unfolding of Lü Dongbin's sword mastery. According to this, he is already an accomplished sorcerer, but finds himself pegged in an impossible situation: he must deal with unworkable demands or else risk serious punishment from Guanyin.

The Coin-Throwing Contest

One day while traveling through Zhaozhou town, Lü Dongbin found himself in a frantic sea of people moving swiftly across town, yelling over and over: "Something horrible has happened! Something horrible has happened!" He followed the people to the bank of a nearby river, lined with lifeless bodies, and observed them mourning their dead. Curious, he asked an old man exactly what had happened. "Yesterday," he explained, "the ferry that carries the locals across the river capsized, resulting in three deaths. Today, the river has claimed the lives of eight more. The rapids are producing powerful whirlpools, and innocent lives are being lost."

The scene touched Lü Dongbin's heart. He walked along the river, deeply saddened by the tragic events. An inner dialogue commenced as he searched for a solution to the dangerous rapids. In his mind's eye, he could see a bridge built across the water, eliminating the need for a ferry and thus resolving local fears and worries. He reassured himself that his vision would become a reality.

Lü Dongbin's pensive stroll had taken him a distance from the accident site. Gradually, he became aware of a faint commotion. He raised his eyes to see where it was coming from and noticed an inn just ahead on the riverside. The closer he came, the more the sounds turned into explosive uproars of laughter. He was bewildered. He could not comprehend how people could celebrate and have parties when there had just been this calamity.

Lü entered the public house to investigate. Huddled around an open bay facing the river, there was a cluster of local officials and wealthy merchants, tossing gold and silver coins outside. They were aiming for a gorgeous woman, sitting in a small boat anchored off the bank of the turbulent river. An old helmsman stood next to the boat baiting the crowd: "Hit this beauty with a coin and she is yours to marry." Many men heaved handfuls of tokens as the others cheered—all except Lü Dongbin. He moved flowingly through the assembly to peer more closely at the lady. Carefully inspecting her with his powerful inner vision, Lü Dongbin recognized her at once: she was in fact Guanyin, while the chief auctioneer was none other than the Buddha's brother. Lü Dongbin was repulsed. He found the entire charade highly insensitive and not at all compassionate. Especially regarding it in contrast with the deaths just having occurred in the town, he was disgusted with the bodhisattva's arrogance and inability to see the suffering of others.

Lü Dongbin turned to face a young man eagerly watching the contest: "What is your name?"

"I am called Wei Tou."

"Would you like the lady for your wife?"

"What? Are you kidding? Of course I want to marry her. She is so beautiful."

Lü Dongbin encouraged him to try his luck but the young man said: "No can do. I am saving my money to build a bridge over this river."

"Don't worry, we will use my money."

Lü then led the young man to the second-tier balcony. With coins in both hands, he started to recite a spell to break Guanyin's protective shield. The Buddha's magic had prevented all objects from penetrating her aura, while the gold and silver coins piled up nicely in her boat. Lü handed the coins to Wei Tou, prompting him to throw the money. He did so with reluctance and was dumbstruck when the coins actually hit and the crowd of onlookers cheered with elation.

The Stone Bridge

At this precise moment, Zhongli Han arrived at the inn. Immediately, his uncanny abilities sensed that something was wrong. He had come to meet with Lü Dongbin and now felt his fellow Daoist in some unforeseen trouble, maybe a mishap he would be held accountable.

Lü Dongbin was perfectly content with his actions while Guanyin was infuriated, scanning the room until she discovered his presence. Displeased by his unsolicited involvement, the bodhisattva ascended into the clouds, transforming back into true form. She then ordered her brother to escort Lü and his co-conspirators into the celestial cloud chamber. Both Lü and

Zhongli went to face the bodhisattva, Zhongli arguing Lü's defense and pleading that the gods might excuse his misdeed. Guanyin was contemplating the matter when Lü decided to speak up himself: "I have done nothing wrong in attempting to find you a husband. I know your Buddha-heart is pure and sincere. I was merely hastening to assist the fulfillment of your wishes." Lü remarks, of course, were close to being contemptuous, audaciously trying to justify his actions as a good deed.

Guanyin was vexed by his attitude and responded with wrath: "To argue with me is futile. I turned myself into a beautiful woman to raise money, so people could build a bridge across the river. You have ruined my plans. Do you realize what you have done?"

Lü Dongbin apologized, pleading ignorance, and reaffirmed his indifference. But Guanyin insisted that it was too late. There was only one chance for Master Lü to redeem himself: "You have until sunrise tomorrow to have a bridge constructed across this river or else you suffer the consequences!"

"I understand," Lü replied.

Guanyin duly vanished. Lü began to laugh. Zhongli Han was surprised and worried by his friend's reaction: "What are you laughing about? This is no joke. If by sunrise tomorrow you have not produced a bridge, you are going to be severely punished. This is no laughing matter."

As if unmoved by the magnitude of the situation, Lü replied nonchalantly: "This has been an eventful day. I need to get some rest. When I awake, I will deal with the task at hand."

Night followed the day and the moon rose in the western sky. Lü was sound asleep on a large stone. Zhongli tried to wake him. When he remained motionless, he nervously began to yell at the sleeping Daoist, urging him to rise. Lü opened his eyes and said calmly: "Don't worry my friend. Everything will be all right." Then he closed his eyes again and resumed his rest.

At midnight, Lü finally awoke from his stream of magical dreams. His mind was clear, and he made his way over to an assortment of boulders that covered the landscape of a nearby mountain. Drawing his magic sword, he began to strike the boulders one by one. Magically, each rock changed into a mountain goat, until they made up a large flock. He channeled them into two lines and maneuvered them down to the river. Along the way, the bodhisattva's brother appeared to check on his progress. Stunned to see him standing among a flock of goats in the middle of the night, he strongly reiterated Guanyin's warnings. "Your time is running out. What on earth are you doing with this herd? If the bridge is not finished by morning, you will be punished."

Remaining stoic, Lü Dongbin proceeded with the herd toward the river. There he guided the two lines directly into the water until they were all wading in the breaking waters. Once they were all properly aligned, he walked waist-deep into the rapids and drew his sword. Striking the lead goat on the head, all the mountain goats changed back into stones, which formed the foundation of the bridge. He then went back to the mountain to repeat the procedure several times more, until the bridge took shape from several layers of mountain stones. When morning came, the eastern sun gave its blessing, shining brightly on the newly erected bridge. Lü's martial prowess reached a new level; he even surpassed Guanyin's skills—a milestone in his cultivation.

Wondrous Feats

By mundane standards, earthly objects such as mountain stones seem impossible to move without the use of extensive machinery, such as a crane, rope and pulley, and cart. Even with this type of equipment, such structures as the pyramids in Egypt cannot be reconstructed to this day. Engineers have speculated for centuries about the methods by which they could possibly have been built, and people in general have looked to the heavens for answers about the mysteries of the ancient civilizations. Some have suggested that higher beings, advanced beyond worldly standards, have aided human evolution and technological advancement. Daoists, however, believe that this is not beyond the realm of possibility. In fact, they have many records of marvelous feats accomplished by the Eight Immortals and other sages, who have traveled to starry cultures beyond our own to learn their technology and ways of spiritual cultivation. To do so, they used Daoist esoteric methods as well as the secret codes of the *Yijing*.

Another theory applied to the construction of marvels such as the ancient pyramids and Lü's stone bridge is the numeric language of nature which makes up the fabric of the *Yijing*. The text has organized the physical world according to laws of change and transformation, described it as the natural flow of numbers and mutable calculations. Every level of life, beginning with plants, minerals, and animals, has its specially assigned number. If one is versed in the numerical combinations, possesses an exceptional store of *qi*, and has good rapport with nature, one can unlock limitless capabilities over and above the laws of physics.

Dr. Wu's teacher, Master Du, once displayed this level of practice to his young apprentice. The two were out on a walk observing nature when they happened upon three large rocks. Master Du said: "These three rocks belong to the White Cloud Temple." Little Wu wasn't totally clear on the meaning behind this statement, so Master Du decided to demonstrate. The old master stood opposite the rocks and turned his body to a forty-five degree angle. Striking a Qigong posture, he addressed them in a numeric language, then explained: "In nature, each living thing has its own numeric code, including humans. Self cultivation enables humans to merge into oneness with the universe, establishing a profound relationship with nature. If versed in the numeric formulas of the *Yijing*, the spirits of these life forms respond to our commands." He concluded the discussion with the promise that by the following morning, the three large stones would find their own way inside the gates of the White Cloud Temple.

Although merely a child, Master Wu would not believe anything unless he saw proof, and he would not accept lessons without first investigation. The next morning he awoke bright and early, and went out to search the monastery grounds for the three rocks. Low and behold, as his teacher had promised, they had in fact arrived. But rather than being amazed, he tried to figure out the most logical method of their transport. Like a crime investigator, he looked for a cart or wagon, but found none. He checked the dusty grounds for track and drag marks, and found nothing. Determined to discover the truth, he proceeded to run outside the gates, looking at the rocks' original location in the forest. Again there were no signs of any physical activity. All the way back home, he kept on looking for evidence, but there was none. When he reached the White Cloud Temple, his teacher was waiting with a smile: "It is true and there is no need to disbelieve. Your mind is limitless."

The Emperor's Formula

The herbal combination known as the Emperor's Formula for Supplementing the Heart (Tianwang buxin dan) is an old and multi-use recipe related to three traditions: Daoism, classical Chinese medicine, and the oral tradition.

The position of the formula in the tradition is not unlike that of the famous novel *Xiyouji*, known in the West as "The Journey to the West" or "Monkey," written by Wu Cheng'en in the late Ming dynasty. The novel features a character named sun Wukong, the Monkey King. Brashly arrogant, he is a Daoist wizard who escorts a Buddhist monk in pursuit of sacred scriptures and gets into a lot of trouble in both fantastic antics and heroic feats. Encrypted in the text are secrets of Daoist internal alchemy. Daoists, however, believe that the original source of this text is the record of Qiu Chuji's journey to Gengghis Khan, also called *Xi-youji* and translated into English by Arthur Waley as *Travels of an Alchemist*. How can we know what is true? There is an original manuscript documenting Qiu's undertakings which predates Wu Cheng'en by over 300 years.

One day, when Master Wu was at the Beijing Medical Institute, he engaged in a conversation with his professor about the true origin of the Emperor's Formula. Master Wu shared with his instructor that the White Cloud Temple has records according to which Lü Dongbin was its original creator. Based on the professor's lifetime of study and research, he had never heard this and was very doubtful. Undeniable, concrete proof would be needed. Master Wu said he could deliver such evidence. The next day, he escorted his professor as the guest of the White Cloud Temple to catch a rare glimpse of the Daoist archives, which are rarely if ever opened to outsiders. Once inside, he presented him with the original manuscript, handwritten by Lü Dongbin and explained to his visitor more details about the legendary recipe.

He expounded on several procedures not currently found in medical records, such as milling the natural ingredients with a large amount of water. He then discussed the wide spectrum of diseases to which the formula could be applied. His professor was surprised, since he had not realized the formula's vast effectiveness and versatility. He asked why the original recipe had a stronger impact on diseases than its current TCM (Traditional Chinese Medicine) versions.

Master Wu explained that this was due to the modern lack of the primary ingredient known as cinnabar (*jusha*), which Daoists had deliberately eliminated from the outsiders' version of the recipe for safety purposes. Cinnabar is a mineral of high toxicity, due to the abundance of lead it contains. It is thus a potential poison, and as such is considered too risky for untrained practitioners and modern medicinal doctors to prescribe: they might lay themselves open to malpractice lawsuits. Still, Daoists still use it in its original version, including cinnabar, but only under controlled circumstances and within its own organizational structures. They also still follow Lü Dongbin's original manual which has a step-by-step detoxification method and use precise techniques to refine the cinnabar to make it medicinally beneficial. They adhere rigidly to these steps and prevent untrained practitioners from using the formula.

The first step is to increase the cinnabar's strength by burying it underground. The longer the duration before unearthing the cinnabar, the redder it becomes, indicating a higher potency. The second step is to substantially reduce the lead content, so that it can be ingested safely into the bloodstream. This process, as mentioned above, involves vast amounts of water; it also necessitates the use of tofu which assimilates the poisonous lead component. And it works with the *Yijing* calculation of seven times seven (forty-nine) in determining the number of days needed for cinnabar purification.

The process is as follows. Beginning with a block of tofu, the top center portion is carefully scooped out. The cinnabar is then placed inside the carved tofu bowl. Afterwards, the removed section of tofu is replaced, resealing the block with the mineral inside. The tofu is then steamed continuously, round the clock, for forty nine days. Water is added as needed and the fire is never extinguished. Any disruption will abort the experiment: the process has to be started over. Every stage in the detoxification is crucial.

When steamed, the tofu's absorbent and assimilative qualities are activated, thereby drawing out the lead toxins. Daoists also use this method to cleanse precious metals and jade, but for lesser periods.

Following the steaming, the cinnabar is withdrawn from the tofu, packed in ice, and frozen for seven days. This allows it to contract and helps to squeeze out any remaining toxic constituents. When finished, the frozen cinnabar is taken out and placed under continuously running water for another seven days, preferably a natural waterfall, river, or stream for the final purging of impurities. Having gone through three mercurial forms of water—gas, ice, and liquid—is then ground into a powder that is deemed lead-free. This process echoes the Great Ultimate (Taiji), similar to Laozi's explanation of the yin and yang of the dragon sword described in the introduction above. Steam is the rising of yang-*qi* into the heavens; ice is the transitional stage in the clouds; water as flowing over the cinnabar is the return of yin-*qi* to rivers and oceans. There are some slightly different other theories in Daoism, but they basically follow the same water way of *qi*, nature's original purification system.

The importance of the formula in Daoism can be seen from its position in the White Cloud Temple's apothecary: it contains 930 herbal concoctions, classified according to greater and lesser. The greater group consists of 560 recipes; the lesser has 370. The formula ranks as number one in the combined divisions; it also serves as the source for approximately seventy percent of Daoist herbal prescriptions. While the heart of the recipe remains the same, secondary herbs can be modified by adding or subtracting from the original construct to tailor it to individual cases and seasonal weather patterns. This approach matches Lü Dongbin's own application of the formula over a millennium ago.

Today, because of the complex purification process described, people don't really use cinnabar in the Emperor's Formula despite its proven healing powers. Master Wu in his life as a monk and a practicing physician has personally witnessed its effectiveness, seeing how monks in the White Cloud Temple were taking it regularly to maintain optimal health with special emphasis on care for the heart. There have hardly been any heart-related problems in the White Cloud Temple over the centuries, especially among those who included cinnabar in their diet.

Even beyond the monastery, in China, Master Wu's use of the Formula has led to spectacular results. Over thirty years of clinical practice, he has applied it in many severe cases, such as cancer, Alzheimer's, and epilepsy. On one occasion, he was treating a patient with cancer in the sinuses and brain. He approached the situation with standard medical techniques tailored specifically for brain cancer, but after several treatments the patient's condition had hardly improved and there was no pain relief. Since the cancer was in its latter stages of progression, with the patient's consent, Dr. Wu prescribed the Emperor's Formula, including cinnabar. After even one prescription, a major symptom disappeared and the patient was again able to speak—prevented earlier due to extreme swelling in his neck. As soon as he took the herbs, his inflamed area shrank and speech became again possible. As this medicine gives hope, extends life, alleviates pain, and helps in the latter stages of life, maybe modern physicians and patients should consider accepting the risk of taking it.

Martial Training

Besides its positive effects on terminal illness, cinnabar can singularly contribute to longevity. The clarified mineral acts as a preservative by slowing down the decomposition process of cells. In ancient times, the emperors' tombs were purposely lined with it to delay decay. Bodies thus preserved have remained intact even after centuries or even millennia. To accomplish the same outcome in the living, Daoist have ingested cinnabar and thereby fortified their bodies. The practice not only enhances health and extends the life expectancy, but is also essential to reaching higher levels of martial skills. This is illustrated in a story from Master Wu's childhood.

At the age of seven, Little Wu was already quite proficient in the practice of the Eight Immortals' Revolving Sword. Master Du encouraged his young acolyte every day to practice diligently in a courtyard right outside his quarters inside the monastery. At the same time, Little Wu also developed a skill called "light practice" (*qinggong*), a light, floating, or jumping form of gongfu.

Starting this practice from the age of five, he worked through the first level, which required the use of a large, round, and shallow basket woven from different tree branches, called *puoluo*. The basket contained red beans about as heavy as he himself was at the time, around twenty pounds. Everyday Little Wu would stand and walk on the outer rim of the basket, the beans in the center acting as a counter balance and preventing it from overturning. He continued for days and weeks until he reached absolute balance: no shuddering or wiggling of either himself or the basket. Once he achieved this, he would stand on the rim and reach inside to grab a handful of beans, placing them outside the *puoluo*. He would then continue the exercise until he reached the same level of balance and stillness with the lesser counterweight. After two years of practice there were no beans left in the basket and he could walk on the rim without overturning it. The practice also demanded taking a strict vegetarian diet, special herbs, and regular qigong exercise.

This accomplishment spawned extraordinary abilities in Master Wu. He had become light and could literally walk up walls and enter windows without making a sound. His speed had multiplied. Without effort, he could run down and catch a rabbit in full stride.

The next level of "light practice" again began with red beans inside the basket about as heavy as he himself. This time however, the monks strapped bricks around his ankles for added weight and challenge. As he accomplished the training, he was expected to leap from the ground into a tree and capture a bird before it could take flight, a technique his older Daoist brother had already perfected. He was duly called Sparrow Li (Yanzi Li San).

Master Wu used the same basket also as his bed, its round shape forcing him to sleep in the fetal position. This was important because, according to Daoist beliefs, sleeping in a curled posture curbs sexual desire and helps gather and store *qi* in the belly. Straightening the body during sleep allows *qi* to disperse and stimulates sexual yearning.

Fighting Experience

During Master Wu's childhood, every weekend in a nearby Beijing park, entertainers, artist, actors, vendors, and other skillful people assembled to show off their art in a boisterous, carnival setting. They came from all over China to display their unique skills for fame and fortune. Trained animal acts playing tricks, flame and sword swallowers were all popular attractions for the children. One day an acrobatic troop arrived, parading with a flag attached to a long bamboo pole waving in the breeze.

Little Wu was drawing water from a well, a forty-minute daily exercise that was a special assignment from his teacher. His younger Daoist brother rushed over to inform him that a band of acrobats had just camped outside the southern gate of the monastery. They were showing their skills, trying to taunt the monastics, themselves famous for physical and martial arts expertise, and hoping to start a competition. The monks usually ignored this type of display, seeing it as arrogant and troublesome.

Wu Baolin jokingly suggested that his younger brother debunk the troop by ripping down their flag. The novice refused, well aware of the monastic rules against such action and fearful of being severely scolded. Little Wu, on the other hand, was not as concerned with the regulations as he should have been and often exhibited provoking behavior. He had not yet realized the purpose and importance of law and order, and that Daoist rules were to protect, not to limit or control. When the younger monk suggested that he himself displace the banner, he accepted the challenge.

Using his newly developed "light practice" skills, he walked up the high wall surrounding the temple compound and perched on the top to observe the acrobats. Near the southern gate, right next to the wall was a tree about as high as the entertainers' flagpole. Without anyone noticing, he quietly jumped to the top of the tree and balanced there. Holding on to a single branch of the tree's crown, he waited carefully for the right moment, then soared out of the tree and snatched the banner off the pole. When he landed and dropped the flag on the ground, the entire troop was stunned and ceased all activities. The adults were incensed by his gesture and got ready to beat the little boy up. They circled around him, jumping up and down and tormenting him.

An elderly man approached, walking over from the troop's tent: "Your martial skills really are excellent. Our troop has celebrated two hundred years of history, and in all that time no one has ever taken down the flag. You are the first. What family do you come from?"

"I come from the White Cloud Temple."

Without replying, the man stepped closer to Little Wu and tapped him twice on the back of his head, between the Hundred Meeting (Baihui) and the Great Hammer (Dadui) points, then gave him a light slap on the back. Instantly, he was overcome by a splitting headache. Gripping his head with both hands and crying out in excruciating pain, he turned and ran for the temple gates. He has no personal memory of what came next, relying on the reports by his fellow students.

When the monks saw him in such great pain from his encounter, seven of them immediately left the gates to investigate and take revenge. Soon they were engaged in combat, easily defeating twenty or more acrobats. Standing about victorious, they saw the elderly man once more coming from the tent, walking toward them in a confrontational manner. The monks attacked, but after barely touching the elder, they were somehow thrown up and away as if by a powerful force. All seven were tossed away like amateurs and it became clear to all concerned that the old man was highly skilled, indeed.

The seven monks retreated to the monastery with various injuries of their own. They checked on Little Wu, watching him as he lay face down with his breath almost undetectable. He was dying. Everyone urged the senior master to notify his teacher, but he was reluctant because Master Du was at the time practicing deep meditation in a nearby cave. He had made it clear that no one was to disturb him for all of his forty-nine days of fasting and complete restructuring and turning of his mind. He was only half-way through and precious time would be wasted if he had to interrupt his practice. However, since it was a matter of life and death, the senior master sounded the special emergency sequence of drum and bell across the city.

Master Du appeared within minutes. After briefly standing over his young student to assess his condition, he turned him over on his back and touched several points on his body, reversing the *qi*-flow and eliminating the negative effects of the harmful strikes. According to the Daoists present, Master Du looked worried and annoyed for the first time ever. The sight of his student had disturbed his peaceful tranquility in a way no one had ever seen before. Uncharacteristic emotions welled up inside him, leading Master Du to release a loud, long, and thunderous yell. Then he literally flew toward the southern gate.

Once outside the gate, Master Du faced the group of acrobats. He requested to see the coward who had taken advantage of a seven-year-old boy. Shaken and surprised, the elderly leader stepped forward, cautiously maintaining a safe distance of about twenty feet from the ancient Daoist. By the fear in his eyes, the old man undoubtedly recognized the likes of Master Du and began to beg for forgiveness shamelessly. His plea was that he did not know the monks, and especially the boy, were his students. "Had I known," he repeated over and over again, "this would never have happened."

Remaining silent, Master Du stood like a mountain, slowly drawing *qi* into his body. Then suddenly and without any warning he stomped once on the bricks below his feet, smashing all of them within a three-foot radius. As the force surged through his body, the elderly man fell to the ground twenty feet away, but Master Du had used just a fraction of his ability. He then turned around and reentered the monastery to rescue Little Wu from the hands of death.

He used various *qi* techniques to revitalize the boy but also placed a large pill the size of a gum ball into his mouth: the original Emperor's Formula. Little Wu took a pill like this on an empty stomach every morning for twelve days, thereby recovering fully, but would pay a high price for his mistake. As Master Du told him and the others who had encountered the elderly man's *qi*-force, the man's force had permanently stunted their growth potential for light practice. From that point onward, they would never be able to improve their jumping skills and had better focus on other types of qigong or martial arts. Master Du was a hundred years old at this time. In his whole life, he had chosen only two students to train every morning in light practice, Li San and Wu Baolin. The latter's training ended right there.

A month after the incident, word arrived at the White Cloud Temple that the elderly man had passed away, due to multiple ruptures in the internal organs. Master Du then informed his students of his true identity: Master Guo had been the senior student of a famous mind boxing (*xingyi*) master by the name of Guo Yunshen. He warned everyone that sooner or later, his other students would seek revenge. When that happened, nobody was to give away his whereabouts.

Challenges

It came about three years later. Wang Xiangzhai had been Guo Yunshen's top student and later became a well-known fighter working as a bodyguard. After hearing of the death of his martial uncle, his master's other senior student, he quit his job to prepare for revenge. He then went to Beijing and publicly announced his challenge to Master Du Xinling. The old Daoist did not respond, but the broadcast reached Little Wu's parents who had known Wang Xiangzhai for a long time since he had once worked for their family. They considered him a genuine friend of the family and immediately tried to deter him from fighting, stating that the mishap was their son's fault. They apologized and pleaded for his forgiveness in an attempt to resolve the issue, but Wang Xiangzhai refused to listen to them, claiming that Little Wu had nothing to do with the affair. He sent out another challenge, to which Master Du Xinling did not respond either.

Tired of waiting, Wang Xiangzhai showed up at the White Cloud Temple, hoping to find his match. The monks were instructed beforehand to avoid any confrontation with Wang and continue with their regular duties. He walked around exploring the temple grounds until he found the abbot's living quarters. He stood at their door and loudly requested Master Du to emerge to discuss the rules of their inevitable engagement. There was still no reply. Perturbed by the silence, Wang Xiangzhai impatiently raised both hands with his palms facing the dwelling. Concentrating his inner resolve, he took three steps back, shattering the glass in the windows. Then he left, breaking every stone he stepped on.

One of Wu Baolin's older martial brothers was incensed by Wang Xiangzhai's disrespectful attitude and went to Master Du to respectfully ask for permission to somehow reciprocate or diffuse this aggression. Master Du gave his permission, but reminded him not to get into a fight.

At Wang's next visit to the monastery, he picked up where he left off. He strolled around the grounds, purposely cracking as many stones as possible under his feet. The older martial brother followed him, carrying two large barrels of water on his back and shoulders. Wherever he stepped, the stones did not just break, but were pulverized, exceeding Wang Xiangzhai's display. Wang was not intimidated but grew indignant. He left a suitcase in the monastery, indicating his lasting determination to return, then came back two days later.

At this point he came to a decision. Since Master Du refused to fight, he would accept the challenge presented by the martial brother and engaged him in a close competition. Both took a brick in the hand and reached them out until they met flush against one another, forming a bridge. The moment the bricks touched, both started to channel their internal energies into them to see whose brick would crumble first. In the end, Wang Xiangzhai's brick was reduced to pieces. He accepted defeat and pledged to come again in two years time to avenge his martial uncle's death. He then packed his bags and departed the monastery.

After Wang Xiangzhai's fires had been quelled, Master Du directed Little Wu to follow him and invite him back in for a meeting. The boy ran as fast as he could to catch up, but no matter how hard he tried, he could not reach him. Luckily Wang stopped to buy a fried sweet potato from a street vendor, and Little Wu caught up with him. Out of breath, he made a proposition: "If you buy me a sweet potato, I will arrange a meeting for you with my teacher." Wang turned to the vendor and bought an entire box of the morsels and carried it all the way back to the monastery.

Little Wu led Wang to a room at the rear of the temple where Master Du was waiting. The two seated themselves before the aged Daoist wizard and listened to his words. Wasting no time with formalities, he spoke: "I know you are the best student of Guo Yunshen and I respect and treasure your martial skills. Had I agreed to your challenge, you would have suffered greatly, but I did not want to hurt or ruin your level of attainment. Now that you have decided to leave our compound, I will show you the genuine martial practice of the White Cloud Temple."

Master Du then summoned a few of his students to bring a large sharpening stone and had them place a large block of tofu on it. Standing over the stone and lightly placing his palm on the tofu, Master Du inhaled deeply, and then exhaled forcefully, making a *hai* sound: the sharpening stone shattered while the tofu remained intact. Seeing this exhibition of internal power, Wang Xiangzhai dropped to his knees and respectfully asked to become Master Du's student. The master acknowledged his sincerity, but declined to accept him as a student of the Dao. Yet he gave him a rare and special gift. He placed twelve pills of the Emperor's Formula in his hands, explaining that he had to combine the fire of his heart with the water of his kidneys before he could reach true greatness in the martial arts. Once integrated, the two forces would join like heaven and earth, and the easiest way to get there was with the help of this medicine.

Persistent in his quest to become a Daoist, Wang Xiangzhai came back to the monastery regularly, hoping to be accepted into the monastic order. This was highly unlikely, since he had such a checkered past, especially during his wanderings as a bodyguard. According to the rules and regulations of the White Cloud Temple, murder was a non-negotiable obstacle. Instead, Master Du allowed him to visit the monastery to practice with his students on the 1st and 15th days of every lunar month. On these practice days, Wang indirectly learned many things from Master Du but he remained barred from the higher levels, mainly for his own future safety.

Master Wu and Wang soon agreed to exchange teachings on these days and over time came to call each other brothers. Thus Master Wu shared with him the complete set of static qigong postures known as "standing form" (*zhanzhuang*), which eventually became Wang's central practice. It increased his energetic power manifold, so that in later years he would be known as the "Invincible" among all the outer schools and around the globe. In return, Wang later gave Master Wu all his notes and writings, collected during a lifetime of martial study and research; he also taught him his ultimate qigong form, called "Great Accomplishment Fist" (Dacheng quan).

The Emperor's Formula developed by Lü Dongbin thus helped and enhanced the powers of many individuals throughout history. Although known primarily as a supreme swordsman, Lü Dongbin was seriously dedicated to the study of natural medicines. As a result, despite all the many names he has been called throughout history, he is known as Master of Medicines (Shuyao) among Daoists who see him as a doctor first and as a swordsman second.

Zhang Guolao, the Old Sorcerer

China's archives contain an ancient scripture called the *Yibai shenxian tongjian* (Comprehensive Mirror of the Hundred Spirit Immortals). Volume 6 describes the immortal Zhang Guolao, originally known as Zhang Guo, who first appeared under the Tang as an old-style sorcerer. His legendary status and official history both describe him as originating from the spirit of a white bat created at the time of creation who lived variously during the time of the ancient emperors. As an immortal under the Tang, he lived for several hundred years, thus the name Lao ("Old") as part of his name. The stories and visual materials, moreover, all show him with a white donkey as companion, which he could ride a thousand *li* (quarter miles) a day. Sometimes he would sit on it facing backwards, but he always after the journey would fold it up and place it into his sleeve or carrying case. Some stories note that the donkey was created from a picture to which Zhang Guolao added water, thereby magically turning it into a live animal. Feats such as these made him a famous magician. In addition, he also possessed a percussion instrument known as the bamboo-tube drum (*daoqingtong*) and also called the fish drum. It came with two small bamboo drumsticks and was commonly used to provide rhythmic underlining during storytelling, singing, and chanting. In the case of Zhang Guolao, however, it symbolized his proficiency to harmonize with the heavenly drum of Dao and thus became his main emblem.

Unlike traditional Daoist transmission through the male, Zhang Guolao received his alchemical arts training from a female goddess named Xuan Yu who was mentioned in the *Tongjian*, was a disciple of the creator goddess Nüwa, the Snail Maiden. Described variously as the spouse of Emperor Fu Xi or as his sister, her extraordinary beauty combined human features with those of a Dragon or a snail's tail. After the emperor passed on, she was known as Nühuang, the Empress. During her reign, Prince Gonggong, the Spirit of Water, was in conflict with Zhuanxu, the Spirit of Fire. In their conflict, they smashed the western pillar of heaven, making a hole in the sky that caused the earth to tilt. Both spirits tried to overthrow Nüwa but her level of qi mastery was higher and she emerged victorious and punished them. She then used her magical powers to patch the hole in the sky with five-colored stones matching the five phases.

When she took on disciples, Zhang's teacher Xuan Yu was the most exceptional. She became famous in her own right due to her superior weaving skills and was in charge of producing the special garb of the celestial courts. Because her tools were silks, ribbons, ropes, sewing needles, and other materials to do with textiles, her martial prowess relied on these, and Zhang Guolao inherited and transmitted them, spreading them variously. Thus, for example, as part of his rope mastery, he taught the herdsman of the Mongolian plain their proficiency in the use of the ropes and lassos, helping them to control their livestock and capture wild horses. He also established the use of long silk ribbons in Chinese traditional dance ceremonies—using them both for aesthetics and to recreate the motions of ethereal *qi* in waves and spirals—a feature that was also adopted in Korean culture. In addition, the use of scarves to protect against the cold, of leg bindings to secure shoes, and of belts to lift up trousers go back to the immortal and his divine teacher.

The Donkey Mystery

Master Wu's early training required reading and memorizing many important books from the temple library, sometimes working through as many as seven books at once while his teacher would play musical tones to stimulate brain waves and unlock inner potential. Reading about Zhang Guolao, his interest was peaked by the mysterious donkey who neither ate nor drank but could travel large distances in a day and was able to be disassembled and reassembled as needed. Having been raised around animals, Little Wu was doubtful: how could this be?

The mystery became clear when he remembered seeing unusual bicycles around the monastery that were only two feet tall and could be collapsed. He brought this thought to his teacher, and Master Du responded with a story from the classic novel *Sanguo yanyi* (The Romance of the Three Kingdoms). Among its leading characters is the artist, inventor, and statistician *Zhuge Liang* who creates something called *muniu liumao*, described as a mule combined with a horse. Although an animal, it does not eat grass and can move heavy objects with ease. Later in the novel, the creature turns out to be something like a wheel-barrow, one of the classical inventions of China. The dynastic histories further describe the invention of the horse-drawn chariot for use in battle and official life as well as of gunpowder, paper, printing, and the compass. This makes it entirely possible that Zhang Guolao's donkey was in fact an early bicycle. Still, most tales describe it as a real donkey and tell how it attained immortality and acquired superior powers.

The Immortality Herb

Once, while transporting goods from village to village, Zhang Guolao and his donkey searched for a place to rest and saw an old temple near the foot of a mountain. As they got closer, they smelled a wonderful aroma stirring in the breeze. Zhang dismounted and walked up to the temple window to catch a glimpse of the dwellers, hoping for a share of their food, but all he saw was a large pot of herbal stew simmering on a fire. Famished, he decided to help himself by breaking off two small branches from a tree and using them as chopsticks. He ate the delicious stew until he was totally full, then fed the remainder to the donkey and emptied the left-overs on a wall outside the temple. Then they went to sleep, blissfully unaware that they had eaten the herb of immortality.

This herb had been discovered when the disciple of a local herb master was walking in the forest and discovered a wandering infant. The baby led him to the far side of a grassy knoll and vanished, leaving him to look at an immense plant radiating outward. The disciple found this fascinating and immediately reported it to his teacher who from the description of the infant discerned that it was the spirit of the immortality herb. Going back to the plant, the master was very excited, had it dug up and placed it into a sack, then returned home to make preparations for cooking it. The next morning he went to the old temple and began the cooking process, but realized that he had forgotten his bowl and spoon. Returning to the village for them, he was sidetracked by a friend in need of counseling. Quite delayed in his errand, he eventually gathered his things and hurried back to the temple.

When Zhang and his donkey woke up from their nap, they noticed a man approaching rapidly up the hill. Judging from his body language and the cooking stains on his shirt, Zhang realized that he was the rightful owner of the stew, coming back for his meal. To avoid a confrontation, he leaped on his donkey and started to ride away, looking back every so often. Suddenly the donkey began floating on air, moving upward: without even realizing it, they had both become immortal. The herb master, on the other hand, wept as his dream lifted off into the sky: he had missed the one opportunity of a million lifetimes.

The branches Zhang Guolao had used as chopsticks grew to be two large trees and the wall on which he splashed the remnants of the stew became as strong as iron. The temple trees were named after Zhang Guolao. The master in his despair told the story of his squandered fortune far and wide, and the legend spread in every direction.

Immortal Teachings

During his ordinary life, Zhang Guolao tended to go to a Buddhist mountain temple for lunch. He never gave a donation and usually behaved rashly. Unaware of his true nature, the monks saw him as a free-loader and a nuisance. To put a stop to his visits and consumption of their rice, three monks plotted to kill his donkey and destroy the bridge he used to cross to reach the temple. Without his donkey they thought, he would no longer have transportation and without a bridge he would not be able to get there.

So one day, after lunch Zhang spent some time chatting with the abbot then stepped outside to find his donkey slain by a tree. Without batting an eye, he looked briefly in the direction of the three monks hiding behind a wall, then gently touched the donkey's head. The animal bounced to its feet, and they rode off toward the gully. Seeing that there was no bridge and riding at full speed, Zhang drew his bamboo tube from his sleeve and flung it across the ravine, transforming it into a bridge. As he galloped across the bridge, the young monks came out from hiding and begged him for forgiveness, which he granted. They learned not to be rude and to be forgiving when needed.

Zhang Guolao also taught martial arts at the White Cloud Temple, establishing a special chamber containing everyday materials useful for self-defense, seize-and-control maneuvers, and the healing arts. Believing that all kinds of soft and pliable materials contained hidden forces useful in self-defense, healing, and the alleviation of psychological dysfunctions, Zhang taught how to utilize everyday resources and clothing as weapons. For example, a towel or ribbon after being dipped in water becomes virtually unbreakable, transforming the material into a lengthy whip, lethal enough to kill and tough enough to withstand a sword's sharp blade. Thus the monks usually wore two belts, one for their trousers and one for self-defense.

Similarly he made use of traditional dance ribbons which, in addition to being beautiful and enticing, can mesmerize and disorient opponents, luring them into defeat. Especially red silk was good for this: when moved about quickly, it can confuse and agitate the mind, a wisdom also shared by the bull fighters of Spain, who use a red cape to agitate and blind the bull, so that it loses its balance and allows the matador to strike. By the same token a woman in red tends to capture men's attention away from all other activities. Leg-bindings are another useful item. Traditionally they were worn in pairs, one to hold the pants in place, the other to be used as restraints. Even the *hada*, the silk scarf Tibetans today offer to visitors and initiates as a sign of blessing, in the old days had a different meaning: it indicated that its recipient was desired dead by hanging or strangulation.

Zhang Guolao also created some unique healing methods with the help of textiles. For example, for weight loss the Chinese prescribe the herb *difuzi* to be taken by mouth. However, by the time the herb's essence has reached the desired body area, its full potency is already somewhat diminished. To speed its efficacy, Zhang employed a six-inch ribbon, contoured in a specific, talismanic pattern along the energetic routes of the body, to immobilize the patient. These bound positions can be uncomfortable, especially when the goal is to reverse or redirect the natural flow of *qi* in order to dislodge internal disease tendencies or digestive issues. The binding patterns tend to represent Chinese characters or talismans for extracting disease—the latter imitating natural patterns and often quite simple. For example, if a home has a rat problem, invite a cat to stay. The cat's *qi*, scent, and even its mere presence is enough to eliminate the infestation even if it never catches a single rat. A talismanic use would be the writing of the stylized character for "cat" in or on the body.

The Eight Immortals Revolving Sword and related qigong exercises all utilize such talismans: they are often drawn on sacred yellow paper in red ink or blood, in a process that involves prayers and incantations and during which the brush must never lose contact with the paper. Following this rule, in ribbon healing, the practitioner has to use a ribbon in one piece to tie the patient, then place the herb *difuzi* on the correct acupuncture points between the ribbon and the patient's skin. He then soaks it with water to propel the herb's potency into the energetic and blood circulatory systems, thereby effecting a more direct and efficacious application.

This style of healing was also effective in difficult cases involving addictions to sex, drugs, and alcohol. It used not only immobilization and herbs but also an external circle beyond the perimeters of the body, on which the distressing factors could be projected. This made whatever the patient craved close yet unobtainable. As the object of desire remains out of reach, the addictive nature—acquired and not inherent at birth—which cannot survive without the stimulus has to leave the body to move toward the object. As the talismanic binds in combination with the herbs stimulate a physical and spiritual purge, they push the addiction outward, making it leave the body. In many ways this is a type of exorcism, separating harmful elements and drawing them out of hiding.

Master Wu once witnessed his Daoist brother, an expert in these techniques of Zhang Guolao, apply this form of healing in a case involving parasitic worms. When neither acupuncture nor herbs could cure the condition, he tied the patient to an apricot tree behind the White Cloud Temple, using talismanic patterns and herbal medicines. Then he placed a large number of live worms in front of the patient and asked him to continuously stare at them. Soon the patient started to vomit worms, thereby cleansing his intestines, a procedure followed by more restorative acupuncture and herbal treatment.

Sexual Addiction

One form of addiction is excessive sexual appetite that leads to various diseases. Daoists as spiritual leaders and as martial masters have tended to be models for society and often were involved with policing. At times they have had to deal with sexual offenders: men with high levels of energy, either inherently or generated by the practice of gongfu, who had been seduced by their own powers and begun to commit crimes such as rape. When the sexual gates of such individuals are open, their qi is like an uncontrollable flood: it does not circulate properly, instead remaining locked in the lower regions of the body and creating lustful urges and psychological disorders.

Offenders of this sort, once known, would be summoned to the White Cloud Temple. If they declined this invitation, they would be taken in for trial and punishment, but not before first treating their condition with Zhang Guolao's method. The individual would be constrained with an herb-infused rope or ribbon and tied to an apricot tree. He was then forced to watch actors, usually hired from a brothel, performing various sexually exciting acts right before him, thereby confronting his inner demons. When the sexual addiction exits the body, it is usually accompanied by a loud, anguished scream and a bout of vomiting. The tormented person cannot bear to view what once plagued him; he begs for the proceedings to stop, indicating success. Once cleansed in this manner, the sexual offender was considered fit to face trial.

Prostitution in traditional China, although legal, functioned according to strict rules. Courtesans and prostitutes, when scorned or mistreated, would reach beyond these rules and disturb the personal world of their clients, launching premeditated attempts to destroy their families and careers, laying charges of sexual deviations. In some instances, these charges may well have been justified, however, they were always audacious considering the women's social position. Also, should the women's testimony be found false, the authorities inflicted severe punishments and often ordered the death penalty. During the Qing dynasty, one form this took was to force the guilty party to mount a horse saddled with a wooden phallus, then sent it off galloping until the woman was lifeless.

Before the authorities caught wind of such potentially damaging behavior, brothel proprietors would take their misguided workers to the White Cloud Temple for treatment. Like the men, they would be tied to the apricot tree behind the monastery with special rope and ribbon techniques. Then dried jujube dates or the herb *tinglizi* would be inserted into their vagina and sexual acts performed in front of them. This helped release the anger and frustration caused by sexual activities, rescuing the women from potentially horrible punishments through the local government.

One may think Zhang Guolao's treatments are cruel to the afflicted individual who is not given any choice and forced into treatment. While this is certainly the case, what alternative is there? Usually the treatment is over in two hours—that's nothing compared to incarceration or death. Western medical methods, too, can be invasive and not leave the patient much choice. During surgery, for example, patient immobilization is standard procedure: a safety measure for the person's own good. This is considered normal especially when invasive steps are necessary. Is it cruel? Not really. It all depends on one's perspective. Just think of the bondage in the Daoist method being applied to the disease or evil *qi*, not the individual.

Why, then, the apricot tree? In fact, it is not essential and any other may do, but the word "apricot" has a linguistic connection to sex, having the same pronunciation (*xing*) as the Chinese word for "sex." Due to this correlation, the apricot tree is seen as a reinforcement of the treatment method, one more soldier to fight, an additional talisman. Chinese has numerous homophones such as this, often reflecting the close connection between human and natural *qi*. For example, the word for the numeral "nine" (*jiu*) has the same sound as the word for "forever" or "permanent" and has thus become a symbol of heaven and eternal life. The word for "wine" or "alcohol" is also pronounced the same way, so that giving a bottle of wine as a gift or displaying it in the home are highly regarded. Then there is a case with strong negative connotations: the word for "four" (*si*) which sounds exactly the same as the word for "death." For this reason, buildings in China may not have a fourth floor, and people tend to avoid having the numeral four in their addresses, phone numbers, and so on. Sometimes this type of thinking is thought nonsensical superstition, but from a Daoist perspective everything in the universe has its own unique purpose. This can be discerned both from simple observation and from *Yijing* study.

At Court

Zhang Guolao lived under the Tang dynasty. His fame as a superior sorcerer earned him two invitations to court under two different emperors, which he boldly refused. Empress Wu (r. 684-705) sent a delegation to deliver a third invitation, but Zhang pretended to be dead when they arrived: he was lying on the floor with worms crawling from his entrails. Hearing of Zhang's passing, the empress ordered a state burial for him, but when the officials returned for his corps, he was gone: he had roused himself back to life and moved into the mountains of Hengzhou to live as an ascetic.

Three decades later people spotted him in the mountains of Hebei. When Emperor Xuanzong (r. 713-756) heard of this, he sent out another invitation which Zhang decided to accept. He arrived at the capital, met with the emperor on several occasions, and became good friends with him. This is what happened.

The emperor had heard much about Zhang Guolao's unsurpassable skills and special gongfu abilities. After arriving in the capital of Luoyang, officials took Zhang to have dinner with the emperor and then planned for him to give a lecture on Daoism at an institution of higher learning. The emperor was looking forward very much to the meeting and was full of respect for the Daoist wizard. However, when Zhang entered the dining hall, his hair was white, stringy, and brittle; his shoulders and back were covered with loose hairs and sprinkled with dandruff teeth; his teeth were few, loose, and rotten. "What a disgrace," the emperor thought.

Disappointed, he asked how someone so great could be so unkempt and decrepit, but Zhang's expression did not alter. He stayed utterly calm, smiling through the wide gaps in his teeth. Then he said: "I am already very old, sire. My skills have diminished considerably over time. Please forgive me." Seeing that the Emperor was discouraged, he decided to cheer him up: he lifted a long white hair from his face and began to poke at his teeth, all the while telling the emperor how he understood his disappointment and would leave as soon as possible. Then his gums began to bleed profusely, turning his mouth a crimson red. The emperor cringed in disgust and ordered the immortal back to his quarters.

After recovering from the incident and giving it some reflection, the emperor decided to try again and once more summoned Zhang to court. This time his appearance was complete opposite: he had rich, black, youthful hair and a perfect set of white teeth. He looked younger and more vibrant than even the youngest courtiers. The emperor was amazed and pleasantly surprised. He offered his compliments with great respect and they enjoyed each other's company.

A little while later, the emperor who was an avid hunter decided to share his passion with the immortal. Accompanied by the royal guard, the posse cornered a beautiful, large stag in a ravine. All escape routes were sealed and the deer was trapped. Planning to feast on the beast for dinner, the emperor claimed the honor of putting an arrow through its heart. He was ready to shoot when Zhang Guolao asked him to wait, stopping the retraction of his arrow at midpoint. He explained that they should not take the life of this amazing creature.

"Why," the emperor asked.

"This is an immortal deer, already a thousand years old," the immortal replied. "Destroying him is an act to be regretted."

"How can you possibly know this?"

"It is quite obvious from the Han coin hooked to its left antler."

The emperor was curious and ordered two riders to take a closer look. Indeed, there was such a thousand-year-old coin, dating from the rule of Han Wudi.

Emperor Xuanzong was impressed beyond measure. He offered several positions to Zhang, hoping to keep him as a permanent member of his advisory cabinet. Though flattered, Zhang Guolao humbly declined the offer and chose life in the mountains where he could practice in peace. The emperor graciously let both Zhang and the immortal deer go to pursue their longevity, but soon thought of another approach to recruit the Daoist wizard.

Imperial Ties

After Zhang Guolao returned to his hermitage, the imperial secretary of affairs paid him a visit, escorted by two eunuchs and an extensive entourage who carried an official scroll sealed by Emperor Xuanzong himself. The formalities of paying respects had barely begun when Zhang Guolao blurted out: "Wouldn't it be terrifying if one had to marry a princess?" He guffawed loudly. His remark was unexpected and completely out of context, catching everyone off-guard. They stared at each other, puzzled and trying to make sense of it.

After some tea and conversation, the appointed eunuch rose to his feet and delivered the emperor's letter. It described the tremendous beauty of his oldest daughter in poetic detail and pointed out how she had been trained in the arts of dual sexual cultivation since childhood. The emperor was offering her hand in marriage to Zhang Guolao. The letter concluded by requesting the Daoist to consider the offer carefully before answering. Zhang waited for about ten seconds, then replied: "I do not deserve her hand. I am not worthy of her royalty. I would hate for her youth to be wasted on an old man." The emperor's gift had been a ploy to tempt the old man with a young woman he could not have otherwise, but it failed to shake the wisdom tree.

The sealed letter had been written in absolute privacy and everyone present, even the secretary and his eunuchs, were highly surprised at its contents. They were even more surprised when they remembered Zhang Guolao's abrupt comment about "marrying a princess." His clairvoyance was startling, and his guests realized the magnitude of his abilities. They delivered his reply to the emperor, then told the story, which spread far and wide. Quite a number of people traveled to the mountains to become Zhang's disciples, but he politely turned them away: he was content to remain a detached observer.

Zhang Guolao is lauded in the history books because of his friendship with Emperor Xuanzong. The books also record that nobody ever saw him eat but only took liquor, wine, and herbal pills which, together with qi practice, was enough to satisfy his nutritional needs. Some records claim that he lived for four thousand years; others tell that he dematerialized into transparency while with the emperor and his senior sorcerer. The emperor could still see him, but the sorcerer could not, nor sense his presence in any other way.

Although Zhang repeatedly declined the emperor's generous offers to join his court, this did not lessen his respect for the immortal. In fact, the emperor ordered a monastery built in Puwu County near Xi'an. It was called Qixia guan and served to commemorate the immortal. The structure is still there today; it remains a house of worship for Zhang Guolao, where people pray especially when they wish for male offspring. Zhang himself, in the meantime ascended to the highest level of the heavenly realms, forever at one with Dao.

Lan Caihe of the Lotus Flower

Lan Caihe, too, lived under the Tang; he was probably the most lively among them, always carrying an efflorescent lotus flower to spread cheerful *qi* as well as a begging clapper (*jieban*) to conjure up magic and play jingles. Those passers-by his amusing spirit attracted usually had a delayed reaction of surprise: Lan had prominent androgynous features, a peculiarity that made him a novelty. The vagueness of his gender together with the entertainment his melodious singing offered made Lan Caihe intriguing, popular, and easily approachable. All members of the Eight Immortals begged for alms, but Lan was the prototypical beggar. He is often portrayed with just one shoe and a blue robe draped over his shoulder, padded and ragged looking—certainly an ironic fate for someone born with a silver spoon in his mouth.

Lan Caihe's is a riches-to-rags story, which unfolded as his inherited opulence evaporated. Before he became homeless, he had been known as Lan Xujian, the heir to an extremely affluent family of laureates, highly successful for many generations. Imbued with the family's pride, he was filled with the determination to follow in his ancestors' footsteps. He took the examination for government office, but failed to make the grade even after several attempts. Although intelligent in his own right, his thinking process was essentially nonconformist.

The following story comes from the White Cloud Temple record, a realistic and accurate account taken from original diaries. It tells of Lan Caihe's path into Daoism and the adversities he faced, notably the poverty he had never even tasted as a youngster. Because of his extreme change in social and material station, he developed a deep-seated compassion for the suffering of all beings, which transformed his heart and gave him a new perspective on the world and human life. He thus became a saint, watching over his disadvantaged fellow men whenever confronted with hardships.

Connecting to Dao

Lan Caihe's father had every confidence that his son would be successful and productive despite his academic failures and figured that he had more aptitude for business than officialdom. To launch him on his first venture, he granted him 200 strings of cash (*dadiao*; 36 coins), which in modern terms equals about three quarters of a million dollars. Well endowed financially, Lan Caihe thus ventured from home to seek fortune in commerce.

One year and several bad investments later, he was flat broke. Having run out of money just before New Year, he returned home worried and distraught, not knowing what potential backlash to expect from his family. His father was indeed upset to hear of his debacle, but took the responsibility on his own shoulders, reasoning that he had sent his son out too early, unprepared and without much practical experience. After careful consideration, on the third day of the New Year, he called him into his study.

The two sat down and thoroughly explored alternative careers. Old Mr. Lan wished for something stable, so that Caihe could support a family of his own, something like teaching or anything else that would allow the boy to use his academic training, even a retrial of the official examination. However, not only did these options have no interest for Caihe, but he most of all wanted to redeem himself in the business world, proving to his father that he deserved his backing. Old Mr. Lan finally agreed and gave him two strings of cash, a lot less than before but a good starting point for making a profit.

Lan Caihe soon embarked on another journey but his investment decisions were no better than before and, like water flowing through the gaps between his fingers, the money ran out very quickly. Finally accepting his inadequacy as an entrepreneur and his obvious ineptitude at handling money, he realized that he could no longer ask his parents, however wealthy, to support to his dealings. After spending his last two coins, he was too ashamed to return home, and his pride forced him to become a beggar in the streets.

As the days passed, Lan Caihe drifted further away from his hometown. With no real skills to speak of, he became a full-time vagabond. He had never been without means and was learning the hard lessons of the street. But suffering through these bitter times, he mellowed into a compassionate individual, performing meritorious acts on behalf of those even worse off than himself. Doing all this, he concealed his true identity, since he did not want to tarnish the reputation and good standing of his parents and extended family.

One evening after soliciting the entire day, Lan Caihe sat quietly, trying to figure out how he could possibly rise out of his predicament and return home a success. Nothing came to him. As he gazed ahead, downtrodden and dispirited, observing the setting sun in the distance, a wise old man walked up to him, holding a steamed bun in his hands from which one bite had been taken. Slowly and deliberately, the old man wrapped the remains of this bun in a clean handkerchief and placed it in his bag. Lan assumed he was a beggar like himself, saving the remaining portion for his dinner, just like he had done himself earlier.

All this occurred in silence. Then the old man unexpectedly asked Lan for a bite of his bun. Lan was caught off guard and stuttered to respond. After gathering his composure, he asked: "How can you be so sure I even have a bun?"

The old man replied: "I not only know you have a cake in your pouch, but also that it has been bitten into like my own." Then he repeated his request.

Out of respect for the elder, Lan Caihe complied, pulled his own bun from the pouch, and handed it over. How could he refuse the old man's request? After all, he had guessed correctly the contents of his pouch.

The old man ate every last crumb, then stood up satisfied. Ready to leave, he said, "Tomorrow I will visit you again at this hour. I expect another bun."

Lan Caihe nodded agreement, though he did not know why. That same night, he wondered who this old, undaunted person might be. How could he possibly know the contents of his pouch? Maybe he had been spying on him, watching what he was taking. His curiosity thus assuaged, he fell asleep.

The next day, just as the sun was floating on the Western horizon, the old man came back. Lan Caihe greeted him and said, "My begging for buns has been unproductive today. I have nothing to give you."

The old man grinned suspiciously and replied: "You are just stingy. I know for sure that there are two buns in your pouch."

Lan Caihe adamantly denied this and kept insisting that he really had nothing. The old man demanded proof and ordered him to open his pouch. Lan thought he had nothing to hide and opened his pouch with ease, but how surprised was he when he found two buns inside, each with a bite taken out! Flustered, he looked all around his pouch for answers, then started to doubt his sanity. Had he forgotten what he had done that day? He really had no idea where the buns had come from.

The old man poked him in jest and insisted they share. After the meal, he got up and walked away—but not before requesting more buns for the following day.

He returned again at sunset. Lan walked toward him, opened his pouch, showed him that it was empty, and asked: "Why is it that I have no buns in here today?"

Amused by his fiery attitude, the old man retorted: "Why was there only one bun in your bag on the first day, and why were there two on the second? Since there are none today, I bid you farewell until tomorrow. Shall we say the same time?" He left Lan standing alone.

Deeply puzzled, Lan Caihe could not sleep that night. He kept thinking and thinking why things had gone the way they did over these three days.

Who was the old man? What was the purpose of the exchange? He had several ideas, such as that there were messages in the buns. But how could they be hidden? Or what could the buns signify? He relived the turn of events one day at a time. On the first day they both had one bun cake with a single bite taken out. Two bites? Two mouthfuls? Then it struck him. The Chinese character for mouth looks like a square: 口. The word consisting of two "mouths," one above the other, is the character for the surname Lü 呂. He became excited.

Reconsidering the second day, Lan asked himself: "How did two buns magically appear in my pouch? Why did they each lack a mouthful?" It became clear to him that the old man was far beyond the ordinary. "Could he be an immortal?" Why was he always made to be host? Why was the old man always the guest? After all, he was a poor, homeless beggar with nothing to offer?

Again he rolled the matter over in his mind time and again, reorganizing the pieces of the puzzle. Finally it all fell into place. The second-day buns were found together; they both had a bite taken out. When placed next to each other, joined at the bites, they would form a hole or cave: spelling the Chinese word *dong*. Then, of course, the word for "guest" is *bin*, revealing the identity of the old man: he was the famous immortal Lü Dongbin or "Cavern Guest," a name he had taken on after a long meditation inside a cave on a mountain near the Yangtze. As soon as Lan Caihe had solved the riddle, a feeling of warmth and comfort spread through him. No longer cold or hungry, he slowly dissolved into a state of bliss under the moon and stars.

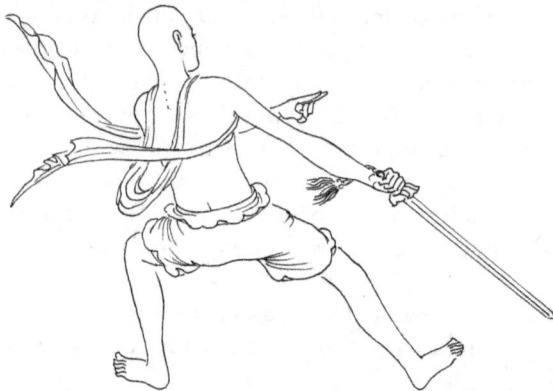

The next day at sundown, when the old man appeared again, Lan Caihe kneeled down and knocked his head to the ground in respect. "How did you figure out who I am?" Lü Dongbin asked. Lan explained his reasoning, and Lü Dongbin complimented him on his cleverness: "Your thinking is close to the Daoist way." Lan bowed again: "Lord Lü, may I be your student?"

Lü Dongbin, impressed by his intelligence and good heart, accepted Lan on the path. "Follow me to Mount Luofu and I will teach you the Way."

Repaying Debts

Lan Caihe was eager to follow, but his responsibility to his family was holding him back. He was an only son, expected to start a family and bear children, so that his family tree could continue. Telling Lü Dongbin all about his business blunders, he made it clear that he needed some sort of resolution before moving on. The immortal listened intently and was moved by Lan's sincere devotion to his parents. Honoring Lan's filial piety, he decided to help resolve his dilemma.

To do so, he made his new apprentice draw pictures of the hundred good deeds of an obedient son as set forth by Confucius, which illustrates the various actions a child can do to honor his parents. For example, one picture is of a dying mother in a destitute family unable to hold proper burial rites: the son sells himself as a servant to pay the funeral expenses. Drawing and copying these pictures is believed to link the heart's affection to one's personal ancestry, moving conventional family life into the spiritual sphere. Lan Caihe obediently drew hundred images—the original scroll still a treasured relic of the White Cloud Temple—and thereby fulfilled his filial obligations.

Next Lü Dongbin helped Lan Caihe rectify his shortcomings in business, realizing fully well that this was crucial for Lan Caihe to regain his confidence. Unless taken care of properly, this failure would come back to haunt him and obstruct his path to immortality. He thus charted a plan which would take one full year to ripen. He instructed Lan to work ten months for a local shop keeper, saving his entire salary for future investments. With his earnings, he then was to purchase an array of fireworks for New Year, transporting them to a remote village in Shanxi's Hongdong county, and there resell them. With profits made from this, he should next purchase a flock of sheep right there, then move them to another town for resale. Once this was all done, Lan would be able to return home to visit his family and repay his debt. At this time he could also inform his parents of his chosen career as a Daoist. Lan Caihe trustingly agreed to follow through—of course, he had nothing to lose since all else had failed.

Lacked Lü Dongbin's foresight, Lan still was locked in a state of ambivalence. He held his teacher in high esteem and followed all his instructions to the letter, no matter how ridiculous and farfetched. The ten months of his initial employment passed quickly, and Lan Caihe went off with his fireworks to the elevated regions of Shanxi. The journey was long and arduous. He had several episodes of frustration along the way, during which he wondered how in the world he was going to make any real profit from this. Most places in China had tons of fireworks for New Year, there was nothing rare or hard to find about them. The price Lü Dongbin set on the product was high and could potentially make Lan Caihe a laughing stock. None the less, he marched on.

Near his destination, the temperatures began dropping rapidly and the snow fell so heavily it covered him up to his calves. When he finally pulled in to Hongdong county, it was New Year's eve and he went directly to the marketplace to set up his sale. The weather was brutal, and the town was deserted, nobody selling or buying anything. Lan Caihe was tired and alone, getting more dispirited and defeated by the minute. Things got so bad he decided to celebrate the New Year all by himself. He started to light the fireworks. Their cracking and bursting resonated around the town, while their lights filled the night air. The town started to wake up, and people came out of their homes to enjoy the celebration. Smiles and laughter flooded Lan Caihe's vending post, as droves of people bought his fireworks at premium prices. He was amazed. The people told him the severe weather had prevented the fireworks from arriving; they were overjoyed that he had made it. He was a hero. During all this excitement, Lan Caihe thought of Lü Dongbin, and from that moment forward believed in him wholeheartedly.

Following the other instructions, Lan Caihe completed his journey and returned to Lü Dongbin. Shaking his head in bewilderment, he asked the immortal: "How did you know I would be so successful in selling the fireworks and then would be able to unload the sheep for such a large profit?"

"The ring around the moon during last year's Moon Festival allowed me to predict the weather and upcoming events for the year. Eventually I will teach you how to do this."

In the following, Lan Caihe immersed himself in the practice of Daoism. After his enlightenment, he thought back on his life as a beggar and decided to do what he could to alleviate the burdens of the underdogs.

Lotus Rising

During his stint as a beggar, principally because of his extensive education, Lan Caihe had been a leader among mendicants. He had gained a first-hand understanding of the hardships of homeless life: illness, hunger, and overexposure to the seasons were common miseries, sometimes reaching a point where they could not even beg any longer and faced starvation. General society thought of beggars as a nuisance, but Lan Caihe saw them as a symptom of turbulent times and wanted to help them re-establish good lives, thereby treating the roots of social problems. He believed that if they were at least able to beg for alms, their extreme suffering could be prevented and worked hard to create solutions to the epidemic of poverty. To this end, he dreamed of developing an herbal formula to improve health maintenance, hygiene, and self-preservation. He accordingly came to accumulate the ingredients for an herbal formula called *Butong yiqi tang*, making special use of the lotus flower.

The lotus, in Daoism and other Asian religions, is considered the original model of human evolution and seen as a reflection of mathematical perfection. Lotus seeds are planted in the lower elixir field and cultivated by practicing qigong as specified in the *Longmen jing*. the Five Centers Facing Heaven Lunar Qigong is a yin practice that germinates seeds and nurtures the process with the *qi* of the moon. It leads to an opening and release of conscious spirit, spurting the growth of the lotus which then rises up and climbs through the body's energetic pathways on its path to the heavens. The practice emulates the nature of the lotus flower and the dragon in concerted action, both closely related to the origins of human life. As a result, Daoists think of people as dragon lotus or dragon tree.

Lan Caihe wanted to concoct an herbal formula that would allow the body to survive without food in case of famine, without heat or shelter in extreme weather conditions, and without other aid in unforeseen emergencies. The formula was supposed to create independence for the beggars. His idea was inspired by an ethnic group called the Nejia Lotus People, mentioned in the classic novel *Xiyouji*, who derive their sustenance directly from the lotus flower. They look like humans, but are not composed of flesh and blood. Instead, they are born of the spiritual core (*ling*) of the lotus, its pure essence. Able to survive without food and drink and only requiring clear water, they stand beyond survival needs and are free from emotions, desires, and ambitions, thus having no inner conflicts.

Lan Caihe experimented variously to engender his new herbal formula. Already a perfected immortal, he used a rather unconventional method: he slowly dissected himself. Slashing and cutting portions of flesh from his body, he opened cavities in which he literally planted lotus seeds packed in soil. As they grew and blossomed, he continued to other sites until the majority of his body was covered with lotus flowers. Doing so, he came closer to the nature of the lotus and managed to make it part of himself, but hidden deep inside he was still essentially human and thus had survival needs and emotional reactions.

Stalled in his progress, he sought out the Lotus Master (Taiyi zhenren), the teacher of the Nejia People. He recommended a spiritual transplant, exchanging Lan's human soul for the spiritual core of the lotus. They agreed, and the Lotus Master deployed a crane to effect the exchange. After the operation, he was closer to being like a lotus, but he still had not reached the same level as the Nejia People, especially being unable to fly. Unlike the latter, he was a lotus immortal, combining the two worlds of humanity and the lotus, since he had been born of a human seed and had a human history that could not be erased. However, he had accomplished his goal, since he no longer required food to sustain his physical body.

Lan Caihe accordingly returned to the ordinary world as a lotus immortal and soon enthusiastically assembled the beggars' leaders for a conference, determined to teach them and all their charges the lotus path of immortality, thus to extinguish suffering. The response, however, was far less than anticipated. The idea of cutting their flesh and planting lotus seeds into their bodies was drastic and absurd to them, and they had no trust in him or faith in the method. The majority of the beggars accordingly failed to follow his instructions and did not achieve anything, looking even more decrepit in the process. As a result, his reputation and credibility suffered and many came to see him as a lunatic. His goodwill, sacrifices, and efforts had been in vain.

The Healing Formula

Soon after, Lan Caihe had the good fortune of meeting the bodhisattva Guanyin and explained his plight. Sympathetic and compassionate, the bodhisattva showered him with wisdom and explained that his approach, although suitable for himself, was not really appropriate for ordinary mortals. His intent was good, but his technique was not practical. How, then, could Lan Caihe help the people? How could he alleviate their inhumane conditions? How could he heal ailments of liver and stomach due to a lack of proper nutrition?

Guanyin observed Lan Caihe's dedication and offered a solution. The bodhisattva invited him to visit the sacred gardens on Mount Putuo, located on an island in the South China Sea and gather the locally growing herb *shengma*, which could help with the treatment of the beggars' symptoms. However, Guanyin added, *shengma* alone would not be enough. The beggars would still suffer from weak immune systems and thus remain vulnerable to many diseases. The bodhisattva recommended that Lan Caihe next go to visit the bodhisattva Dizang (Ksitigarbha) on Mount Jiuhua to obtain another plant called *chaihu*. From there he should move on to Mount Wutai, the sacred mountain of the bodhisattva Wenshu (Manjusri) in northern China. He would provide him with an herb called *huangqi*. After this, he had to go to the fourth disciple of Sakyamuni Buddha, the bodhisattva Puxian (Samanthabhadra) who would give him the herb *chanpi* that grows on Mount Emei in Sichuan. In this manner, he would collect four potent and effective medicinal herbs that would combine to cure the beggars' conditions. In addition, all the other members of the Eight Immortals each donated an herb to Lan Caihe's formula, bringing the total number to eleven. These eleven ingredients, then, formed the base of the formula *Butong yiqi tang*, with which he was able to cure the ailments of many struggling beggars.

Unlike this Daoist version, which credits Lan Caihe with the medicine, the historical records of traditional Chinese medicine claim that the formula goes back to the Chinese countryside, where it was a common and highly valued remedy. Its main master is commonly described as Lü Dongyun who played a major role in spreading it, standardizing the recipe, mass-producing the medicine, and distributing it even to the furthest regions of China.

Butong yiqi tang most fundamentally acts as an immediate energy enhancer with hunger curbing qualities. It is an excellent dietary supplement for either losing weight or maintaining a desired level. Regular use of the herb under the care of a knowledgeable physician makes it possible to gain sufficient nutrition from a single bowl of rice without losing nutritional essentials. This is the most beneficial and predictable aspect of the formula, and thus most useful for the underprivileged, such as beggars.

What few people know is that the formula is also very effective in liver diseases, such as hepatitis, particularly in the later stages. The key ingredient for this is *shengma*, which works as an anti-inflammatory and reducer of infection, but should generally be avoided since it leads to increased blood pressure. In Daoism, however, it is considered a wonderful substance, and the monks of the White Cloud Temple tended to take it in thirty-gram doses. Although at first sight alarming, this heavy dosage has tremendous effects in dissolving toxins in the body and is thus a must for purification, but only under the guidance of a trained physician.

Cultural Impact

Lan Caihe's involvement with lotus and with beggars has had a wide cultural impact. For example, lotus leaves, another important component of the formula, act as a catalyst in medical terms but according to the popular tradition, they are a memorial of Lan Caihe and his dedicated efforts. In fact, he made their use popular: his disciples were the first to use them to collect alms as opposed to the traditional wooden bowls; they wrapped and stored their food in them; and they utilized them as umbrellas and roofing materials. Eventually, this rubbed off onto the marketplace, so that even in the larger society lotus leaves came to be used to wrap meats, rice cakes, buns, and so on.

Another aspect of Lan Caihe's tradition is the use of lotus root, today common in Chinese cooking, mostly in soups. One recipe in particular calls for lotus root in combination with pig's feet; it is well known to help produce an abundance of mother's milk and believed to chase away evil spirits and misfortune during the cooking process. Lotus root and pig's feet both act as a talisman summoning the presence of Lan Caihe for protection— lotus root reflecting his practice and pig's feet reminiscent of the beggars who are always on their feet.

Lotus root, moreover, has several holes or chutes. Traditionally, those with larger holes are called "Lan Caihe's root": their emptiness reminds us that Lan Caihe was not of pure lotus spirit. On the other hand, those with small and meaty holes are called "Nejia root," referring to the completeness of their lotus spirit.

Another cultural feature associated with Lan Caihe is found in the tattered, torn openings on beggars' clothing. They are added by design, reflecting the holes Lan Caihe needed in his clothes when he had lotus flowers growing from his body. Although few disciples committed wholeheartedly to the lotus immortality practice, they still emulated its ideas and cut similar holes into their dress. On the other hand, there are a few who did commit to the practice, which has thus survived over time.

Master Wu in his childhood had the chance to witness the effects of human lotus cultivation with his own eyes. One year, a visiting Daoist came to stay at the White Cloud Temple: he had a red-rooster flower growing from his right shoulder. The inquisitive youngster asked his teacher about it, and Master Du explained that this was the Daoist's particular way of cultivation, reflecting his own belief system. To him, a follower of the immortal Lan Caihe, the lotus practice helped quiet his heart so he could attain the Dao.

Considered a true saint, Lan Caihe is still actively worshipped even in today's modern society. His good deeds and sincere interest in the underprivileged classes have continued to create a legacy of compassion and blessings, a cornerstone of Daoist culture. He never neglected people of lower status, but believed that being lowly was the inevitable starting point of the quest for human perfection. In this, human unfolding resembles the growth of the lotus: both pass through three stages. The first is earth: the lotus seed sinks into the murky water and takes root in the mud of a lake or pond. After a brief period of hibernation, the seed sprouts, turning upward until it breaks through the mud in its search for heaven. Next, comes the human phase, when the shoot opens into the water: in its effort to gain strength, it is challenged by flowing waves and hungry water creatures which feed on the sprouts and stems of the young seedlings. These are the dangers and uncertainties of human life. Third, the bud reaches beyond the water and into air: it has advanced to the heaven phase. In this stage, the lotus can blossom into a thousand pedals and finally realizes its true unadulterated nature. It releases new seed pods into the water, and the innate process begins again!

Three Kinds of Emperors

Chinese traditionally speaks of three kinds of emperors, a fact not commonly known. The first is the emperor of the country, the leader of the ruling class, commonly called the Son of Heaven (*tianzi*). The second are the monks of the main religions, known as the Masters (*shizi*). More surprisingly, the third kind of emperor are the beggars, named Flower Sons (*huazi*). All three are "sons," sharing the title *zi*, a respectful additive signifying status and formally used when addressing people of high rank.

Daoists, moreover, claim that the universal law of reincarnation operates a rotating system through the three kinds of emperors in society, leading people from one to another in a system of three stages. Thus, the life of the *tianzi* is the most demanding and extreme, because major decisions and responsibilities for large organizations, such as an entire country, rest squarely on their shoulders. In this view, the title is not limited to the emperor alone, but can also be used on a lesser scale to refer to the president of a company, the principal of a school, or even the head of a household.

People on the level of *shizi* are called upon to dispel the evils of nature and, with the help of spiritual power, learn to control or police the cryptic realms of negative energies. Their lives are full of very hard work; they make noble sacrifices for the whole of society. Monks and other religious specialists cannot indulge in the bittersweet, sensual enjoyments of a normal life on earth. They have to remain within the order of heaven, working to balance the forces of yin and yang.

The complicated social connections and responsibility of the *tianzi* and the solitary yet arduous life of the *shizi* in due course give way to the third stage, the life of a beggar. Although transients, homeless, and mendicants appear to be at the lowest rung of the social ladder, yet in actual reality they possess unequaled freedom. Beggars do not answer to anyone or anything except Dao: exempt from conventional work, they can sleep whenever they desire, go wherever they please, do what they like. Rather than as a punishment in life, Daoists see this as a form of gratification. It is the Dao's way of rewarding a soul: it allows the soul to rest before moving it again into positions of intense responsibility or spiritual discipline. It is not a perfect life, but then again how many really are?

Also, beggars rely on the kindness and compassion of their fellow men to survive. Their station is like that of elderly people who have worked hard for their entire life and now rely on their offspring or social services for care. From this angle the three kinds of emperors can also be seen as stages in a single lifetime: reaching from a level of deep involvement in social activities through spiritual cultivation to a period of retirement and dependence.

The Eight Immortals often cleverly disguise themselves as beggars to test people's hearts and compassion. Lü Dongbin did this with Lan Caihe— had he refused the immortal's request for his bun, he would have lost the opportunity of many lives. In other words, in the world of the ten thousand reflections things are not always what they seem.

Han Xiangzi, the Gentleman

Han Xiangzi or Han Xiang was the grand nephew of Han Yu, the famous novelist, poet, scholar, and official of the Tang dynasty, best known for writing and editing documents for the imperial government. Han Xiangzi benefited greatly from his expertise, developing superb writing and cultural skills much like Lan Caihe. The difference between the two immortals' writings was one of popular connection: Lan Caihe, due to his humbling years as a beggar, wrote in a more simple, folkloric style, using poetry and rhymes consistent with catch phrases to spread the essence of Daoism. Han Xiangzi, on the other hand, studied directly with his famous relative Han Yu and, at age sixteen, passed the second level of the imperial examinations. A true prodigy, he gained a strong literary foundation and eventually reached senior government positions, also publishing an extensive body of books and essays on Daoist thought.

Despite his lofty academic and political achievements, whenever Han Xiangzi is first discussed, his striking good looks stand in the foreground. Always perceived as the most handsome of the Eight Immortals, he is a genuine *junzi*, a righteous gentleman. Even nowadays, people say, "Trust me and do not worry—I am a *junzi*." This applies perfectly to Han Xiangzi because of his attractive features and because of his exemplary honesty. His candor went so far that the records only know of one incident in his entire life when he did not tell the complete truth.

Flowers and Music

Along with his good nature, elegance, and honesty, Han Xiangzi is characterized by his intimate connection to the finer arts of life as expressed in flowers and music. He is frequently shown adorned with colorful peony flowers and always accompanied by a magical bamboo flute. Historical records affirm his exceptional musical talents, and he has been honored as the patron saint of musicians. But there is no consensus about which type of bamboo flute he played: was it *di* or a *xiao*? A *di* has its blow hole on the side and is held horizontally, while a *xiao* has a specially carved mouthpiece and is held vertically, not unlike the clarinet. The discussion about this issue has lasted for centuries, and the White Cloud Temple even held a conference on this issue.

A key goal of Daoism is to align human beings with nature—music does much the same. Daoist music thus follows the sounds produced in the natural world. Based on the paradigm of the five phases, it recognizes five tones, which it defines and puts to unique use. This is where the subtle difference between the two kinds of flute comes in—the horizontal having slightly less of a connection to nature than the vertical one. Based on the study of tone variances and after careful examination, the members of the White Cloud Temple conference thus concluded that Han Xiangzi played the *xiao*. It produces sounds in immediate harmony with the five pure tones of nature and thus opens the essence of Daoist cultivation.

Master Wu sees yet another important factor that indicates the choice of flute being the *xiao*: Han Xiangzi was a highly skilled Feng Shui master and wrote several books on the subject (today at the White Cloud Temple). Thus in correcting environmental energetic imbalances, Han Xiangzi used the exact placement and angling of his flute to redirect and conserve positive *qi* while releasing stagnant *qi*. Even today it is well known in Feng Shui circles that hanging a bamboo flute in a house will help blunt sharp edges and pool positive energy by balancing any unevenness of yin and yang. This fact, then, lends further support to the monastery's conclusion that Han Xiangzi played a *xiao* rather than a *di*.

Among the Eight Immortals, Han Xiangzi and Lü Dongbin were the only ones with Feng Shui skills, Han being the more advanced practitioner. In fact, he attained such a high mastery in the practice that his methods came to constitute a separate branch. Master Wu, who also practices Feng Shui, stands in the direct line of Han Xiangzi's style. During his training, he had to memorize many works by the immortal and became particularly fond of one story that demonstrates the powerful impact a bamboo flute can have on environment and destiny.

Clearing Vision with Feng Shui

Huayuan is a common practice among Daoist and Buddhist cultivators: it is a form of begging or rather fund-raising in that one persuades wealthy individuals or families to donate money to help the less fortunate. The donations may also go toward building temples as service centers for the community and the increase of Daoist and Buddhist social functions. For example, during the Tang dynasty, Daoist knowledge had not yet reached the cultural mainstream and few people had heard of Laozi and his teachings. To get the people to listen to the Dao, activists arranged dinner parties and other events, funded through *huayuan* collections. Socially open, such events created the perfect setting for casual mingling and intellectual conversation, and all attendees were subtly exposed to Daoist philosophy over meals and entertainment.

On one occasion, Han Xiangzi went to visit Jinan in Shandong. On the way, he practiced *huayuan*, but contributions were few and far between, and people tended to give food and clothing instead of cash. Lü Dongbin was traveling closely behind, supervising him. Since the takings were so meager, he advised Han to discontinue his quest and return to the mountains. Han Xiangzi refused and continued on alone.

The next day, he happened upon the family home of Lord Jiang, a wealthy silk merchant. The merchant had been blind for over two years. Though without vision, he had an acute sense for the divine and, from the content of their conversation, he believed Han Xiangzi could be an immortal. The silk merchant decided to make him a lucrative offer. If Han Xiangzi could restore his sight, he would grant him whatever he asked. They struck a deal.

Han Xiangzi strolled in and around the estate observing the layout in terms of Feng Shui. In the front yard he noticed a tall post standing alone on the right: its position was problematic and raised several questions. Han Xiangzi casually interviewed the lord, prying into his past and the history of the property. He had received his high title not only for his wealth and fame in commerce, but also because he was a respected man adept in literature. In addition, he was familiar with the mystical workings and mechanics of Feng Shui theory and had made sure that his home was situated and designed according to its principles. The only misplaced item on the land, in Immortal Han's opinion, was the post in the front yard. As he discovered, Lord Jiang had gone blind shortly after the house was completed.

They continued to talk about this and other issues. Eventually Lord Jiang revealed that he himself had dabbled in fortune-telling and admitted that he had at one point made a calculation for himself which foretold the arrival of an immortal but did not tell whether he could cure his affliction. Lord Jiang believed that Han Xiangzi's arrival fulfilled the prophecy and he was planning to test the immortal's powers. If he was able to cure his blindness, he would not only pay lots of money but would become a full-time devotee of Daoism.

Han Xiangzi's analysis of Lord Jiang and the home's Feng Shui was promising. The main difficulty was the lone post, which had led to the loss of vision. Lord Jiang suggested eliminating the post, but Han Xiangzi found that things were not that simple. If it were eliminated, it would take the lord's life along. Instead, Han Xiangzi proceeded to hang his flute on it and ordered the household to leave it there for seven days and nights, by which time Lord Jiang's sight should be completely restored.

After the appointed time, Han Xiangzi returned to the estate to find the silk merchant fully healed. Jiang was utterly amazed at the success of the flute remedy and wanted to know just how it had restored his sight. Han Xiangzi explained that a post in or around the house would create an obstacle and lead to an obstruction of personal *qi* flow, which would eventually manifest as a physical ailment. Without fresh *qi* irrigating and replenishing the body, disease is inevitable. Since the post was barring the right front window and windows are the eyes of the house, the lord's vision was impaired. The flute, on the other hand, acted as a conduit for the natural *qi* to penetrate the post and flow through it, thus unblocking the obstacle and restoring the faculty of the lord's eyes. Now that his vision was revived, the post could be taken down without mortal danger.

The Post-lifting Contest

Lord Jiang immediately became a firm believer. He asked Han Xiangzi to name his price. The immortal asked for all of the goods found in his yard, including the post. In addition, he asked for Jiang's assistance for fundraising in his hometown, where he was well known and highly respected. The lord agreed with enthusiasm, offering any service within his power. The two loaded up a horse-drawn cart and transported the articles and post into the city of Jinan. Han Xiangzi sold the merchandise and had the post set up in a central location. He then ordered posters drawn and had them placed all over town to announce a public contest: the first to lift and carry the post to a spot some forty miles away would collect a generous cash prize. The people's response was immediate.

Lord Jiang's curiosity led him to ask what the immortal's ultimate objective was. Han Xiangzi answered that the local people were unaware of the practice and power of Daoist cultivation. Since most were illiterate, they had never read the works of the sages, unlike the lord who was a rare exception. To expound the teachings of Daoism without first establishing trust would be futile; in order to preach Dao and *de* or virtue, the applied principle and moral potency of the Way, faith and trust were essential. Han Xiangzi's ploy was to use the post to spread Daoist ideas.

Han Xiangzi also told Jiang about his own ideal path. His first step was to truly cultivate his spirit, he should perform virtuous deeds, dedicate himself to good causes, and give selfless service to his community. The second step was to separate himself from all his belongings, to rid himself increasingly of possessions. This is because, having too many possessions to worry about and create emotional ties, the cultivator's heart is filled and his concentration preoccupied, thus preventing getting any closer to Dao. The Dao, as Zhuangzi says, gathers in emptiness alone.

Lord Jiang realized that this commitment was being tested and accepted the challenge with vigor. That very day, he burned the deed to his house, donated his collection of precious antiques to charity, and forgave all debts the townspeople and the city owed him—including almost fifty percent of the municipal budget. As a result, his life and health improved measurably, but he still had to get through the post-lifting contest. As Han Xiangzi made it clear, the key to maintaining his eyesight depended on the successful outcome of the contest. If nobody showed up to move the post, Lord Jiang would permanently lose his sight.

The lord was anxious that no one would be able to perform this feat, but Han Xiangzi told him not to worry, assuring him that the right person would come along. It all depended on how much he wanted to pay. As the proverb says: "If the money is there, the right person will appear." The immortal therefore took the liberty of setting an astronomically high cash reward. Unbeknownst to the public, this would be paid out of Lord Jiang's pocket.

Soon thousands of people from all over the greater area flooded the streets of Jinan. Few could budge the post, let alone lift it or carry it for forty miles. After three days of failure after failure, a huge lumbering mountain of a man came to try. Intuitively, everyone knew that he was the one. He hoisted the post onto his shoulders with ease and delivered it to the required destination within a few days. Before several hundred witnesses, Han Xiangzi paid him the full cash prize. From this moment on, the people of Jinan and its surrounding regions respected and trusted him for being a man of his word. Having won the people's trust, he was then able to educate them about the wonders of Dao, improving the lives of many. Lord Jiang, moreover, kept his eyesight and enjoyed a fruitful life of spreading and observing the magic and beauty of Dao.

Han Xiangzi / 115

What Han Xiangzi accomplished here was a high level of *huayuan* cultivation. This breakthrough gained him an audience and allowed him to spread the main teachings of Laozi. He also emphasized the *Yijing* and its hexagrams, giving explanation on the constantly evolving changes in all aspects and stages of nature and human life. He was thus able to open up the highest qualities of Daoism and share them with innumerable people, clarifying the key concepts of fate and destiny, encouraging people to take charge of their role in the greater cosmic sphere, expand their wisdom, and improve their lives.

Fate and Destiny

Nowadays, some believe firmly that the road to long life, prosperity, and good fortune depends solely on a person's internal drive: motivation, ambition, and hard work. For example, someone hoping to get into a prestigious university will show strong determination in his studies yet will also expect to succeed through his connections, just like people born or married into a wealthy and prominent family will make use of their background. Which is it—effort or social situation? The answer is both, but neither work ethics nor circumstantial factors, although important, are ultimately the determining factor in shaping a person's destiny.

As the *Yijing* outlines, without disqualifying effort, social setting, and free will, human destiny is to a large degree predetermined. About half of what happens to an individual in life is due to the combination of internal attitudes and their external reflections in society in combination with the natural, social, and political environment. That is to say, the *Yijing* claims that we have control to affect or change our fate only to about 50 percent. The other half is firmly predetermined and remains unchangeable.

For instance, who your parents and siblings are is predetermined. Being born male or female is predetermined, even though these days there may be surgical alteration. Will you be married? How many times? Will you have children? How many? All these are predetermined and provide the essential framework of a life. To understand it better, think of a house that is already built: it cannot be completely reframed and its fundamental structure remains, key beams have to stay in their original location. On the other hand, the way it is decorated and used depends on personal preference and taste: which room you decide to designate for what purpose, what colors and paints you use, what style of furniture you obtain and where you put it, what pictures you hang on the wall. There is, thus, quite a bit of flexibility in one's personal life-style and career choice, where fate and destiny can be changed—enhanced or diminished. This is the controllable body of destiny.

Daoist cultivation is a key method to appreciate and improve the underlying patterns of destiny, and the tools best suited to work on the undetermined half of one's destiny, the section that is within personal reach, are the sword practice and qigong. Over millennia of study, Daoists have experimented with duplicating the natural cycles as outlined in the *Yijing* and compressed their knowledge into these mental and physical exercises. The practices emulate the universal pattern of change and thereby recalibrate the course of perception, destiny, and fate within the microcosm of the human body.

Through these energetic practices, the personal *qi* field is enhanced, repaired, and renewed. As it gets fully integrated, the inner truths of the psyche emerge. Thus entrance into Dao, no matter how deep or shallow, opens the opportunity of discovering the hidden aspects of long life, prosperity, and good fortune in ones personal destiny. Joining the flow of nature, one gains a heightened intuition, which can then be used to capitalize on opportunities or reduce (or even avoid) misfortunes, even if they are part of one's predetermined destiny. This is a great gift for all evolving individuals. However, the question remains: "Would this not have happened anyway if I were not cultivating *qi*?" After it is all said and done, the Dao remains mysterious and enigmatic.

Master Wu learned about all this from Master Du, who taught him about this aspect of the *Yijing* by referring to a parable from the teachings of Han Xiangzi. He said: "Everyone is like a leaf on a tree. Eventually each leaf will fall. Some leaves fall on the main road; others fall into the gutter. Those that fall on the main road will meet with success; those that fall into the gutter will not. Yet the leaf had no choice where it falls. The wind decides where the leaves are blown. Individuals are just like leaves: their direction has only little to do with their wants and needs. They may ask: Is this what is meant by 'destiny'? The *Yijing* says that destiny's answer is: 'I do not know.' Instead, destiny says: 'I am like the wind. I blow, but I have no idea which leaf is going to fall where.' Now, if you are the leaf, you will never know where the wind is coming from or when it will start blowing."

Proper *Qi*

Daoists number the various opportunities one may encounter in the course of a lifetime to 84,000. They come in all kinds: big and small, favorable and unfavorable. And they correlate to the 84,000 pores of the human body, known as ghost gates (*guimen*). This is a huge number of potential doors to be opened, of positive chances in a single lifetime, matched by an equal number of possible misfortunes and tragedies.

Major ups and downs of opportunity occur less frequently than minor ones, but they tend to have longer lasting effects. For instance, if you purchased Coca Cola stock thirty years ago, you have received immense dividends so far and will continue to do so for years to come. If you did not make such a purchase but had the chance to do so, you missed an opportunity. Similarly, you may regret that you married a certain partner or regret that you let someone else slip away. Along the same lines, in the course of a lifetime you may encounter different diseases of major or minor significance. Is this life threatening? Or is it simply a string of common colds? Is it due to a sports accident or a car crash? All these can redirect the path of your life for better or for worse. Even a minor inconvenience such as a fender bender on the way to work may be the cause of some unexpected good fortune. You never know from where the wind will blow and where the leaf will fall. But in order to maximize the odds in your favor according to the ancient esoteric wisdom of Daoism, it is essentially important to open the ghost gates.

In Daoist theory and *qi* practice, the body skin, understood as a microcosm of the lungs, is trained to breathe in the same fashion as a frog. When the ghost gates of the pores are opened and cleared and move in unison with the breath of the universe, proper *qi* from within moves outward to surround the body's aura, thus attracting the proper *qi* of nature. This in turn provides a refractive sheath, an aura of light which protects from evil energies. Once you have this, you will experience a heightened awareness and be able to intuitively sense good opportunities and unwanted misfortunes.

According to the teachings of Han Xiangzi, this heightened perception obtained through enhanced proper *qi* is the secret of Feng Shui analysis and the apperception of the deeper mystical realities of the universe. To cultivate this *qi*, you must develop honesty and faith in your practice: in its most effective stage, you have to have a pervasive attitude of truth over illusion. In one of his books, Immortal Han discusses the importance of developing proper *qi* to attain the Dao of Feng Shui. He says: "One must first possess proper *qi* inside, then one can merge it and communicate with the proper *qi* on the outside. When inner and outer come together, the profound blending of righteousness becomes the key to arriving at the highest caliber and unveiled clarity of Daoist Feng Shui analysis, interpretation, and practice."

To maintain and protect righteous energy within, one has to cultivate the stillness of the heart and learn to realize the mind and heart as one. Because the heart houses the spirit, it is the seat of all feelings and intentions. Maintaining a balanced disposition while passing through all sorts of positive and negative agitations in everyday life one can preserve one's internal heart-mind energy. It is said, "The heart must remain in stillness like a perfect moon reflected on the surface of a placid lake, then one will not lose sight of Dao." It is difficult to avoid many wind-induced ripples and waves on the water's surface; it demands deep concentration. Tranquility is found by turning the eyes inward away from the indulgence of images in the colorful and chaotic world. Images and questions will then arise in the mind's eye, where they can be sorted and settled with control. This is the key prerequisite to all Daoist exercise. It will allow the practitioner to deal with unsolved issues sharply and swiftly, with a single stroke of the mind's sword dissolving them in both conscious and subconscious states. The solutions reached may not necessarily be permanent, but they are concrete in the moment and help in keeping the mind's galloping thoughts and emotions at bay.

Daoists tend to discourage questions about the why, how, and what if of the world of destiny and recommend keeping to the center of internal stillness. Too many queries become a danger zone, leaving too few outs in precious moments of time when decisions are essential. Trying to rationalize fate keeps the mind away from intuition, seals off the present, and prevents forward progress and the acceptance of the brighter side of destiny. "No matter whether the waters are calm or stormy, the ship's helm must be manned!"

Destiny and Self

Laozi said: "My destiny is in my own hands; I do not depend on heaven." What does he mean by this? He wants to inspire people to dedicate themselves to the practice of gongfu. His ultimate purpose is to support heart-mind practice and enhance its impact on people's way of looking at the images of the colorful world. The eye of wisdom and insight, guided by a heart-mind in deep stillness, maximizes people's chances of doing the best with the moldable half of their destiny. It pierces the illusions separating human beings from self-realization. However, Laozi's statement does not mean that people have preeminence over life or can gain absolute power over the universe—as it has been read on occasion in the course of history. Laozi never intended complete attainability or control, which would mean having full dominion over the entire universe. This is impossible. No single human being can possess this kind of power.

To correct this misconception, Qiu Chuji of the White Cloud Temple notes that most people are unable to handle or manage even half of their own personal responsibility, let alone control the universe at large. A hundred percent control would also include other worlds, unfathomable galaxies and creations. Qiu thus provides a perspective, from which we can appreciate the small responsibilities that are our burden for the minute activities they are. It gives the bird's eye view and opens us to comic relief.

Perfecting half of destiny is almost impossible. Even Han Xiangzi, a realized immortal, with all his ambitions cannot claim this perfection. He maintains that he was a genuine gentleman of his word, but even this is only accurate to ninety percent, and even Han Xiangzi lied once in his lifetime when speaking about marriage. Lü Dongbin called on him, accusing him of hypocrisy and being a false gentleman. However, people say if you have lived eighty percent of your life as a gentleman, then you deserve the title. In the sword and qigong practice, reaching eighty percent or more in terms of spiritual refinement is also a point of arrival, called "achieving gongfu excellence."

Cao Guojiu—Full or Empty, or Both?

Over the years, followers of Daoism have found it a challenge to embrace or reject the complex demeanor of Cao Guojiu—depending on which stage of his personal history they gravitate to. Is the glass half full or half empty? Each one has to decide for himself.

Cao Guojiu was born Cao You, one of four children born to General Cao during the Song dynasty. He and his two brothers were undisciplined and even delinquent, mightily flexed their brawn and intimidated innocent people just for fun. They abused their father's military status and immense wealth to the vulgar edges of tyranny. His only sister married the Renzong, the fourth Song emperor, who was originally named Zhao Zhen and later became Empress Dowager. After she had given birth to imperial children, family members called him and his brothers Imperial Uncles Cao, allowing them to penetrate more deeply into the inner circles of imperial power and thus further corrupting them.

However, this is just one side of the story. Many other records describe Cao Guojiu as a civilized and even-tempered man with exceptional skills in numerous areas, from archery and music to scholastic and political endeavors. In any case, his official position as Imperial Uncle allowed him to maneuver behind closed doors to influence politics at court and promote various special-interest groups. People either feared or respected him, but he was never challenged—that is, until an incident took place in the countryside that gave him a heavy dose of his own medicine. It was a humbling situation that presented him with an ultimatum and offered a great giant opportunity to change and reverse course. Would he seize the defining moment of his life? Although there are few historical accounts, either official or popular, of Cao Guojiu's life, this popular tale had a strong impact and given inspiration to anyone who believes that it is never too late to change.

Making Amends

One day while living the carefree lifestyle of wine, women, and song, Cao Guojiu and his two brothers along with their peers decided to go hunting. On their way into the forest, their horses ruthlessly trampled over the crop fields and herb gardens of local farmers and country folk. They ravaged a wide stretch of countryside, but nobody in his right mind dared to complain or challenge them and their actions. Their gang hunted all day, killing much more than they could consume, then set up a base camp near the main road to the city. Shaded by the wide canopy of large trees, they kindled a fire and cooked a spectacular feast. One of Cao Guojiu's cronies served as lone sentry overlooking the main road. Just before the sun was setting, he alerted Cao and his brothers that people were approaching. As they came into view, they turned out to be two well dressed jewelry merchants who often traveled to the capital for business. More than likely they were carrying precious metals and gems to sell in town. Immediately the group was taken over by greed.

Cao Guojiu ordered part of his entourage to the crossroads as a welcome committee, inviting the merchants for a friendly drink. However, they politely refused, stating that they had an important appointment in the city. The gang reprimanded them for rejecting their hospitality and insisted that it would be disrespectful to refuse an invitation from the Imperial Uncles. Unable to refuse, the merchants apologized and agreed to join the group for a little while.

The gang cheered them as honored guests and encouraged them to drink heavily. They soon became drowsy, passed out, and died, aided into the otherworld by poison the gang had put into the wine. Their heartless laughter rang out widely as they stole and handled the precious goods. At the same time, a heavy storm began to arise, blowing in every direction and forming an electrically charged atmosphere. The wind was so powerful that it raised whirls of dust, clumps of earth, and even large rocks, forcing everyone to close their eyes and cower on the ground. It stopped as quickly as it had started and settled into a dead calm. When the storm cleared, the gang rose to find to their dismay that the dead merchants and their valuables had mysteriously disappeared. Enraged by the loss of this fat profit, Cao Guojiu and his cronies drank themselves into a stupor.

That night, he had a nightmare followed by a crystal clear vision. He was tightly bound in a bathtub among a horde of demons who were dissecting his body and torturing his soul. Then he heard a commanding voice, ordering the demons to leave and let him go. Cao Guojiu rose to face an ancient Daoist master. He knelt before him, thanking the immortal for his rescue. The immortal told him that if he changed his behavior from bad to good, he would be able to escape retribution. With these words of wisdom clearly in his mind, Cao Guojiu woke up, gasping for breath. Scared witless by this vision revelation, he determined to change his ways once and for all.

Using his personal resources, he began to funnel all his wealth, power, and influence into making amends through charitable contributions. On one occasion a large flood had washed away a vital bridge on which the livelihood of many people depended. The local government did not have funds to reconstruct it, but Cao came to the rescue, donating a thousand cash strings of gold and silver. Once its construction was well underway, he sponsored a medical center of the highest quality, providing the finest doctors and most excellent herbs of the region to facilitate healing. Those who sought medical attention, regardless of social class or background, were never turned away or charged for services or medicine. After every good deed performed, he felt his life becoming more and more like a dream, as if dark clouds were being lifted from his eyes. He could see and feel the world in a compassionate way like never before.

One year, a drought had devastated the local crop, leaving the farmers with little or nothing to harvest. The community had no money and not even food for themselves. With the New Year festivities approaching and rations alarmingly low, Cao Guojiu again used his resources to aid the farmers and local villagers, spending several thousand strings of cash to clothe and feed them. What had threatened to be a bleak festival instead became a wondrous celebration of life. In one of the villages, he set up a major facility, where food, clothing, and other goods were manufactured and distributed where needed. Branching out from this, he also launched home care and live-in communities for the elderly, all without charge. To honor the Daoist immortal who had so mercifully saved his life, moreover, Cao Guojiu erected a temple in the village, giving people a place of worship where they could thank the heavens for their abundant blessings.

Cao Guojiu thus turned his life around completely, forging a positive spirit that brought blessings to innumerable lives. In the beginning, the locals were suspicious of his caring attitude and philanthropic efforts since they knew him as spoiled brat full of nasty, violent behavior. It took some time, but eventually the villagers embraced him well—unlike his own family members.

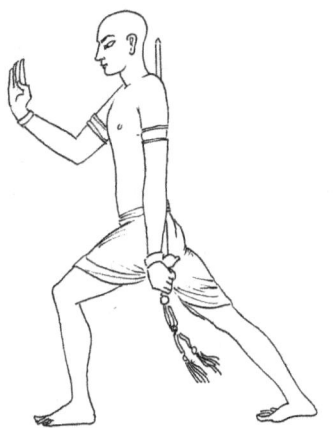

Life Events

His two brothers never had a dream revelation and thus changed little. They openly opposed his new path and constantly complained of what they called his frivolous wasting of the family fortune. They wanted to stop him from doing his charitable work and secretly conspired to disgrace him. One day, the brothers sent an unauthorized delivery of food to a local village on behalf of Cao Guojiu's foundation. Unknown to the courier, the food was laced with poison, leading to the sickness and even death of many innocent people. The news traveled back to Cao Guojiu who was deeply saddened by the loss. After a careful investigation, he traced the culprits, finding his own flesh and blood responsible. Since Cao Guojiu at this point was a public figure of high visibility, he had few options on how to pursue the case. Eventually, he personally ordered their arrest and execution: the toughest decision of his life and the final measure of his righteous transformation. Afterwards, he was well respected and trusted even by those who still held reservations regarding his sincerity.

According to another record, his two brothers were also at the center of a murder story. In an act of blind passion, the younger brother Cao Qingchi killed an aspiring scholar. He was deeply attracted to the mesmerizing beauty of the scholar's wife and in his romantic fantasy believed that she would fall madly in love and marry him once he had gotten rid of her husband. When the woman failed to obey Cao Qingchi's wishes and threatened to report his wrongdoing to the Imperial Guardian of Morals, Pao Laoye, he imprisoned the innocent widow and, on the advice of his elder brother, threw her down a well to eliminate all connections to his first murder. However, she was rescued from the well by an immortal and given refuge until they could contact Pao Laoye's office. The younger Cao was sentenced to death for his crime of passion; his older brother was pardoned.

Cao Guojiu himself continued to serve in government and as public benefactor for twenty years, then decided to leave all worldly affairs and retreat to the mountains to pursue immortality. According to some legends he was on his way to a sacred Daoist peak when the immortals Lü Dongbin and Zhongli Han came to test his true intentions. Ready to cross the Yellow River, Cao Guojiu stood on the shore waiting for the local ferry. When the two ferry operators asked him to pay in advance for their services, his old personality reared its ugly head. He flashed his golden imperial identification tablet to the ferry captain as if to say "I ride for free." The operators' response was unexpected: completely unafraid, they easily resisted the brash rudeness of the politically privileged. They just laughed out loud and made what could be construed as blasphemous gestures. At this point Cao Guojiu becoming aware of his misbehavior and was embarrassed at his pretentious attitude. He paid the ferry men, gave up his rank of imperial uncle, and tossed his gold ID into the river, letting go of the final vestiges of his ego.

Impressed by his sincere actions, the ferry operators greeted him with warm smiles and revealed their true identity: Lü Dongbin and Zhongli Han. The immortals quizzed Cao Guojiu on his knowledge of the Dao to see if he had learned something during his life and asked him about his destination and future intentions. He told them that he wished to pursue the Dao in the mountains and hoped to find an immortal teacher who would transmit it.

The immortals asked: "Where does the Dao reside?" Cao pointed up to indicate heaven.

"Where, then, can heaven be found?" He pointed to his heart.

Pleased with his answers, the immortals laughed with joy and praised him highly, noting that he was well on his way to enlightenment. Next, Lü Dongbin tossed a pair of jade tablets on the river's surface, using them to get himself and Cao to the other bank while Zhongli Han rode on a large palm leaf. Once safely on dry land, Lü gave the jade tablets to Cao as a set of spiritual talismans, showing that he was a newly initiated student of the Way. Cao Guojiu eventually fully attained Dao at the age of seventy two, then departed from this world of dust and entered the light of the heaven, his heart empty and free.

Youxin Wuxin

What do *youxin* and *wuxin* mean? The word *xin* 心 alone literally means "heart-mind," and it has an interesting history. Ever since Kangjie invented Chinese characters on the basis of birds' tracks, the character was written without its central, high dot. Only Confucius, the master thinker and culture teacher, took the liberty of adding the dot to the center of the word, shaping its modern form. He intended to increase the meaning of the "heart-mind," to enhance the spiritual purpose of the ongoing journey of human experience. He believed that inside the heart-mind, feeling and thought was essential for exercise and growth. However, the addition of the central dot has affected innumerable people negatively, which of course Confucius never intended. They focused too much on the center of the heart-mind, becoming completely involved in movement, activity, thought, and emotions. Daoists think that if the dot were removed the heart-mind would once again be light and free, able to let go the weight, stress, and frustration of life's thoughts and worries. Thus *youxin* is "heart with dot" or "having mind," "intentional" thinking and acting; *wuxin*, in contrast, is "empty heart," "no-mind," "unintentional" or "spontaneous" being and doing.

In 1958, Master Du went to Beijing's Tongzhou district to visit an iron pagoda at the request of some concerned government officials. He was to examine a report that the enormous building was no longer perfectly erect, tilting slowly to one side. In order to properly assess the situation, Master Du had to examine the structure with his own eyes. He duly gathered a group of his students together for a field trip, also taking Master Wu along. Next to the pagoda was a small restaurant, where the group took time to rest and drink tea. While they were all sitting down, Master Du explained the implications the leaning tower might have on the city of Beijing and the entire country: its leaning was a sign that pointed to various underlying issues that might lead to disaster and chaos. The leaning tower was an omen of events to come; it had to be righted as soon as possible.

Master Du further told the group that the pagoda in terms of longitude and latitude was specifically placed on the vectors or portal lines between the human and the ghost world. It had been designed and constructed by Liu Bowen, the top *Yijing* and Feng Shui master of his generation, under the Yuan dynasty when Beijing had just been chosen as the new capital of China. Liu had great skills in the human realms as well as power and control over the underworld. He utilized these to capture all the ghosts, evil spirits, and negative energies in city and country, then placed them underground, crushing them with the iron pagoda and sealing their route of escape. In addition to the pagoda, Liu Bowen also drilled a well underneath a bridge to contain evil spirits. As legend has it, just before closing the well, one of the demons asked: "When can I come out again?" Liu replied: "When the bridge breaks." After this conversation, Liu Bowen sealed the well and named the bridge Beixin Qiao or "Forever New Bridge." He wrote the name on the bridge himself to serve as a talisman of protection, keeping it forever young. He also did this with the iron pagoda.

To rectify the impending situation of doom, Master Du had brought the sword of Lü Dongbin along. After their rest in the tea house, the group walked around the iron pagoda. They strolled along its perimeter, thereby giving the sword the opportunity to sense the area's vibrations and allowing it to detect potential havoc. Any energetic or negativity leaks from the pagoda's foundation would cause the sword to issue a warning by shaking, jumping, or emerging from its scabbard and taking flight—just like it used to protect the monastery from intruders. Fortunately, the sword remained perfectly still, but Master Du, sensitive to very subtle qi-vibrations, perceived some disturbances. Concluding the test, the Daoists went back to the restaurant to eat before returning home.

At the table, the Daoist apprentices focused on Master Du as he explained the history of Liu Bowen and told many tales about how people in the past had exorcised the ghosts and goblins trapped in the wells. The restaurant owner, overhearing the lecture, greeted him respectfully and told him about his personal difficulties: many people were abandoning the district surrounding the pagoda because of the tower's mysterious nature. The leaning tendencies had led to a considerable decrease in his business, a downward spiral he was not recovering from. He himself was thinking of moving away, but he was deeply attached to the location and had many old friends there, so it was a difficult decision. He concluded by asking Master Du for help or advice.

Master Du nodded in agreement and requested ink, brush, and paper. He promised to write some special words to hang on his wall and assured him that the talisman would bring business back. Not to worry! The word he wrote was *xinzi*, using the character for "heart-mind" without the central dot. Following Master Du's directions, the owner immediately hung it on the wall closest to, and facing, the iron pagoda. It symbolized a new beginning for him, but despite his gratitude, he could not resist asking if these simple two characters would be enough. Master Du convinced him that the writing was deceptively simple and had quite a bit of power. On that note, the Daoist group gathered their belongings and headed back to the White Cloud Temple. On the walk home, Master Wu himself was as unsure about the talisman as the owner, unable to imagine its significance.

Sometime later in the month, word traveled back through the grapevine that the restaurant business was improving and had begun to boom. People entering were fascinated by the writing on the wall and came back often, wondering why the character was missing the central dot. They came less for tea and food and more to study and discuss the "empty heart" and the refined style of calligraphy. Still, while having their discussions, they ordered tea and food.

Master Du's writings were extraordinary because he was so deeply concentrated in his preparation. He always practiced several hours of sword and qigong before ever lifting a brush, which caused his words to be heavily laced with *qi*. This added a special sparkle like that of a crystal ball to his brush strokes, expression of the universal *lingqi* of nature, harnessed and passed through him into ink and paper. His work thus exhibited a unique, high level of artistry, which caused the fascination of countless viewers. The restaurant continued to be busy for years to come.

Further Lessons

In 1964, Master Du gathered his students once more to investigate the status of the iron pagoda and monitor the situation of its neighborhood. Much to the students' amazement, the pagoda had returned to a perfectly vertical position, which in turn had stabilized the erratic energetic vibrations in the area. After the Feng Shui examination, they went for lunch in the same restaurant. The owner greeted Master Du with enthusiasm and showered him with expressions of gratitude and appreciation.

Although satisfied with the talisman and his thriving business, however, the owner had never been able to come to terms with the truncated "heart-mind" character. His curiosity had become an obsession, and he had developed quite a variety of ideas and theories about its meaning. He was not the only one. Thousands of people had passed through his doors to appreciate, analyze, and debate the profound message of the "empty heart." The owner was convinced that if Master Du ever added the final dot to the center, his business would become even more successful and asked him to do so. Master Du complied immediately, adding the dot without hesitation. The Daoist group departed, but they soon learned that the tea house business was again plummeting.

On the verge of closing down, the restaurant owner desperately rushed into the city to ask Master Du for help. He recounted that, as soon as Master Du added the dot, the place virtually ceased to operate. Master Du explained that in its new version the character was no longer unique and had no more novelty value: it was as common as any other calligraphy. People no longer found it interesting, and therefore his business suffered. So, now the owner pleaded with Master Du to please remove the dot once again, but Master Du explained that, like an acupuncture needle inserted and removed, it was quite impossible to establish the previous status quo. What had been done could not be undone. Plus, it was the owner's fate as also confirmed by *Yijing* divination that prosperity was his only for six years: it was his destiny that the Daoist priest appeared on his doorstep in 1958. Master Du also told him that, if he looked at the iron pagoda, he would find it once more perfectly upright. Thus the restaurant owner came to understand the bigger picture, seeing his own fate and business in the context of the energy patterns linked to the pagoda.

The final lesson for Master Wu and the other students, as Master Du explained, was that the "empty heart" talisman had never been meant to create equilibrium or success for the restaurant owner nor had it been placed there as a balance force against the leaning pagoda. Rather, it served as a vessel for righteous energy to come in and accumulate. Only after

100,000 people had asked the question about it, could the light brilliance of universal *qi* move the pagoda back to its upright position. Master Du's intention had been to lure people in to view the pictograph and gather their heart-mind energy there, using their intense imaginative and wishing power. This was the fulfillment of the central dot. Master Du used this one dot, this inner power, this strong aspect of universal *qi* to slowly shift the iron pagoda back upright over a six-year period. We call this method Creation Feng Shui. A self-creating method, as opposed to the active rearrangement of structures or furniture, it is considered the highest level of Feng Shui and relies heavily on outside factors, such as time, place, and people. They must all be in perfect synchronicity and in close alignment with destiny and fate for this force to be active.

Even a leaf from a tree can ruin your life by changing the position of the universe. The leaf itself does not know when it will fall, which way the wind will blow, or where it is going. The wind does not know which leaf will fall. They are perfect strangers.

He Xiangu, the Lady Immortal

> Those with wisdom do not accumulate.
> Because the wise serve the people, they gain more:
> The more they give to others,
> The greater is the wisdom they retain.
> —*Daode jing* 81

The womanly virtues of grace and compassion play a large role in Daoist practice, but rarely are they visible in the form of a female deity. The eighth and final slot of the circle of the eight trigrams belongs to the immortal lay He Xiangu, whose maiden beauty and warm-hearted nature are held in high regard amongst worshipers. Among the trigrams she represents Kun (earth), the receptive and pure yin. It consists of three broken lines, positioned at the western gateway, and needs a female to fill it accurately, making sure of the proper *qi* placement in terms of yin and yang. As regards art work, she is mostly portrayed with a lotus flower in her hand, a symbol of her open heart and grace.

He Xiangu was born in Guangdong province in south China around the year 700. Most people have to suffer, work hard, and make big sacrifice in attaining the Dao, but their plight is minor in comparison with He Xiangu's desperate struggle of surviving her unbearable family circumstances. The lady immortal, much like the blooming lotus she carries, grew from the muddy and murky waters of a misplaced destiny.

According to history, her parents forced He Xiangu into an arranged marriage to cement an alliance with a wealthy family of land owners. She was a *tong-yangzi*, a child bride more or less sold into her husband's family. He Xiangu performed this duty, going against her own deepest wishes, and married the land owner's son who was himself still a young boy. This was common: the grooms were small children or even infants, and teenage wives were nannies to their husbands as well as caretakers of their new family long before ever becoming an actual wife. Once grown and matured, it was not uncommon for the husbands to find their wives undesirable, since they had come to think of them as older sisters. Uneducated and by then well past their prime, these women ended up as lowly housekeepers.

Unfortunately for He Xiangu, fate had joined her with an evil mother-in-law, who dictated her every move and did not appreciate her warm humanitarian sentiments toward the local farmers and beggars. She made He Xiangu, barely a teenager at the time, do the most filthy and difficult tasks from dawn to dusk, day after day. The future immortal's almost unbreakable willpower somehow still managed to maintain compassion and spiritual endurance. In this manner she was tested in her heart and soul to the brink of death, then raised into enlightenment.

Pure Heart

One evening, after a long day's work, He Xiangu lay her head down to rest. Her sleep was her most precious possession, in fact her only possession, an escape from a tortured life. On this night, the immortal Lü Dongbin visited her by entering her peaceful dream world to convey an important proposition. In a rousing sermon, he offered a method in which she could shed her imprisoned life of slavery. If she could perform and accumulate no less than ten thousand good deeds, he told her, she would be lifted to the realm of heaven and receive immortal blessings. The day before this call, Immortal Lü had randomly used his special perception to glimpse into her heart. What he discovered beneath her calloused exterior was an extraordinarily compassionate and nurturing softness. He Xiangu was the type of person to place others before herself like a mother first feeding a child, even if it meant going hungry herself. Because of these qualities, Lü Dongbin believed she had the capacity to transform her reality. When she awoke the next morning, a glimmer of hope shone from her eyes.

As everyday He Xiangu cooked and cleaned for everyone in the household, but now she began, during the few spare moments of her day, to follow Lü Dongbin's instructions. Her mother-in-law disagreed with her acts of kindness and forbade her from giving away anything from the family home. This created limitations. It was a constant sabotage against He Xiangu who owned nothing and was left no choice but to bank on her own resources.

At the end of her long days, therefore, she went door to door to beg for alms, raising money, food, and clothing to give to the less fortunate. Even on her lunch break, she begged for rice to distribute to the town beggars. There was no rest for the weary maiden whose salvation seemed to rely on this mission. One day, to slow down her pace, the mother-in-law made her move a heavy piece of furniture alone and without assistance. The feat resulted in a broken bone, an excruciatingly painful injury. Still, He Xiangu managed to beg at over one hundred homes per day. This continued for three years.

She lived under the Tang dynasty, right outside the city limits of what is today Xinyang in Henan province, in an area periodically subject to floods, droughts, and other natural disasters. Sometime after she had completed her three years of serving the people, a severe drought fell upon the area: not a drop of rain fell for over a year. Dry, parched, cracked soil was everywhere—all over the land as well as on the faces of the people. The rivers barely trickled from the mountains and several wells had run dry. The local administration ordered food rationing since there were no harvested crops in the region. Begging for alms had declined substantially, and many people died due to dehydration and starvation—a scary, difficult time. In desperation, people knelt and prayed to the gods for rain, but their pleas remained unanswered.

Throughout all this, Lü Dongbin kept a watchful eye on He Xiangu from a distance while also monitoring the drought situation. As the land and its inhabitants wasted away, he decided to intercede and pray on his own to help resolve the suffering. Still no rain fell, and even Lü Dongbin's powers were surprisingly ineffective. He was left no other alternative but to rise above the clouds and pay homage to the court of the Jade Emperor.

At the audience, the Jade Emperor was initially sympathetic to Lü Dongbin's request, however, as it turned out, the situation was more complicated than just a matter of rainfall. When the celestial deities allocate rain, they also take the people's behavior and past actions into account. The amount of rainfall per season thus depends on the quality and effect of their deeds, positive or negative. The area, then, was in dire straits for a good reason: the locals had accumulated so much bad karma that it outweighed the good by a great deal and fell short of the heaven-required minimum quota. So, as it turned out, the Jade Emperor was sympathetic to the people's plight and agreed to help, but he himself was bound by the rules and therefore set certain conditions before ordering a change in the situation:

"He Xiangu," he said, "is the one and only untainted, pure heart and soul in the entire area. If she kneels down to pray, her sincerity will effect a response and this may lead to the dispersal of rain." He further explained that, since her good deeds had saved thousands over the years, she had such a large reservoir of righteous *qi* that she could save the whole. Only her voice was worthy of the gods' attention.

Lü Dongbin returned to earth and organized a town assembly by the bridge over the shallow local river. He relayed the gods solution to the predicament to the people: "If you truly want rains to fall, you have no choice but to ask He Xiangu to pray for you." As if one, the people turned and moved toward He Xiangu's house, kneeling before the beautiful maiden. This was an ironical turning of the tide: everyone, including all the proud and wealthy, were begging from the beggar and pleading for her prayers. He Xiangu was entirely agreeable to help, but she was not exactly sure how exactly to proceed: should she read from a book of sutras or maybe recite a special article? She was confused and nervous—her early marriage had forced her to give up any hope of education and she was illiterate. The people encouraged her to do whatever she felt was right, reminding her that details were unimportant. What really counted was that she pray with a sincere heart, so the gods could hear her loud and clear.

The Rains

The people led He Xiangu to the best location for her prayers, a place selected by Lü Dongbin and supported by the other members of the Eight Immortals. The area had been infested by plagues, murderous acts, and deception, for a number of years, leading to many violent deaths. Its destiny now lay squarely on He Xiangu's shoulders, now empowered to wash away every person's sins. She dropped to her knees and linked her palms together in whole-hearted sincerity. With every breath she pleaded that rain and healing be granted to the people, the land, and all its creatures. She continued to implore the heavens over a hundred times, but there was still no rainfall.

The people turned from her to glare at Lü Dongbin, wanting to know why no rain was falling as he had promised. Immortal Lü himself was bewildered. He had followed the Jade Emperor's instructions to the letter. Did the gods break their promise? To get to the bottom of things, he drew his sword and lifted all the immortals, including He Xiangu, onto a fast-moving cloud rising toward the heavens. As they ascended, they encountered Guanyin, the bodhisattva of compassion, and Immortal Lü Dongbin asked her for an explanation. She said that only a portion of the necessary work had been completed so far, but did not know what else to do.

The immortals continued on their quest, and eventually got Lord Lao to lead an investigation into the matter. He proceeded to question the Wind Lord, the Duke of Thunder, and the rain-making Dragon King. Their reply was that under the command of the Jade Emperor, they had done what they could to bring rain to the stricken area. Unfortunately, for reasons they did not understand either, their powers were rendered useless. The Dragon King noted that there was a dark ominous cloud and fire over the region. Apparently, an evil hold was in place. The quandary could not be resolved by the various gods, but Lord Lao managed to disentangle the impasse with his wisdom eye.

He explained that this particular region was the largest producer and distributor of sesame oil in the country. The overplanting of sesame had seriously damaged the earth, absorbing its vitality and diminishing the spirit of the soil, thereby harming the *qi* of the entire region. Thinly scattered nutrients barely supported the crops, many fields hardly produced anything anymore. The reason for this was that the producers of sesame oil who were selling it to all reaches of the country had allowed greed to sway their integrity. For many years, about half of the barrels they sent out contained a goodly portion of water underneath the sesame oil, which is lighter then water and naturally floats to the top. Thus they created the illusion of 100 percent pure oil and in fact cheated on their customers. Their malicious intent was discovered and incensed a great many people across the country. As a result, a heavy cloud of negative thoughts from all directions had arrived there and was casting a curse of fire and brimstone over the region. Even the Jade Emperor could not lift it and was unable to assist any further.

After the immortals had learned all this information and returned to earth, He Xiangu ran home to grab the broken begging bowl she had used for the previous three years. She returned to the bridge, bowed down, held the bowl above her head, and began to pray. She told the Jade Emperor that it was all true: many people had deviated from goodness and deserved to be punished. However, in addition to the obvious criminals, there were still many harmless and righteous people who did not deserve to suffer. He Xiangu then promised the heavens that each and everyone present would perform 10,000 good deeds. No one argued. In fact, the immortals seconded the motion. As officers of heaven, they agreed to oversee this task, ensuring compliance and completion.

Suddenly, the ominous dark cloud of malicious intent dispersed and thick white rain clouds accumulated. It rained! Then radiant sun rays filtered through the clouds, and a beautiful rainbow arched from horizon to horizon. The people rejoiced greatly. He Xiangu's prayers had been answered and she had emerged as a savior. Her heart of gold was able to change the fate of an entire region and to this day she is worshipped and respected in her home province.

Womanly Wiles

This next story shows the effects of He Xiangu's accumulated wisdom gained from her thousands of good deeds. Around the middle of the Tang dynasty rebels rose to overthrow the government, leading to an opportunity for He Xiangu to raise her spiritual level. She had completed exactly 9,999 good deeds and needed only one more before she could enter perfect Dao, the heavenly realm of immortality. To reach this pinnacle, He Xiangu employed a woman's wiles, a craft unique to the female perspective of the world.

As the government fought to put down the rebellion, many stretches of country suffered from random acts of violence, thickening the already negative atmosphere. It was getting harder and harder to distinguish between good citizens and rebel bandits, and extensive cloak-and-dagger activities placed national security on maximum alert. Across the river from the capital, the rebel population grew steadily along with their store of food, weapons, and livestock, leading the revolutionaries to assume a threatening stance and making war inevitable.

All around the country, the rebels had concentrated on stealing horses for several months, hoping to gain speed and position. They believed that having large numbers of fighters on horseback would increase the maneuverability of their troops and make them able to fight the better equipped and thoroughly trained imperial guards. Horses were thus crucial to their venture. The rebels also relied on the emperor's growing concern for innocent bystanders who would be in harm's way once battles began. To accentuate this inherent diversion, the insurgents deployed small units of soldiers to wreak havoc on the population. Using a scorched-earth strategy, they ravaged villages, burned homes, and destroyed crops to weaken the Tang resources and force the army to create safety zones, shelters where they could supply provisions for the victimized.

Lü Dongbin had offered his services to the emperor as an advisor with the intention of resolving any large-scale conflict before it even commenced. Prior to doing so, he had consulted with He Xiangu, reminding her that one good deed remained to be done for her to reach the goal of ten thousand. He stressed that if she could in fact figure out a way to diffuse the potential war, a great many blessings would be her reward. He Xiangu embraced this task. She positioned herself at the river bank opposite the rebel forces, systematically analyzing their actions. After several days, she became aware of their horse maintenance routine. Depending on the weather, every second or third morning at sunrise, they brought their entire stock of horses to river for watering and grooming. In her report, she also emphasized that the rebel force without horses would be like a fly on an elephant's back.

Guided by Lü Dongbin, a secret meeting was convened with the royal guard to discuss and coordinate He Xiangu's discover and come up with a scheme to dissolve the threat of war. The plan's first order of business was to round up every single horse in the region, no matter whether military or civilian, young or old, fast or slow, and bring them to an agreed rendezvous point near the river. With everyone's cooperation, all the horses in the city and its outlying areas were rounded up in a single day.

He Xiangu insisted that all the horses be taken outside of the city wall close to the river. Her next order was to separate the mature stallions from the mares and take them to a remote location, away from the river. Among the remaining mares, only those that had recently given birth were kept together with their colts and fillies. All others were taken to pasture. He Xiangu then announced that by the following morning, the potential of war would be gone. The Tang troops were not entirely informed of the plan, just in case there were any rebel spies among them.

He Xiangu and the guards waited patiently as the brilliant sun rose in the east. As predicted, the rebels came to the bank to lead their horses to water. When over half of them had reached the river, He Xiangu ordered the guards to separate the young from their mothers and take them to a designated area behind the city wall next to the river. At the same time, orderlies herded the mares slowly away from their young down toward the water. Soon their maternal instincts came forth as they were forcibly redirected: they kept turning their heads and whisking their manes, trying to catch a last glimpse of their disappearing young.

On the other side of the wall, still in earshot, the fillies and young colts cried out miserably for their mothers, attempting to break through to them. This all caused a huge commotion, a highly emotional ruckus. As a result, the mother mares all started to cry out loud, neighing uncontrollably. The stallions on the rebel side of the river, hearing all this, instinctively perked up their ears, listening carefully to the sound of the distraught mares. Drawn by the sounds of yearning and passion, they broke free from the group, galloped to the river, and began to swim toward the whinnying mares. To them the distress signal sounded just like a mating call. The rebel mares, moreover, without hesitation followed their stallions studs across the river, fearing that they would lose their mates.

Completely taken off guard, the rebel troops made a desperate attempt to control the horses, but their large numbers and strong vigor made this quite impossible. Desperate to catch their valuable horses, they mounted on the rides they still had and followed them across the river, hoping to catch and bring them back. The royal troops under the authority of He Xiangu waited patiently. As soon as the rebels reached their side of the river, they launched a powerful ambush, confiscating all the horses and capturing the majority of the unprepared rebel troops. This eliminated the risk of war: any battle with the remaining rebel troops would have been a suicide mission. He Xiangu's plan had worked to perfection and she did her ten thousandth good deed. Her wisdom was celebrated in the heavens and on earth.

"Womanly wiles" in general form a major kind of war tactics in China. Used variously in battles and political conflicts, they helped shift power during critical crises. He Xiangu adapted the tactic by employing mares instead of women, conceiving of a truly brilliant plan that used Daoist methodology in that it applied nature's magnetic attraction patterns of yin and yang. She saved innumerable lives, setting a phenomenal example of profound wisdom.

Punished for Doing Good

Another story that characterizes He Xiangu's life began on the doorstep of her husband's home. Conditions with her mother-in-law were a complete nightmare, since the older woman scrutinized her every move and continued to heap verbal and sometimes physical abuse on her, with and without justification, constantly finding fault whatever she did. However, He Xiangu did not allow these pressures to affect her ultimate decisions when it came to matters of the heart and humanity.

One day, the mother-in-law left the house on business and was not expected back until late afternoon. She left He Xiangu with the task of preparing a dinner centering on freshly made tofu, a favorite dish of the house. While she was pouring soy milk into a tray where it would gel into tofu, she heard a knock on the front door. Opening the door, she found six Daoist monks standing before her. Their clothes were dirty and unkempt, draping their malnourished bodies like wind-tattered flags. One appeared to be crippled. He stepped forward and begged almost pathetically for half a bowl of soy milk, whose scent was permeating the house. He Xiangu responded without hesitation and filled his bowl. Immediately, the other five raised their bowls, pleading for soy milk to warm their bodies. She turned around and closed her eyes, shivering at the thought of her sadistic mother-in-law throwing a tantrum and beating her for handing out the soy milk to strangers that had been planned for dinner. Stricken with fear, she looked at the Daoists ready to refuse, but then was overtaken by her motherly instincts, knowing that their needs outweighed her fears. As the Daoist drank from the bowls, He Xiangu began thinking out loud, mentioning that she would rather be beaten by her mother-in-law then ignore her heart. As she said this, the monks exchanged glances. They finished the milk, thanked the gracious maiden repeatedly, and said goodbye.

The sun was well into the western sky, when her badgering nemesis returned from her errands, coming directly into the kitchen to inspect He Xiangu's cooking preparations. She found a single small block of tofu on the kitchen table and immediately asked why there was so little when there should have been six times as much. Outraged, the madam demanded an explanation. He Xiangu stuttered but could not find the words or the courage to explain. Trying to force her to speak, the women lay into He Xiangu with intense force but the young woman's silence held true. Her mother-in-law's eyes turned fiery red and she threatened to break both her legs if she did not tell the truth that very instant. She meant it, too, so He Xiangu confessed. She was punished further and then sent out to retrieve the six beggars to repay the mistaken charity.

He Xiangu left the house a nervous wreck, crying uncontrollably. Her vision was blurred by tears. She did not even remember in which direction the monks had gone, wondering how on earth she could ever find them. She knew for a fact that they were not locals and worried herself sick, thinking that they had already left the village. Restless with fear, she kept walking around, unsure of where she was going. She walked about for over an hour, scanning every object in her sight until she fixed her gaze on a hillside in the distance: there were the monks, contentedly resting and settling in for the night. He Xiangu set out for the hillside. As she got closer, she tried desperately to stop crying but when she began to explain her predicament, she wept. The Daoist noticed the welts on her body and upon hearing of the rash behavior and conditions set forth by her mother-in-law, they agreed to return with her and promised to replace the soy milk.

Waiting impatiently at the front gate like a starved guard dog, the mother-in-law spewed a barrage of obscenities at the returning group, demanding that they immediately return her soy milk. Flailing her arms about, her body language showed that she had not even the slightest iota of clemency. The Daoists politely listened to her ranting. When she finally ran out of steam, they silently exchanged glances, faced the cold woman, and as if one started to throw up the soy milk. The projectile streams splashed onto the ground before her, soaking her shoes and spotting her garb with regurgitated liquid. The six Daoists then wiped their mouths and walked away.

Infuriated by the insult, the outraged woman snatched He Xiangu by the collar and pushed her head down to the ground, forcing her to drink the vomit as a penalty for her benevolence, but He Xiangu refused to swallow. The putrid remains covering her face, she rose up, a firm yet subtle act of revolt which sent her mother-in-law into a frenzy. The woman was totally beside herself. She reached into her topknot and drew out a long bamboo pin, letting her hair down past her shoulders. She walked into the kitchen and set the pin into the oven's fire until scorching hot and then vengefully used the glowing spike to burn He Xiangu's face and hands. At this point, He Xiangu only wanted to die.

Immortal Transformation

Many hours later, after the pandemonium had settled, He Xiangu walked back into the kitchen and grabbed a bowl from the cupboard. On the table sat a pot with the gelling chemical that was needed to transform soy milk into tofu. Added to hot soy milk, it congeals and allows the tofu to firm, but by itself it is poisonous, especially if taken in large amounts. He Xiangu filled her bowl to the brim and drank it down. Waiting to die, she found her senses fading, but decided she did not want to pass on in the house of a witch.

She lifted herself up from the chair, moved past the door, and shuffled toward the river. She stopped at the bank, standing completely still as if already dead. Overwhelmed by sadness, hot tears fell from her eyes into the speedy current, further rippling her reflection. Finally she drew her last breath and leaped into the water. She was swallowed by the turbulent waves of the river, tossed and turned in unrepeatable patterns. Conformed to waves and whirlpools, she became part of the rhythmic cycle of water.

Seventy-two hours later He Xiangu was still unconscious. She had failed to die from drowning or poisoning. A small river boat pulled up next to her buoyant body and hoisted her aboard. The captain placed an herbal pill in her mouth to dissolve. Shortly thereafter she awoke: standing above her staring down at her was her savior. Focusing her eyes with some difficulty, since they had not been open for several days, she recalled a familiarity in the man's eyes, but could not place him.

Noticing her struggle, introduced himself: Lü Dongbin, one of the six Daoist she had fed earlier, had come to her rescue. He thanked her on behalf of all of them for the soy milk and described her seventy-two hours in the river: the waters had washed out the poisons from her blood stream and had been purified by a pill called "Tianwang buxin dan." She was reborn and out of danger.   Immortal Lü gently laid his palm on her forehead and anointed her as divine immortal with a transference of his heavenly *qi*. She rose a new person, bowing her head on the deck and grateful to be alive. Birds flew above encircling the vessel, guiding it to a quiet section at the center of the river. There, in the subtle flow, grew a beautiful lotus flower. Lü Dongbin reached down and plucked the lotus, handing it to He Xiangu. This was her gift from the bodhisattva Guanyin. He Xiangu was now a Daoist immortal. The news of her transformation spread quickly and she became well known in the vicinity. Her mother-in-law was livid. Soon thereafter, a mysterious disease struck the old woman: she died a slow and painful death.

Practice

Basic Set-up

Equipment

Type of Sword: To practice the Eight Immortals' Revolving Sword, use a Chinese straight or taiji sword. Spring-steel is ideal, given the blade's added flexibility and strength. A well-crafted sword can be bent back onto itself in a curve, and the reverberation of *qi* at the tip of the blade can be seen when held. Combat-steel, straight swords are also acceptable, but should not be sharpened to avoid injury.

Size: When measuring for the appropriate length of a sword to suit an individual, take perfect measurement from the top of the iliac crest or naval to the heel of the foot or the ground while the sword is drawn from the scabbard. One or two inches difference, either longer or shorter, is still acceptable, especially if the sword is of exceptional quality.

Choice: When making the final decision on a sword, the only and most important criterion is is that you like it and have a personal connection to it. The same way you feel when choosing a puppy from a litter or in the way in which you gravitate toward people. There should be a good feeling, a mutual affinity. It is always better to choose a sword in person.

Weight: As a beginner, the weight of the sword should feel comfortable in your hand. If you feel it is strenuous to move the sword around or lift it overhead, it is probably too heavy for you or not properly balanced. After some years of practice and as the body gains internal strength, you can also use heavier swords. This is one indication of achieving levels in sword cultivation.

Clothes: Wear loose, light, and comfortable clothing; add layers during extreme cold weather to prevent illness. Avoid clothes that are oversized or baggy, so you do not snag or entangle different parts of the sword in them during practice. This will disrupt concentration and increase the risk of injury. Silk clothing is a natural conductor of *qi*.

Shoes: Shoes should be flat, so that the heels (roots) of the feet are well grounded and in contact with the earth. However, make sure the soles of the shoes are thick enough to protect your feet from bruising or puncture from miscellaneous objects on the ground. Try to avoid slippery soles and raised heels such as in dress shoes and running shoes. Rubber soles and flexible uppers are usually the best material for practice.

Safety: If you have never undertaken this kind of exercise, take certain precautions: consult a physician and receive a complete checkup to make sure that there are no health issues. Also, if you are not comfortable moving the steel sword around the body, use a substitute, such as a light-weight, collapsible or a wood sword, both without sharp edges. They are not difficult to find. Please do not use sharpened blades during practice to avoid being cut. There are some movements in the form which require the sword's blade to be held in hand or pressed against the body.

Mindset

Clear Mind: Before practice, make sure your mind is clear and without distractions. Establish tranquility by turning the eyes inward, away from the indulgence of images in the colorful, chaotic world. Let the images and questions arise in the mind's eye so they can be sorted and settled with controlled conviction. Do this as a prerequisite before commencing Daoist exercise. Also, answer all unresolved dilemmas curtly and swiftly, using the sharp stroke of the mind's sword, thereby dissolving their presence in both conscious and subconscious states. The solution you find this way are not necessarily permanent, but they will keep the mind's wild horses and emotions at bay for the moment. When the mind becomes more or less quiet, start the practice.

Thought *Qi*: Daoist exercise is not without thought as some people claim. It could not be called exercise or meditation without them. The kind of mindful ideas you have determines the type of *qi* you develop in the body. Straight thoughts or devious? Easy or complex? Caring or full of greed? Relaxed or anxious? Many movements of the Eight Immortals' Revolving Sword sequence require some mental enhancement to activate the different expressions of the internal life force. They help you to stay on the big road of what Buddhists call "right mindfulness." They are also important in executing the techniques correctly and building your spiritual confidence.

Warm-up

Qigong: The practice of qigong is the most suitable warm-up exercise for the internal martial arts and goes hand in hand with them. It is the mother of all Daoist exercise. Qigong allows you to gather, circulate, centralize, and store vita energy and blood in body and joints. This grade of energy is different than that gained from food and drink, and qigong practice is like adding high-octane fuel to a vehicle before driving. All other fuel sources are of lower quality. To learn appropriate Daoist qigong exercises, please read Dr. Wu's *Qigong For Total Wellness: Increase Your Energy, Vitality, and Longevity with the Ancient 9 Palaces system from the White Cloud Temple* or contact the Beijing Chinese Medical Center.

Walking: Walking is a great way of increasing the circulation of the body and filling the muscles with blood. It is recommended over running to lessen the risk of injury and also to keep the heart rate from going too high. The heart will receive a steady sufficient aerobic workout during sword practice. One hundred paces is the recommended distance, best done after every meal to help digestion.

Easy Stretches: Generally, qigong and walking increase muscle elasticity and help relax and store energy in the main joints of the body. This is equivalent to stretching if done properly and for an extended duration. Although stretching is helpful, when the body becomes older there is a higher risk of injury to the joints, ligaments, tendons, and muscles. On the microscopic level, tiny capillaries and muscle fibers break and tear easily: thus we recommend only light stretching.

Breathing

Regular Breathing: Breathing during practice is best done by inhaling through the nose and exhaling through the mouth. Inhaling belongs to yin (kidneys) and exhaling belongs to yang (lungs). When practicing the sword movements, inhalation is a closing procedure or contraction while exhalation is an opening procedure or expansion. There are specific instructions and accurate guidelines on when to inhale and exhale. They are not absolute, as each individual has his or her own body rhythms and breath counts.

Pore Breathing: There are no detailed instructions on pore breathing in this book. With regular practice, there may be instances when proper *qi* moves above the surface of the skin through the pores and mingles with the external energies of nature. At this point they reach unison and you will feel a sensation of effortless movement. You can achieve it by connecting to the expansion and contraction of the universal breath.

Natural Breathing: Whenever the instructional portion of this book does not specify a breathing pattern, just breathe naturally. If you get to a place in your practice where you are no longer conscious of your breathing habits and instead feel immersed in natural, uninhibited breathing, this is a sign of the harmonious relation between internal organs and external influences.

Environment

Location: Finding a suitable location can sometimes be challenging, especially in the city. A good spot depends on many factors. A location with ample trees, flowers, natural flowing water, birds, or other wild animals will produce, support, and enhance a positive *qi*-field. If you find animal excrement in a potential practice area, skirt it by all means, since this is dirty *qi* that can cause disease. If there is none and the various creatures appear frequently to play, then it is a good place to practice. Overall, the area should have a good balance of yin and yang. The place has to be both easily accessible and convenient. If practice areas are scarce around your house, best try to find a good place on your way to or from work. This way you have a better chance at practicing regularly. For more tips, see Dr. Wu's *Lighting the Eye of the Dragon: Inner Secrets of Taoist Feng Shui*.

Surface: The surface of the practice grounds should be flat and even. Check the area thoroughly to make sure there are no cracks, holes, or depressions in the ground to eliminate any chances of spraining an ankle and or a knee. Be sure the surface is dry to avoid slipping on wet ground. If the area has grass, make sure it is short and not too soft, spongy, or wet.

Windy Days: The best weather to practice Daoist sword are windy days. By surrendering to the wind during practice, you and the sword gain sensitivity to *qi* so that, if ever forced into combat, you have the advantage over your opponent whose every motion and thought relates to the wind element. Let the wind guide your movements, so that you are going with the flow of nature.

Mountains: To develop the top martial *qi*, practice in an environment where you have mountains and some rocks or stones. This will help to build a rock-solid foundation. Mountains last forever, so they also contribute to longevity as well as good ethics.

Water: Practicing near a river, stream, lake, or the ocean helps to enhance your yin energy and contributes to the fluidity of your motion. The ocean is also a source of wisdom and fortune.

Timing

Sunrise: Early morning practice is best around 6 am, when the darkness gives way to the sun. This is an excellent time to create changes and redirect destiny through the open window between yin and yang.

Noon: During the hours from 11 am to 1 pm, the sun is directly overhead and peaks with yang energy. If you are lacking this or would like to pursue longevity, this is a great time to practice.

Evening: The early evening hours from 7 to 9 pm are a supreme time to practice the Eight Immortals' Revolving Sword or other martial arts. The magnetic field of the earth is strongest during these hours and helps to develop the internal spring force of the body.

Midnight: The period from 11 pm to 1 am is the peak of yin: a peaceful and quiet time to practice sword. Afterwards you can enjoy a deep, restful sleep.

Birth Time: Another optimum time for practice is during the time of your birth. This is a unique opportunity to align with your higher self and receive vital information from the universe. That specific time of the day is like the numbered combination of a lock: only that exact sequence of digits can unlock the channel.

Sun and Moon: A wonderful time to practice sword cultivation is when the sun and moon are out together, sharing the same sky. This is a powerful way of gathering these energies simultaneously from the strongest sources of yin and yang in our solar system.

The Elixir Fields

Lower: The lower elixir field sits in the center of the belly, slightly below the navel. From here *qi* is distributed to every place in the body during practice. At the conclusion of any Daoist exercise, make sure to always return the *qi* to this area for storage. A "field" is a place where farmers plant seeds and harvest crops; in the body it is the area where the fetus grows and the spirit body develops. It is also where the sun resides in the microcosm of the human body.

Middle: The middle elixir area is located right between the nipples, on the vertical line which separates the right and left halves of the body, at a point called Central Platform (Tanzhong). This is the heart *qi*-center, the place of the moon in the body's microcosm.

Upper: The upper elixir zone is in the center of the head, reached by moving inward between the eyebrows on the forehead, through a point called Hall of Yin (Yintang), also the source of the Heavenly Eye. Moving *qi* into this area triggers the inner components of the brain, such as the pituitary and pineal glands, resulting in the penetration of inner vision. This is the residence of the stars in the microcosm of human anatomy.

Movement

Waist: The waist separates the body's lower half from the upper. Taiji quan texts descibe it as two round mill stones, such as those used in grinding soy beans for tofu or wheat for flour. They turn in different directions to grind the beans or grain very fine. When they are turning, it is difficult to stop their momentum. For this reason, they are considered a great source of power. Thus we understand the generating power through the waist and lower elixir field. Movements in the Eight Immortals' Revolving Sword utilize this concept.

Joints: There are thirteen major joints in the body: neck, shoulders, elbows, wrists, hips, knees, and ankles. They all are satellite storage areas of *qi* power. Practice helps them to remain open and fluid, so that one never gets arthritis or injury from lack of strength. The joints should never be fully locked or perfectly straightened during practice, so that *qi* can flow freely and you can easily absorb any impact from oncoming forces during combat. One poorly conditioned joint will effect the rest: "A chain is only as strong as its weakest link."

Linkage: The joints move together like a chain. Whenever you swing a chain or use it to tie or tow an object, it moves one link at a time. The last link never reaches its full range or potential unless all others are active, which means the first has to engage the second, the second the third, and so on. When studying or observing a practitioner's movements, we are not so much concerend with his or her techniques, i.e., the precion of the form, but look most at the joints and the way in which they join and activate the rest of the body. This is the true measuring stick of the internal force and level of practice. You can also think of this as a string of pearls, always joined and moving together. The interconnected joints help the body to move as a whole in a effortless wave.

Speed: Practice your sword exercises at a slow speed and increasingly allow internal energy to direct your movements. The mind directs the *qi*, and the *qi* moves the body. If you have ever studied or even observed taiji quan in action, you will know the reality of this statement. Make short transitional pauses between each movement, so short that they are undetectable—like the continuous flow of clouds, which seem to be locked in stillness yet never cease to move. Thus continue to flow through the form from one posture to another, unless otherwise specified in the instructions. Remember: those who practice say, "Sometimes the sword follows you and sometimes you follow the sword." This will influence the speed of your practice.

Practice Key

Bagua: The directions of the eight trigrams are key to all movements and directional changes in the form. The lowest trigram in the arrangement is to the south. The first standing posture of the form begins facing this direction.

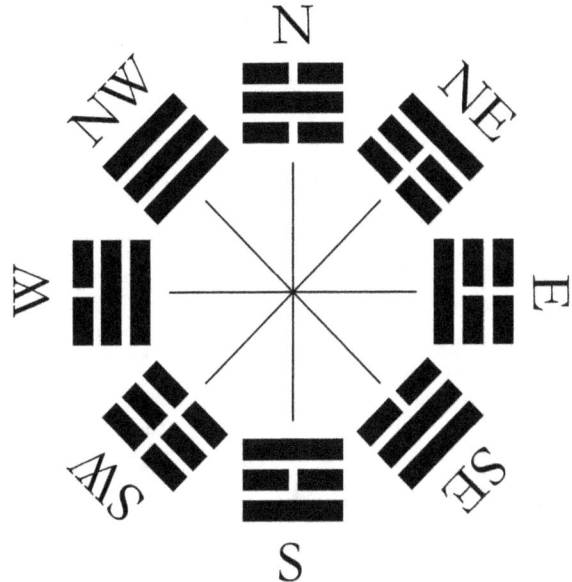

Anatomy of the Sword

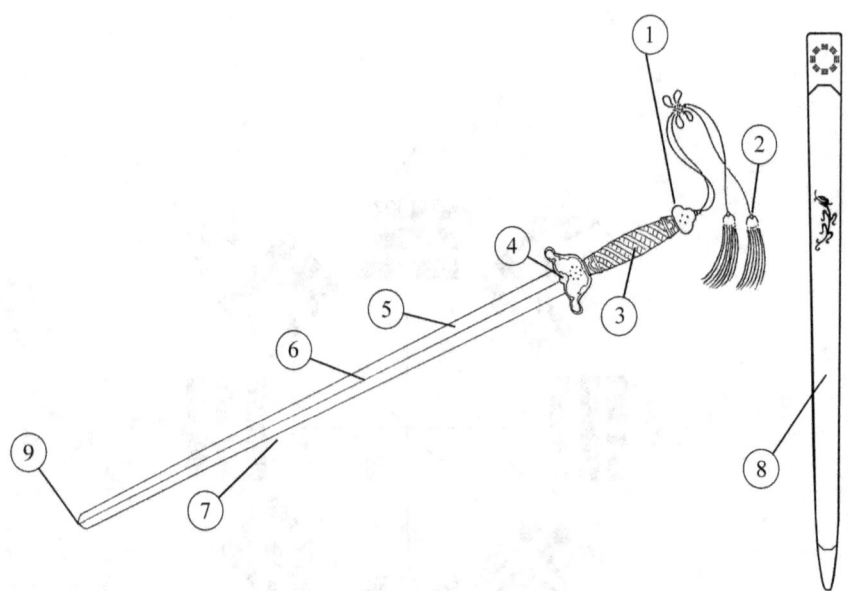

1. Pommel
2. Tassel
3. Handle
4. Guard
5. Blade
6. Spine
7. Edge
8. Scabbard
9. Tip

Instructions

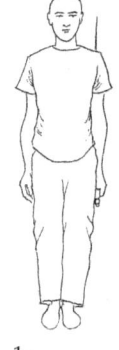

(1a) Start by facing south. Human beings are thought to be born in the north and walk south toward the sun and destiny. The heels are touching and each foot opens outward, away from the centerline at a 25-degree angle. The right hand rest on the right side, the middle finger lightly touching the Fengshi point along the outside of the thigh. The left hand holds the sword vertical, the cutting edges pointing north and south. The hand grip is inverted, index finger and thumb closest to the nearest pommel. The edge of the blade is firmly pressed between the left shoulder blade and the deltoid muscle, against the Jianzhen point; the left inner elbow supports the blade's flat side. The back is straight, the waist relaxed, tailbone gently tucked. The knees are slightly bent, and the chin is one vertically placed fist away from the clavicle or upper chest. Hold this posture until the mind becomes quiet. Breathing is natural.

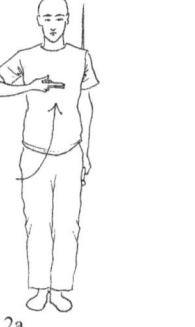 

(2a) While still resting on the side of the leg, the right hand forms a sword-mudra by uniting thumb, ring finger, and pinky. The thumb covers the other two fingernails, acting as a clip to keep them in place. Index and middle fingers join side by side and become straight like a sword's blade. Begin with a long, slow inhale through the nose, as the right sword-mudra floats up the front centerline of the torso, palm-up, until reaching the point between the nipples at the center of the chest. This moves *qi* from the lower elixir field into the middle elixir area.

(2b) The right hand turns palm down, simultaneously exhaling and sinking to the lower dantian, freezing at this position. The *qi* has been returned to the lower elixir field.

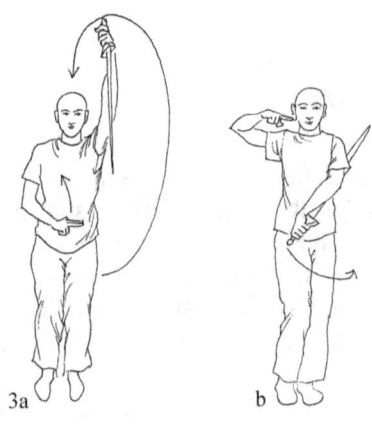

(3a) Just as the right hand sword-mudra finds rest at the lower elixir field, the left hand holding the sword lifts off to the left side of the body, palm down. It forms an arc that continues overhead and down the centerline of the face and torso while you inhale through the nose. On the downward part of the arc, begin exhaling through the mouth. At the point where the left hand passes the eyebrows, a lever action commences as the right hand sword-mudra, palm down, moves up close to the body.

The sword handle and mudra pass one another at the tan zhong acu-point, moving in opposite directions.

(3b) The sword handle completes a full 360-degree arc at the original starting position on the left side of the body; the right hand sword-mudra hovers above and slightly forward of the right shoulder. As the right hand moves toward the shoulder, the right foot adjusts, pivoting on the heel to a 45-degree angle to the right along with the waist, while you slightly bend the right leg. Begin inhaling during this transition.

(4a) The left foot steps forward, landing heel-to-toe in a left front bow-stance, both heels forming a straight line while exhaling. Almost immediately, release the right hand sword-mudra, straighten and lift all five fingers, and make a right hand stroke, using the lower outside heel of the palm to push down along the lower rib cage and up in front of the middle elixir area. As you turn the waist, you generate power. Keep the elbow bent to form a half circle from the shoulder to the hand, and the left foot angled inward. The left knee should not go forward beyond the big toe to avoid injury. Sink into the position. Weight is 70% front, 30% back.

(5a) When the right hand stroke reaches the position in front of the middle elixir area, begin inhaling and lift the left hand holding the sword off toward the left side of the body, palm down. Near the point where the arm is extended and level with the shoulder, the sword hand changes direction, moving forward on a horizontal plane. The sword is horizontal, flat, and parallel to the ground; it remains braced against the inside of the left elbow.

As the sword traverses inward, toward the open palm of the right hand, the left elbow bends and the right hand catches the backside of the left hand in front of the middle elixir area. Keep the eyes focused, looking down along the sword's spine and to the tip of the blade. The elbows are pointing north and south, the right heel of the palm applies light pressure to the sword's pommel so the blade remains flat and fixed to the left elbow.

(5b) After the right hand has caught the back of the left hand, the momentum of the horizontally held handle continues up and back, around and above the right shoulder near the right ear. Shift your weight into the right leg and continue the circular orbit of the sword as the arm moves down, forward and just under and ahead of the middle elixir area. The majority of the weight has shifted with the circle, this time into the left leg, and the entire body moves in unison. A second circular orbit of the sword begins back and up toward the right shoulder and ear, shifting the weight into the right leg. Continue to inhale. As the directional arrow indicates, the sword becomes vertical in the next movement.

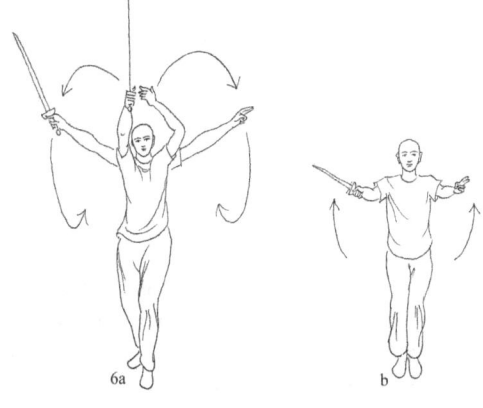

(6a) The momentum carried to the right shoulder continues into a smaller orbit. As the sword begins to descend forward, the majority of the weight remains on the back leg. The heel of the right hand, resting on the pommel, pushes down, sending the tip of the blade vertical into the beginning of two large circles. In this transition, the left hand relinquishes control of the sword to the right

The body opens front to face south while subtly drawing the left foot back a half step into a left empty stance. Weight is 90% back, 10% front. In this exchange, the right hand takes hold of the sword handle with the index finger and thumb closest to the guard. The left hand forms a sword-mudra by joining the thumb, ring finger, and pinky. The thumb print covers the other two fingernails, acting as a clip to keep them in place. Index and middle finger join side by side and become straight like a sword's blade. Both palms are facing one another: this rotates the sword blade to face north and south. The motion does not cease during the change of grip, and both sword and mudra climb skyward like two pillars. When the two reach their peak, they stretch out to the sides going down and back behind the shoulders to create two circles along the sides of the body. Begin to exhale.

(6b) When sword and mudra pass by the right leg—at which point the palms are once again facing each other—the right leg should feel as if it is being picked up by the sword and carried forward, stepping and settling next to the left foot. Both feet are now parallel and touching, with knees slightly bent. However, sword and mudra continue forward to complete the two circles, finishing with both blades pointing south and parallel to the ground. The hands are a bit wider apart than the shoulders, palms facing. Elbows and wrist are slightly bent to avoid rigidity, so the blades are angled downward approximately two inches. Sink into the position. When the sword is close to reaching this posture, begin to inhale to prepare for the next movement.

(7a) Let the sword blade fall while exhaling, creating a circle on the vertical plane along the right outer half of the body. The right wrist rotates down and around, assisting the sword to complete the circle. The left hand sword-mudra does not move. When the sword swings by the right leg and begins its ascent forward, it uproots the leg with the energy and momentum generated, making it hop forward as far as the sword will take it. The sword finishes the circle at the same time as the right foot hits the ground again, sword and mudra pointing south once more. When the right foot is down, the left leg has already begun to follow.

(7b) After the left foot crosses the plane of the right foot, both the sword and mudra perform a small elongated circle in front of the body—like the arms that turn the wheels of an old locomotive. This is synchronized with the left foot coming forward into its final position, landing one step ahead of the right foot in an empty stance (weight is 90% back, 10% front). The sword and mudra continue their forward motion to complete the two elongated circles, finishing with both blades pointing south and parallel to the ground. The hands are a bit wider than the shoulders, palms facing. Elbows and wrists are slightly bent to avoid rigidity, so the blades are angled downward approximately two inches. The left knee and toe angle inward to cover and protect the vital areas.

(7c) Inhaling, step forward and place the right foot next to the left. Simultaneously point both sword and mudra straight up by bending wrists and elbows. Palms are still facing. Both feet are now parallel and touching and the knees are slightly bent.

(7d) Continuing to inhale, bring the right palm holding the sword to face the middle elixir area, and let the left hand sword-mudra rotate upward next to the left temple with the palm facing forward.

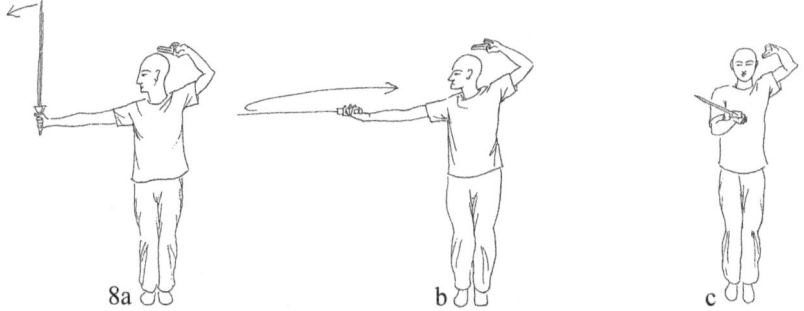

(8a) Exhale and unfurl the arm and sword to the right side of the body extending the arm out to the west. The eyes follow the blade in the unfurling. Maintain the vertical position of the sword while doing so. After the arm reaches full extension, the wrist releases, letting the blade fall and cut down until it is parallel to the ground. Do not allow the tip of the sword to dip below this level. The left hand sword-mudra remains in position at the left temple, palm facing forward.

(8b) Once the sword has become parallel to the ground, turn wrist and palm up toward the sky. The sword's blade is now flat and the eyes are fixed on the tip of the sword blade. As the arrow indicates, the sword traverses inward, toward the centerline of the body in the next movement.

(8c) Start to inhale with the eyes locked on the tip of the sword. Eyes and head follow as the blade begins to slice across to the left, moving from the shoulder with the arm still extended. The waist helps this process almost effortlessly, until the sword is pointing due south and positioned parallel to the ground. The left hand sword-mudra remains in position at the left temple. Both feet are still parallel and touching; knees are slightly bent.

(9a) Exhale and let the sword blade fall downward, creating a circle on the vertical plane along the right outer half of the body. The right wrist rotates down and around, assisting the sword blade to complete the circle. (The left hand sword-mudra does not move until the sword comes back around 360 degrees.)

When the sword swings by the right leg and begins its ascent forward, it propels the leg using the sword's energy, making it hop forward as far as the sword will take it. The sword completes the circle at the same time as the right foot hits the ground again. When the right foot is firm, the left leg has already begun to follow.

(9b) When the left foot crosses the plane of the right foot, both sword and mudra, now pointing south, perform a small elongated circle in front of the body, like the arms that turn the wheels of an old locomotive. This is synchronized with the left foot coming forward into its final position, stepping ahead of the right foot in an empty stance (weight is 90% back, 10% front). The sword and mudra continue their motion forward to complete the two elongated circles, finishing with both blades pointing south and parallel to the ground. The hands are a touch wider than the shoulders and the palms of the hands are facing one another. The elbows and wrist are slightly bent to avoid rigidity, therefore the blades are angled downward approximately two inches. The left knee and toe angle inward to cover and protect vital areas.

(9c) Inhale and pivot on the heel of the left foot outward to a 45-degree angle, shifting the body weight from right foot to left, simultaneously moving the sword into a vertical position (arm extended out in front of the right shoulder and chest), while rotating the left hand sword-mudra to the position opposite the left temple (ca. 8-12 inches from the head) with the palm facing left and away from the body. At the same time that the left foot settles into position, the right foot is stepping forward and hooking inward.

Both heels of the feet are aligned and the eyes are staring straight ahead through the blade. Weight is 80% back, 20% front.

(10a) Begin exhaling and continue to step through with the left foot into a left twist stance while releasing the wrist and letting the blade fall with your arm extended, so it cuts down until it is parallel to the ground. Do not allow the tip of the sword to dip or angle below this level. The left foot and sword arrive to their intended positions together. The left hand sword-mudra remains at the left temple. The feet are perpendicular and the weight is evenly distributed. The left foot is flat on the ground and the right foot is planted on the ball (Note: Continue exhaling until you reach the final posture of movement: see Fig. 10f)

(10b) Step around the twist stance with the right foot until it becomes parallel and even with the left foot. The feet are shoulder-width apart in a natural stance. Fully extend and arc the sword and mudra from right to left, side by side across the sky, like the hands of a clock. The right palm holding the sword faces the body; the left palm faces away. The body is turned to the east. The eyes look up, following the sword all the way across to the left side of the body. The weight is evenly distributed.

(10c) As the sword and mudra reach the horizon on the left side of the body and begin to form the lower half of a circle, the left palm rotates inward to face the body and both arms pass in front of the legs. Both arms are extended and continue to circle toward the original starting point. The eyes never leave the blade.

(10d) When the sword begins to move across the original starting point of the circle to the body's right, without changing the directions of the palms which now both face you, let the body naturally follow the sword and begin to twist to the right at the waist.

(10e) Pivot on the heel of the right foot for 180 degrees and swing the left foot around until it is parallel and even with the right foot. The feet are shoulder- width apart in a natural stance while you continue to extend and arc both the sword and mudra. They are now going from left to right, side by side across the sky, like the hands of a clock. Both palms face away and the body is turned to the west. The eyes look up, following the sword all the way across to the right side of the body. The weight is evenly distributed.

(10f) As the sword and mudra reach the horizon on the body's right, just prior to forming the lower half of the circle, there is a directional. When the sword is parallel to the ground, the right wrist turns the palm upward to face the sky, thus turning the blade flat. The left hand sword-mudra turns palm down toward the earth. The waist starts to turn the body to the left while you pivot on the heel of the left foot. Both arms extend out from the shoulders in front, elbows slightly bent. Sword and mudra pursue the horizontal and circular direction of the waist, and the entire body moves as one unit. The eyes follow the blade.

(10g) Pivoting on the heel of the left foot for 180 degrees, swing the right foot around until it is next to and touching the left foot. This occurs in unison with the upper half of the body, which now faces east. The feet are joined and the knees slightly bent, while both arms are extended outward from the shoulders in front of the body, elbows slightly bent. The right palm still faces skyward with the blade flat; the left palm with the sword-mudra, during the 180-degree pivot, has rotated to face in toward the right hand. Settle into the posture and start inhaling.

(11a) Still inhaling, let the sword blade fall downward, creating a circle along the right outer half of the body. The right wrist holding the handle rotates down and around, assisting the sword blade to continue and complete the 360-degree circle. The left hand sword-mudra does not move.

(11b) Once the sword has made its full circle, immediately draw the hands in toward the middle elixir area, palms up.

(11c) Cradle the right hand holding the sword with the open palm of the left hand, as the sword's blade stays flat and level. Simultaneously draw the right knee upward in the direction of the middle elixir area while folding the leg. Exhale and prepare to extend the limbs forward.

(11d) From the position at the middle elixir area, both hands holding the sword fully extend out in front, while the right leg fully extends back with the sole facing up and the toes pointed. The back must be flat like a table top, and the joints of both legs and arms locked. The eyes are raised and focused on the end of the sword to maintain complete concentration. Hold this position for five seconds. Breathe naturally.

(12a) Start inhaling and begin to slowly bend the left leg at the knee, allowing the spine to return to a vertical position. At the same time, separate the hands and retract the right leg. The weight is still fully on the left leg.

(12b) The left hand again forms a sword-mudra and rotates to the position opposite the left temple (ca. 8-12 inches from the head), palm facing left and away from the body. The right hand holding the sword draws down and back at a 45-degree angle near the right hip. Top of the right foot finds a nest behind the bent left knee. Eyes and body now face southeast.

(13a) While still inhaling, take one step back with the right foot, simultaneously bending the right elbow inward. The left hand sword-mudra stays in position.

(13b) Step the left foot behind the right into a right empty stance: weight is 90% back, 10% front. Wrap the sword around the left side of the body, palm down. The blade is flat and the inner edge lightly touches the left ribcage. Apply a gentle torque to the left of the waist. The left foot is at a 45-degree angle. The left hand sword-mudra stays in position.

(13c) Begin to exhale as you shift your weight forward into the right leg and draw the sword away from the left ribcage to point it forward. In the process, turn the sword over, palm up. This begins a two-step explosion of internal force similar to that of a coiled snake striking out.

(13d) The left leg steps ahead of the right leg, catching up to the bottom of the sword handle at the right ribcage.

(13e) Trot toward the southeast, then lunge forward with the right foot and plant it with an inwardly rotating thrust of the sword at a 45-degree downward angle. The left foot drags behind and stops approximately 18 inches behind the right. It finishes on the ball, with the heel off the ground. The right foot is angled in to protect the vital areas and the left hand sword-mudra stays in position. Weight is 40% back, 60% front.

(14a) Inhale and pivot the right foot on the heel to the left while lifting the right arm and sword in an overhead motion. The left hand sword-mudra waves over to the left, synchronized with the pivoting and sword movement. Both palms are facing away from the body.

(14b) Continue the movement overhead until the sword handle is positioned over the right shoulder, arm held vertically, with the blade parallel to the ground, tilting down two inches. The left hand sword-mudra extends from the shoulder, palm facing inward. After this 180-degree transition, settle into a left empty stance facing northwest. Focus the eyes on the point where the tip of the blade and the sword-mudra's line intersect. Weight is 90% back, 10% front.

(14c) Take the left foot and step back behind the right into an empty stance while rotating the left hand sword-mudra up to the left temple (ca. 8-12 inches from the head), palm facing away from the body. At the same time, as if carving the inside of a melon, draw a half circle with the sharp edge of the sword, until the palm faces upward and the pommel of the sword is in front of the nose, the blade's edge skyward. Weight is 90% back, 10% front.

(14d) Begin to exhale as you roll forward into the right leg, followed by the left foot stepping forward. The sword and left hand sword-mudra remain in place. Trot toward the northwest.

(14e) Let the right foot lunge forward and set down with an inwardly rotating thrust of the sword at a 45-degree downward angle. The left foot drags behind and stops approximately 8 inches behind it, finish on the ball, heel off the ground. The right foot is angled in to protect the vital areas, and the left hand sword-mudra stays in position. Weight is 40% back, 60% front.

(15a) Inhale and shift your weight onto the right foot. At the same time, as if carving the inside of a melon, draw a small half-circle with the sharp edge of the sword (see Fig. 14c) until the palm faces skyward and the sword pommel is in front of the throat, the blade's edge skyward. At the same time draw up the sole of the left foot and rest it flat on the inside of the right knee. The left hand sword-mudra stays next to the left temple (ca. 8-12 inches from the head), palm facing away from the body. Bend the wrist upward, so the sword is vertical and both, palm and sword edge, face the chest.

(15b) Exhale, hold the stance, and let the sword blade fall forward, creating a circle along the right outer half of the torso. The right wrist holding the handle rotates down and around, assisting the blade to complete the circle. Neither stance and nor mudra move.

(15c) When the sword completes the circle, it is again vertical, except the palm now faces forward, ahead of the body. Without pause, let the sword blade fall forward and begin a second circle, this time on the inside of the right arm and under the armpit.

(15d) End in a vertical position, with the edge of the blade firmly pressed between the right shoulder blade and the deltoid muscle against the Jianzhen point. Step back behind the right foot with the left foot while starting to drop the left hand sword-mudra, palm down, along the left side of the body.

(15e) Release the mudra and turn the palm up. Continue the body turning 180 degrees toward the southeast by pivoting to the left on both heels. Finish in a forward bow-stance, facing southeast, left hand shoulder high, palm open and in front of the body in a striking pose. The left foot is angled inward and the right foot is at a 45-degree angle. The left knee bends forward but not beyond the big toe to avoid injury. Weight is 70% front, 30% back.

(16a) From the left forward bow-stance, step forward onto the toes of the right foot next to and even with the left foot while rotating and inverting the left palm to face skyward overhead. The left elbow is slightly bent to form a rounded structure. Weight is 95% left, 5% right.

(16b) Inhale slowly and raise the right knee until the thigh is parallel to the ground while simultaneously pressing skyward with the left palm until the elbow is almost locked. In the one legged stance, the left foot is relaxed and allowed to rest and hang down.

(16c) From the one-legged stance, exhale and extend kicking the right leg out from the knee, slapping the top of the right foot with the left palm out in front of the body. The left foot stays planted and flat on the ground and the sword remains cocked inside of the right arm with the edge of the

166 / Practice

blade firmly pressed between the right shoulder blade and the deltoid muscle against the jian-zhen acu-point.

(16d) After kicking out the right leg, the right foot will quickly retract stepping back and behind the left foot. The sword is also quickly released and drawn out from under the right armpit being led by the handle traveling upward. When the sword is drawn, the right arm and wrist twist inward causing the right elbow to lift and the right palm to face away from the body giving the blade a clear avenue to pass through between the torso and arm.

(16e) With the right foot planted one step behind the left, draw the sword handle upward to its highest point. Then let it continue the motion in an arc (see arrow). The left hand forms a sword-mudra and follows the right with the sword, like the hands of a clock.

(16f) As the sword reaches the high point of its arc, the feet transition to the northwest. However, the waist continues to turn to the right, redirecting the destination of the sword. The left elbow and sword-mudra begin to bend and fall into position close to the left temple.

(16g) The body thus twists back to face southeast but the feet remain pointing northwest. In synchronized motion, kneel on the left and let the left hand sword-mudra fall into position near the left temple (ca. 8-12 inches from the head), palm facing away from the body. The sword slices down, pointing southeast. Although the lower half of the body faces northwest, head and eyes are turned southeast, looking down the fully extended right arm and sword.

(17a) Inhale and turn the right wrist palm up, so the sword is flat. As the wrist turns, waist and sword naturally rotate back around to the left. Rise slowly to your feet, keeping the eyes fixed on the sword.

(17b) Rotate back to the left, allowing three contacts to come together and arrive in front of the body at the same moment as if attracted by magnets. As the sword points northwest, left index and middle fingers of the mudra make contact with the right forearm at the Kongzui point. Simultaneously set the left foot forward into a transitionary twist stance.

(17c) Continue rotating left in this position by stepping around and bringing the right foot parallel to the left, temporarily facing southwest. Keep your eyes fixed on the sword.

(17d) Continue rotating to the left by stepping around with the left foot.

(17e) Set it back and behind the right to the northwest, while the sword smoothly glides around the perimeter. Keep your eyes fixed on the sword.

(17f) Immediately step with the right foot toward the northwest, redirecting the momentum of the circle and allowing the sword to go linear and forward. Halt and shift just over 50 percent of your weight into the right leg. The sword remains horizontal and flat, while the left hand sword-mudra keeps contact with the right forearm.

(17g) Shift the weight into the back leg and go into a right empty stance, both feet flat on the ground. At the same time bend the right wrist, palm facing the body's center, until the sword is perfectly vertical and the blade's edge faces the chest. Weight is 90% back, 10% front. Begin inhaling.

(18a) While still in the empty stance and facing northwest, exhale and let the sword fall forward, creating a circle along the right outer half of the body. The right wrist holding the handle naturally breaks and rotates down and around, assisting the blade to complete its circle on the vertical plane. The left hand sword-mudra maintains contact with the right forearm.

(18b) Without halting the momentum of the sword, turn the right wrist and sword inward directing the tip of the blade to dive down and across the body at a 45-degree angle, simultaneously stepping forward with the left foot planting into a right angle, left heel to right toe. The power is generated and assisted by turning the waist. The left hand sword-mudra maintains contact with the right forearm.

(18c) Make a complete vertical circle with the sword along the left side of the body by lifting and turning the right wrist outward, back over to the right (see arrow). Let the blade glide near the body's surface to complete a figure of eight that connects both sides of the body. You generate power by turning the waist. The left heel to right toe stance does not alter. The left hand sword-mudra maintains contact with the right forearm.

(18d) As the sword returns to the right side of the body, begin the second of the three figures of eight, twirling once again along the right outer half of the body as the arrow indicates.

(18e) In the same instance, the right foot steps forward and around the left foot to form another right angle, right heel to left toe. The left hand sword-mudra maintains contact with the right forearm. Breathe naturally.

(18f) Turn the right wrist and sword inward, directing the tip of the blade to dive down and across the body at a 45-degree angle. Simultaneously step forward with the left foot and place it at a right angle, left heel to right toe. You let the diving sword make a complete circle along the left side of the body by lifting and turning the right wrist outward, back over to the right (see arrow). The blade glides near the body's surface to complete a figure of eight that connects both sides of the body. The left hand sword-mudra maintains contact with the right forearm. Breathe naturally.

(18g) When the sword returns to the right half of the body, begin the final figure eight, twirling once again along the right outer half of the body as the arrow indicates. In the same instance, the right foot is stepping forward and around to the left foot to form another right angle, right heel to left toe. The left hand sword-mudra maintains contact with the right forearm. Breathe naturally.

(18h) Turn the right wrist and sword inward.

(18i) Directing the tip to dive down and across the body at a 45-degree angle. Keep your feet fixed at right angle, right heel to left toe. The left hand sword-mudra maintains contact with the right forearm. Breathe naturally.

(18j) Let the diving sword make a complete circle along the left side of the body by lifting and turning the right wrist outward, back over to the right.

(18k) Simultaneously, turn the left hand sword-mudra palm up, disconnecting from the right forearm but stays inside of the right forearm. Begin inhaling.

(18l) With the body now facing northeast, take one step back with right foot into a left empty stance (weight is 90% back, 10% front). At the same time spreading the right and left arms into a majestic pose: emanate the grandeur of a lion, opening the heart energy for all to see. Keep the palms slightly angled skyward. Continue to inhale.

(19a) Still facing northeast, step back with the left foot into a right empty stance (weight is 90% back, 10% front) while bringing the sword handle out in front and in line with your nose and keeping your elbow bent slightly. The left hand sword-mudra falls into position next to the left temple (ca. 8-12 inches from the head), palm facing away from the body. Hold the blade vertically, palm up. Continue to inhale, coiling a spring force into the back leg.

(19b) Explode forward while pressing out of the stance with the right foot.

(19c) Step into a quick trot with the left foot.

(19d) Continue forward with the right foot stepping into a wide lunge.

(19e) Move into a forward bow-stance and simultaneously inwardly rotate and thrust the sword at a 45-degree downward angle, pointing northeast. The left hand sword-mudra stays in position next to the left temple. Weight is 70% front, 30% back.

(20a) Take a big step with the left foot behind the right, to the northeast (see arrow). At the same time let the left hand sword-mudra follow the same pattern along the lower half of the body. This pulls the sword 180 degrees in an overhead motion, the blade edge slicing down toward the southwest.

Imagine the sword as a bullwhip to properly perform this move.

(20b) At the exact same time, let the left foot settle into a side horse-stance with the feet parallel and turn the left hand sword-mudra palm out near the left temple. The sword is level, pointing southwest with head and eyes fixed in the same direction. Weight is 55% back, 45% front.

(20c) Begin inhaling and step forward with the left foot into a transitional left twist stance. The feet are perpendicular, with the left foot flat on the ground and the right planted on the ball of the foot. Sword and sword-mudra do not move.

Instructions / 171

(21a) Continue stepping ahead with the right foot, heel to toe, and as if skipping.

(21b) Step behind the right foot with the left foot onto the ball of the foot.

(21c) Let the right foot lightly leap forward and the left to step in its place.

(21d) Let the right foot land on the ground, then lift the left leg forward into a straight front kick, tapping the toes with the fingers of the left hand which is flat and open.

(21e) The kick pushes the sword up indirectly, moving it overhead toward the right side of the body (northeast). Begin to exhale. The sword and reformed left hand sword-mudra glide across the sky like the hands of a clock, palms facing away from the body. The left foot after its kick comes down to the ground (see arrow).

(21f) The sword slices down into a horizontal and level position, while the left hand sword-mudra falls into place next to the left temple (ca. 8-12 inches from the head), palm facing away from the body. Head and eyes are facing northeast. Weight is 60% back, 40% front in the modified stance.

(22a) Inhale and curl the right arm in and across, wrapping the sword around the left side of the body with the palm down. The blade is flat and the inner sharp edge is lightly touching the left ribcage. The sword handle and forearm are positioned slightly ahead of the body. When the sword has made contact with the body, lower the left hand sword-mudra to the opposite ribcage with the palm down, lightly touching the right side of the torso with the index finger. The sword blade and the left forearm rest lightly on one another to form a cross. For women, the left hand sword-mudra makes contact with the top of the right hand.

(22b) Turn the waist to the left while slowly exhaling and begin stepping back, around and behind the right foot with the left toward the northeast to start a 540% degree leaping and turning powered by the waist.

(22c) When the left foot touches ground, it immediately acts as a spring,

(22d) elevating with added trajectory, the entire body in the direction of the northeast.

(22e) Both feet are off the ground while the body is still turning to the left.

(22f) This 360-degree airborne finale plants down on the ground with the right foot first,

(22g) and is then followed by the left foot.

(22h) The waist turns the body to face northeast in a forward bow-stance. Throughout the 540-degree lift off, the positions of the sword and sword-mudra remain in place at the ribcage(s). The left foot is angled inward and weight is approximately 70% front, 30% back. The left knee bending forward should not go beyond the big toe to avoid injury.

(23a) Inhaling, step forward facing northeast and place the right foot parallel to the left foot with the right heel off the ground and knees slightly bent, while simultaneously uncrossing the arms. When opening like a pair of scissors, exhale as the sword-mudra glides, while almost touching, above the sword blade. The sword is drawn down and to the right side of the body at a 45-degree angle and the left hand sword-mudra goes up and to the left at a 45-degree angle, both reaching full extension together.

(23b) With the right foot heel still off the ground, begin inhaling simultaneously guiding and slowly thrusting the sword vertically along the center-line of the body as the left hand sword-mudra, palm down and horizontal, moves equally as slow in the opposite direction and is positioned inside of the sword closest to the body.

(23c) When the right arm nears full extension above the head and the left hand sword-mudra approaches position at the lower elixir field, the right heel of the foot drops making contact with the ground and straightens the body and legs, creating a gentle thrust of both arms into their intended positions, ending the exhale. The feet are side by side and parallel.

(24a) Inhale and raise the right heel off the ground, bending both knees while simultaneously turning the right palm down and slowly lowering the sword straight across until it becomes horizontal and flat. Let the edge of the blade be even with your brow and third eye, approximately one foot in front of them. The left hand sword-mudra turns over, palm up, as the right heel is raised, but it remains fixed in position at the lower elixir field.

(24b) Lower the right heel to the ground and begin a long slow inhale through the nose. Let the left hand sword-mudra, palm-up, float up along the front of the torso to the middle elixir area right between the nipples at the center of the chest. Lift and cross the right foot and leg over the left thigh which bends down until it is parallel to the ground.

(24c) While in this one-legged posture, inhale and cross both arms as if hugging a tree, bringing the sword just over and behind the left shoulder. The handle of the sword rests on the deltoid muscle, while the left hand sword-mudra crosses under the folded right arm and the fingers are set vertically on the outer side of the upper right arm.

(24d) Maintain the one-legged stance, begin opening the arms like a pair of scissors. Exhale as the sword glides above, without touching the fingers of the sword-mudra that slides underneath the sword's blade. Draw the sword down and to the right side of the body at a 45-degree angle while letting the left hand sword-mudra go up and to the left at a 45-degree angle. Both reach full extension together.

(24e) Still on one leg, inhale and lift the sword overhead so that the blade is horizontal and points northwest. The palm faces forward ahead of the body and the blade's edge is skyward. The left hand sword-mudra at the same time moves down to a horizontal, level position on the left side of the body, palm facing forward. Eyes and head follow. Turn your head and fix your gaze on the northwest. Inhale.

(24f) Release the right foot from the upper left leg and take one step toward the northwest while pivoting on the sole of the left foot. Right then direct the sword in the same direction, arcing and diving down, apparently coming in toward the body (see arrow). The left hand sword-mudra drops along the left leg.

(24g) Take a step forward with the left foot to the northwest into a left twist stance with the feet perpendicular. Redirect the sword by turning your right wrist outward, twisting the right forearm until the palm faces up and the blade's edge is skyward. The sword points northwest. The left hand sword-mudra circles up into the position 6-12 inches from the left temple, palm facing away.

(24h) Step forward with the right into a right forward bow-stance, extending the sword with a gentle thrust spurred by the momentum of the steps and stances. The right foot is angled inward; the weight is approximately 70% front, 30% back. The right knee is bending forward; it should not go beyond the big toe to avoid injury. Back leg is slightly bent.

(25a) Step forward with the left foot into a left twist stance, while bending and lifting the right wrist to make the sword stand vertical, palm facing the body. The left hand sword-mudra stays fixed. Breathe naturally.

(25b) Continue by stepping forward with the right foot into a right forward bow-stance, while lowering the right wrist down until the sword is parallel to the ground with the blade's edge skyward. The left hand sword-mudra stays fixed at the left temple.

(25c) Step forward again with the left foot into a left twist stance, bend and lift the right wrist to make the sword stand vertical, palm facing the body.

(25d) Step forward and around the vertical sword and the left leg which remains anchored in place by hooking both sword and left leg with the right foot. Turn the body 180 degrees to face southeast, pivoting on both feet into a transitional empty stance. Continue flowing by taking one step back (northwest) with the left foot (see arrows).

(25e) Simultaneously pull the sword down by the right hip and raise the sword-mudra up and overhead, palm skyward.

(25f) Continue walking back with the right foot behind the left, stepping and settling into an empty stance.

(25g) Begin exhaling and arch the spine back, simultaneously following the contour of the posture with the sword, up and over, extending it like a bridge past the crown of the head. At that moment, the left hand sword-mudra presses down, palm down, along the centerline of the body. It stops at the lower elixir field.

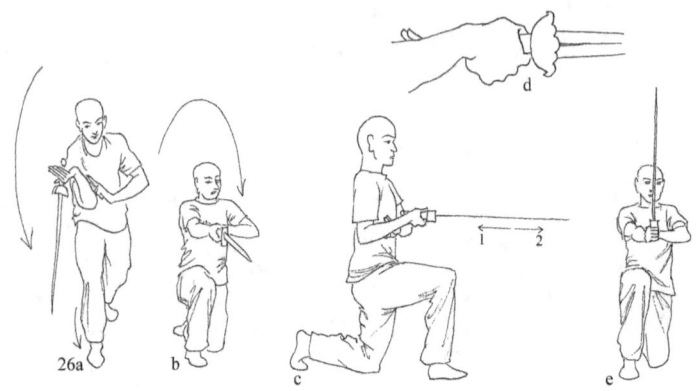

(26a) Take one full step back with the left foot, while bringing the sword down and forward to create a circle on the vertical plane along the right outer half of the body. The right wrist holding the handle rotates out and around, assisting the sword blade to continue and complete the circle. The left hand sword-mudra has shifted near the right forearm.

(26b) Step on the ball of the left foot, then bend the right leg and kneel down on the left leg as the sword completes the top half of the circle in front of the body with the blade parallel to the ground, leaving the right arm almost fully extended. The knee touches the ground just as the sword blade becomes horizontal and the left hand sword-mudra makes contact with the right forearm. The body still faces southeast.

(26c) Turn the right wrist palm-up, making the sword blade flat. Inhale and slowly pull the sword handle in toward the body, bending at the elbow. Exhale and extend the right elbow, pushing the sword back forward with the blade still flat.

(26d) Turn the right wrist so the palm faces in, making the blade's edge skyward once again.

(26e) Bend the right wrist upward, standing the sword vertically while sliding the fingers of the left hand sword-mudra against the base of the right thumb at the wrist. Begin inhaling.

(27a) Still kneeling, exhale and let the sword blade fall, creating a circle on the vertical plane along the right outer half of the body, simultaenously standing up on the right leg, then taking one step forward with the left. The right wrist holding the handle naturally breaks the form and rotates out and around, assisting the sword blade to complete the downward circle. The left hand sword-mudra briefly loses contact with the right wrist during the twirling of the sword.

(27b) The sword completes the circle, slightly raised at a 45-degree angle. The toes of the left foot step on the ground ahead of the right leg, forming a left empty stance. The left hand sword-mudra reconnects to the right wrist. Weight is 90% back, 10% front.

(27c) Inhale and separate the hands, slowly spreading the arms out like wings. Pivot on the heel of the left foot and turn the waist to the left.

(27d) Continue to turn the waist, with both feet remaining on the ground, thus building a wind-up tension.

(27e) Release the tension by lifting the right foot two inches off the ground thereby swinging the foot around to the left in a circular pattern, while pivoting on the ball of the left foot. The arms remain spread.

(27f) The right foot travels around 360 degrees until setting down in its original starting place.

(27g) The waist continues to turn the body leftward, pivoting on the feet. The arms, right on top of left, begin folding in across the front of the body, bending at the elbows, palms down.

(27h) The waist continues to turn until the front of the body faces southeast once again settling into a crouching low left empty stance and the arms, right on top of left with the palms down, have folded across the front of the body structuring a window to peer through.

(28a) Exhale and unwind from the crouching empty stance, turning the waist to the right and pivoting on both feet while simultaneously unfolding the arms outward, palms down and blade flat.

(28b) Continue pivoting on the feet 180 degrees to face northwest, allowing the arms to fully extend and reach their limit at the sides of the body. Both palms turn to face up.

(28c) Inhale and slide the extended arms forward to meet each other in front of the body. Both sword and left hand sword-mudra point northwest. Step the left foot forward next the right foot.

(28d) With palms up, bend the wrist so the palms face the torso, raising the sword and sword-mudra to a vertical position. The elbows may bend slightly but the emphasis is on the wrist bending.

(29a) Step forward with the left foot into a left bow-stance (weight is 70% front, 30% back). Release the left hand sword-mudra, fingers straight and upright, and deliver a left hand stroke down along the lower rib cage and up in front of the middle elixir area, using the lower outside heel of the palm. The right hand turns palm in to face the left elbow with the sword still vertical. The left elbow remains bent to form a half-circle from shoulder to hand. Lower and guide the blade section near the guard of the sword (see arrow), between the thumb and index finger of the left hand. Do not allow the sword blade to make contact with the hand.

(29b) Draw the sword and right elbow back as if drawing a bow with arrow, shifting the majority of your weight into the back leg.

(29c) Release the tension of the draw and allow the sword to pull the body forward, stepping the right toes next to the left foot. The right hand turns palm up, the sword blade is flat, with the pommel out in front of the neck. The palm of the left hand faces skyward above the right shoulder. From here begin exhaling while raising the right knee to form a one-legged stance. Thrust the sword up and forward, palm up, in front of the third eye, while pushing the left palm skyward and fully extending the left arm.

(30a) With the palm still up, gently rock the sword down and to the left in a half circle. Simultaneously kick to the left with the bottom of the right foot and sway the left palm to the far left reaches, away from the body.

(30b) Gracefully switch hand positions with the sword on top, palm down, and the left open hand underneath the sword, palm up. Sway back to the far right side of the body, repositioning the right leg in the original one-legged stance. Continue rocking to the right side with both arms.

(30c) From the right side, gently retract the sword in front of the forehead and the left open palm in front of the heart. Thrust the sword and the left hand and make a right heel-kick straight ahead, fully extending all three limbs to the northwest.

(31a) Step the right foot behind the left, pointing southeast. Bend the elbows, drawing them in closer to the torso, sword and left open palm.

(31b) Plant the right foot a full step behind the left and begin pivoting to the right on both feet. Turn the waist to the right and position the sword blade horizontally, palm down, across the chest with the blade flat.

(31c) Continue turning the waist, shifting the weight of the body forward and facing southeast, into a right forward bow-stance. Simultaneously exhale and deliver a left hand stroke that goes under the sword's blade, using the lower outside heel of the palm out in front of the middle elixir area. Weight is 70% front, 30% back.

(32a) From this right forward bow-stance, turn the waist to the right, swaying the sword (palm down) and the left hand (palm up) over to the right side of the body like floating lotus petals. Feet remain planted.

(32b) Unwind the torque of the waist to the left while leaping forward at a 45-degree angle with the left foot. Float the left open palm above and away to the left side of the body, palm up, across the lower left torso.

(32c) Step the right into a transitional right empty stance (weight is 90% back, 10% front) as the waist torques to the left and sword and left palm continue floating to the left.

(32d) Reach the limit and turn the sword palm down so it can take the higher position. The left open hand turns palm up to take the lower position. Simultaneously unwind the waist to the right.

(32e) Leap the right foot forward and to the right at a 45-degree angle as sword and left open palm float over to the right side of the body.

(32f) Step the right foot into a transitional left empty stance (weight is 90% back, 10% front) as sword and open palm continue floating to the right.

(32g) Reach the limit, turn the sword palm up and let it take the lower position. The left open palm turns left and away, taking the higher position. Simultaneously unwind the waist to the left and leap the left foot forward and left at a 45-degree angle.

(32h) Step the right foot into a transitional right empty stance (weight is 90% back, 10% front) as the waist torques to the left and sword and left palm continue floating left.

(32i) Reach the limit, turn the sword palm down and let it take the higher position while turning the left open hand palm up to take the lower position. Simultaneously unwind the waist to the right and leap the right foot forward and right at a 45-degree angle as sword and left open palm float over to the right.

(32j) Step the right foot into a transitional left empty stance (weight is 90% back, 10% front) as sword and open palm continue floating to the right. Breathe naturally.

(33a) Unwind the torque of the waist to the left while leaping back at a 45-degree angle on the left foot. Let the left open palm float above and away to the left side of the body while the sword, palm up, floats across the lower torso also to the left side: both are like floating lotus flower petals.

(33b) The left foot, followed by the right, steps into a transitional right empty stance (weight is 90% back, 10% front). The waist torques to the left; sword and left palm continue floating left. After the left palm and sword reach their limit, the sword turns palm down and takes the higher position; the left open palm turns palm up, taking the lower position.

(33c) Unwind the waist to the right and leap back at a 45-egree angle to the right with the right foot as the sword and left open palm float to the right side of the body.

(33d) Plant with the right foot into a transitional left empty stance (weight distribution 90% back, 10% front) as the sword and open palm continue to the float right.

(33e) Unwind the torque of the waist to the left while leaping back at a 45-degree angle with the left foot, followed by the left open palm which floats above and away to the left side of the body and the sword, palm up, floats across the lower torso also to the left side. The left foot, followed by the right foot, plants into a transitional right empty stance (weight is 90% back, 10% front) as the sword and left palm continue floating left while and the waist torques to the left.

(33f) After the left palm and sword reach their limit, the sword turns palm down and takes the high position and the left open palm turns palm up, taking the lower position. Lift the right knee in preparation for a directional change.

(33g) Step back right behind the left foot to the northwest while the sword, palm down and horizontal, draws near the chest and the left open hand, palm up, draws near the lower elixir field to start the formation of a ball.

(33h) After setting the left foot down, begin to turn the waist to the right while pivoting on both feet.

(33i) Continue to pivot into a right forward bow-stance facing northwest, aligning the center of the sword's blade with the center of the chest. With the left open hand, palm up, cup the lower elixir field. Weight is 70% front, 30% back. Breathe naturally.

(34a) Inhale and shift the majority of the body's weight into the right leg. Turn the right wrist out to the right, positioning the sword vertically, and let the waist gently turn to the left. The left open palm stays fixed at the lower elixir field.

(34b) Step the left foot around the right to the northwest and moving into a right transitional twist. As if attached by a string, let the left foot draw the sword from above in the same direction.

(34c) Move it in an arc, palm facing away from the body. The left hand forms a sword-mudra, palm up, in front of the lower elixir field.

(34d) Continue pivoting to the left, unwinding into a transitional horse-stance with feet parallel. The sword at the same time completes the lower half of the circle in front of the waist, the right palm facing the body and the left hand sword-mudra leading the way northwest. Begin exhaling.

(34e) Continue pivoting to the left, moving into a left forward bow-stance facing northwest. Let the sword and right wrist corkscrew clockwise, twisting the right forearm muscles until the right palm faces skyward. The sword is now horizontal, with the blade's edge skyward. The left hand sword-mudra rotates up near the left temple (ca. 8-12 inches from the head), palm facing away from the body. Weight is 70%, 30% back.

(34f) While in the left forward bow-stance, lift the right wrist so that the right palm faces the torso. Move the sword into a vertical position, pointing skyward. Wrist and forearm are still twisting.

(35a) Let the sword fall forward while unwinding the right wrist and forearm.

(35b) Let the sword point toward the ground while leading the blade in toward the body, catching it underneath the right armpit and behind the shoulder. At the same time shift your weight back into the right leg. The left hand sword-mudra starts to mirror the right arm, extending out from the shoulders.

(35c) Inhale and without pause, shift the weight back by taking another step back with the left foot. Then let both hands drop smoothly on either sides of the waist.

(35d) Settle into a right empty stance (weight is 90% back, 10% front), facing northwest. Finish with the arms continuing their motion out to the sides of the body to form wings with both palms facing forward.

(35e) Exhale and take the arms in reverse to the front of the body while simultaneously stepping forward with the left foot into a left empty stance (weight is 90% back, 10% front).

(35f) Bring the heel of the left foot in toward the right foot and form a tight left twist stance, the right toes touching the outer edge of the left foot below the ankle. Bend both knees and lower the body. At the same time, lower the sword handle to the right side of the waist, turning the sword vertical and pointing skyward. The tips of the index and middle fingers of the left hand sword-mudra contact the right forearm at the Shousanli point. Push the sword up as the arrow indicates and gaze over the right shoulder at the tip of the blade by bending forward at the waist a few degrees. Begin inhaling.

(36a) Unwind from the left twist into a natural stance, feet shoulder-width apart. Draw the sword from the cradle of the right armpit in a circular motion (see arrow). Do not lose contact between the left sword-mudra and the right forearm.

(b) Exhale and continue the sword motion up and over to the right side of the body toward the southeast, ending with the sword perfectly horizontal. Still maintain contact between the left hand sword-mudra and the right forearm. The eyes gaze southeast; the front of the body faces northeast.

(36c) Take a half step to the left with the left foot while raising the sword overhead. Release the left hand sword-mudra and catch the upper portion of the blade between the left thumb and the open left palm. All fingers and thumb of the left hand are pointing skyward.

(37a) Inhale and begin a 180-degree leftward turn by pivoting on the left heel.

(37b) The waist and upper body follow; still hold the sword over the head.

(37c) Let the right foot and body swing around the left foot (see arrow) into a natural stance, facing southwest with feet parallel.

(37d) Lower the sword handle to the right side of the body; again form the left hand sword-mudra and place it opposite the left temple (ca. 8-12 inches from the head), palm facing away from the body.

(37e) Step back with the left foot and behind the right to the northwest. As if attached by a string, the left foot pulls the sword in the same direction. Begin a 360-degree circle of the sword on a vertical plane.

(37f) Exhale and turn the waist to the left while pulling the sword overhead in an arc.

(37g) Cut downward and settle into a left forward bow-stance, facing northwest. The sword is horizontal with the blade's edge skyward; the left hand sword-mudra is fixed at the left temple. Weight is 70% front, 30% back.

(38a) Quarter-turn the right wrist to the right, so that the right palm is up and the sword's blade flat. Let the left hand sword-mudra move to the right upper ribcage below the chest, palm down, lightly touching the right side of the torso with the index finger.

(38b) Inhale and step the left foot back and behind the right, moving southeast.

(38c) Set the left foot down and smoothly turn waist and body to the left. Arms and sword stay fixed.

(38d) As the body faces southeast, hop the right foot in front of the left, vaulting both feet into the air and starting a 360- degree turn.

(38e) Turn the right wrist over and swing the left foot ahead of the right.

(38f) Set the right foot down, then the left; the left is in the lead. The sword dives down and across to the left, palm facing the torso.

(38g) Turn the waist to the left and quarter-turn the right wrist to the right, so the sword becomes flat, palm up.

(38h) Exhale and settle into a left forward bow-stance, directing the sword blade ahead of the body to the southeast. The sword-mudra stays fixed under the right chest muscle, palm down. Weight is 70% front, 30% back.

(39a) Flip the sword back and over the outer left shoulder, along the torso and leg by turning the right wrist upward.

(39b) Continue flipping the sword until it comes back around, centering in front of the body with the right palm facing forward, rotating the right wrist until reaching its limit. Simultaneously, the right foot begins to step forward and the left hand again grasps the sword at the guard.

(39c) Step the right foot next to the left while inverting the right hand, again grasping the sword handle near the pommel.

(39d) Bending knees to let the body sink down; thrust the sword down with both arms, slightly angled forward.

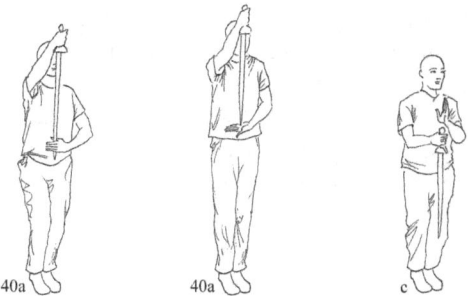

(40a) Inhale and draw the sword upward with the right hand, allowing the left hand to slide down as if lightly wiping blood from the blade between thumb and palm. The flat side of the blade faces the body.

(40b) When the left hand reaches the end of the blade, the palm turns up underneath the tip of the sword to collect the blood, then moves out from underneath the sword to the left.

(40c) Exhale and lower the sword straight down, turning the handle so that the blade's sharp edge faces the body. At the same time, raise the left palm up along the sword until it gets to above the sword pommel in front of the middle elixir area. Form a one-hand prayer-mudra with fingers and thumb set vertically. The outer edge of the open palm and the blade's sharp edge are aligned.

41a

b

c

(41a) Inhale, step the right foot back and around behind the left, moving north. Tuck the sword behind the right shoulder, the blade firmly pressed between the left shoulder blade and the deltoid muscle. The hand grip is still inverted with index finger and thumb closest to the pommel; the right inner elbow supports the flat side of the blade against the Jianzhen point.

(41b) Turn the waist to the right and pivot on the feet. The left hand remains in front of the middle elixir area; the sword stays locked in position.

(41c) Continue to turn the waist to the right into a right forward bow-stance, facing north. Exhale, let the heels form a straight line and execute a left-hand stroke, using the outside heel of the palm to push out from the middle elixir area, fingers straight and upright. Generate power by turning the waist. Keep the elbow bent to form a half-circle from shoulder to hand. Angle the right foot inward and have your weight 70% front and 30% back. The bent right knee should not go beyond the big toe to avoid injury.

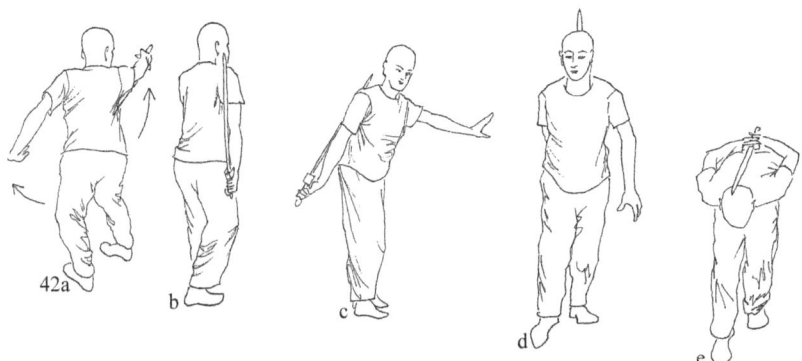

(42a) Shift the majority of your weight from the front to the back leg and move into a transitional right empty stance. Raising the sword handle from the right hip, moving it ahead of the body in a horizontal position. Lower the left hand, palm down, next to the left waist.

(42b) Step the left foot forward into a left empty stance while lifting the left hand, palm up, in front of the middle elixir area. Returning the sword handle to the right hip, making the sword vertical again.

(42c) Pivot on both feet and turn the waist to the right to begin a 180-degree transition.

(42d) Roll the guard and handle of the sword over onto the sacrum at the base of the spine, the right palm holding and facing the body. This aligns the flat portion of the blade and spine with the backbone, now pressed against one another for support. The weight is evenly balanced, with the right leg in front facing south in a modified stance.

(42e) Again grasp the sword near the guard with the left hand, taking over from the right—the grip is still inverted, with index finger and thumb closest to the end of the pommel. Bend forward from the waist until your back is flat, parallel to the ground. Eyes stare at the floor, and the neck is flat. Use the index, middle and ring fingers of the left hand to push up from the bottom of the pommel. The sword slides up the spine and the back of the head several inches. Breathe naturally.

(43a) The right leg is still one step ahead of the left leg in a modified stance facing south, with the weight evenly balanced. The left hand maintains control of the sword; the right hand pushes the pommel. Inhale and separate them at the lower back moving toward the lower front of the body. The back is still flat and parallel to the ground.

(43b) The hands come to meet and exchange the sword: the right hand takes hold of the sword handle, index finger and thumb closest to the guard. Slowly lift head and torso.

(43c) Step ahead with the left foot to begin another 180-degree transition. Both hands remain in contact, halfway through the turn. The spine is almost fully erect.

(43d) Set the left foot down and continue turning the waist to the right, pivoting on both feet as the sword and left hand separate. The left hand forms a sword-mudra.

(43e) Exhale and turn the waist to the right until the torso faces north and the weight is to 90% on the back leg in a right empty stance. Simultaneously spread both arms out to the sides above the shoulders, palms down.

(44a) Inhale slowly and take a small step with the right foot in front of the left.

(44b) Start pivoting left on the right foot. The waist also turns left and both arms close in as if to hug a tree, the left hand sword-mudra crossing on top, palm down, the sword closing in below, also palm down.

(44c) Continue turning left by stepping the left foot behind the right to the north. The arms steadily close inward, the left hand sword-mudra going over the right shoulder and the sword wrapping around the left ribcage below the left shoulder.

(44d) Pivot on both feet into a left forward bow-stance facing north. Both arms hug the body tightly, wrapping around the torso to create a spring like tension using the waist. Weight is 70% front, 30% back.

(45a) Exhale and unwind the body by turning the waist right and pivoting on the right foot for a 360-degree transition that allows the arms to uncross.

(45b) Let the arms open wider and the left foot swing around.

(45c) Set the left foot down in the south and continue the transition back around to face north.

(45d) Keep turning the waist to the right until the torso faces north and the weight is back 90% in a right empty stance. Spread both arms like wings above the shoulders, palms down.

(46a) Inhale and rotate the right wrist to the right until the palm faces up and the sword blade is flat. Slide the right arm and sword horizontally across to the left, in front of the body, until the pommel is aligned with the third eye. At the same time, the left hand sword-mudra moves into position opposite the left temple (ca. 8-12 inches from the head), palm facing away from the body. Bend the right elbow slightly by pulling the sword a few inches closer to the body. Simultaneously draw the right foot a few inches closer toward the left.

(46b) Begin drawing an S-formation with the sword in front of the body by first gliding the blade over to the left. When the blade has reached the left side of the body, the right wrist turns the sword over, palm down, to reverse direction to the right (see arrow).

(46c) Guide the blade over to the right on a slightly lower level. When it reaches the right side of the body, the right wrist turns the sword over, palm up.

(46d) Reverse direction, going back to the left (see arrow).

(46e) Guide the blade over to the left on a yet lower level, palm up. As it reaches the centerline of the torso, the right wrist bends up, standing the sword vertical. Lift the right foot in the process.

(46f) Exhale and let the momentum continue to move vertically as the right arm begins to extend skyward thrusting the sword upward. Lift the right knee behind as if it was attached by a string.

(46g) Raise up on on the ball of the left foot and let sword and right leg lunge up and forward to the north.

(46h) Land in a right forward bow-stance, the right arm fully extended with the sword horizontal, palm up, and the blade flat, held as high above the head as possible while maintaining this said form. The left hand sword-mudra remains fixed at the left temple. Weight is 70% front, 30% back.

(47a) Inhale and drop the right hand to the shoulder height, arm fully extended. Stand the sword up vertically by lifting the right wrist, so that the blade's edges are in line with the right arm. The left hand sword-mudra remains fixed at the temple.

(47b) Lower the blade to a horizontal position and rotate the right wrist to the right until the palm faces up and the sword blade is flat. Slide the right arm and sword horizontally across to the left by turning the waist.

(47c) Bring the right foot over, next to the left so that the entire body faces west and the sword points west, the end of the pommel at the same level as the upper chest. The left hand sword-mudra still stays at the temple.

(48a) Exhale and let the sword blade fall forward, creating a circle on a vertical plane along the right outer half of the body.

(48b) The right wrist holding the handle naturally rotates down and around, assisting the sword blade to complete the downward circle. The left hand sword-mudra does not move. The feet remain side by side.

(48c) Twirl the sword a full 360 degrees. Turn the right wrist and arm inward and allow the sword to dive down in front of the body.

(48d) Turn the right wrist to the right, palm up.

(48e) Redirect the sword by standing the blade vertically, moving upward and lifting the right foot in the process. The right palm faces the body.

(48f) Continues to move vertically. The right arm begins to extend skywardly, thrusting the sword. Lift the right knee behind as if it was attached by a string. Reached the vertical peak and raise up on the ball of the left foot.

(48g) Lunge the sword and right leg up and forward to the west, landing in a right forward bow-stance. The right arm is fully extended, with the sword horizontal, palm up, and blade flat. Hold it as high above the head as possible while maintaining this posture. The left hand sword-mudra remains fixed at the left temple. Weight is 70% front, 30% back.

(49a) Inhale and shift your weight into the right leg, bringing the sword and left hand sword-mudra to form an X in front of the throat. The left hand sword-mudra is on the inside, palm facing away from the body; the sword is on the outside, palm facing the body.

(49b) Step the left foot north, behind and to the right of the right foot, landing on the ball. Spread the arms apart and exhale slowly. The sword crosses the left foot to the north and moves along the right hip; the sword-mudra uses the blade as a guide, moving upward and toward the south.

(49c) Set the heel of the left foot down in what is now a right transitional elongated twist stance with the feet perpendicular. Fully extend the left arm and sword-mudra upward at a 45-degree angle, palm facing away from the body. Extend the right arm to the north at a 45-degree downward angle, eyes following it and fixed on the tip of the blade. It stops next to the inner heel of the left foot.

(49d) Unwind from the twist, turning to the left. The sword and sword-mudra reverse their directions (see arrows): raise the sword to point up and drop the left elbow, lowering the left hand sword-mudra.

(49e) The body fully unwinds into a horse stance facing east with the weight evenly distributed and both arms extended to the sides, slightly rounded forward. The sword points skyward, palm facing forward; the left hand sword-mudra also points up, palm facing forward. (This position can be held in meditation with the eyes closed for any desired duration while breathing naturally.)

(49f) Inhale and step in left foot next to the right, simultaneously lowering and rotating both arms inward, as is if your were closing two doors, palms facing the torso. Forearms are parallel; sword and sword-mudra stand side by side pointing skyward.

(49g) Shift your weight into the right leg, while moving the left foot around and behind the right (see arrow). Bring the sword and left hand sword-mudra to form an X in front of the throat. The left hand sword-mudra is on the inside, palm facing away; the sword is on the outside, palm facing in.

(49h) Step the left foot south, behind and to the right of the right foot, landing on the ball. Spread your arms apart and exhale slowly. The sword follows the left foot to the south along the right leg and hip; the left hand sword-mudra uses the blade as a guide when moving upward and toward the north.

(49i) Set the heel of the left foot on the ground in what is now a right transitional elongated twist stance with the feet perpendicular. Fully extend the left arm and sword-mudra upward at a 45-degree angle, palm facing away from the body. Let the right arm fully extend to the south at a 45-degree downward angle; eyes following and fixed on the tip of the blade: it stops next to the left inner heel.

Instructions / 197

(50a) Inhale and unwind from the twist stance, turning the body to the left. Let the sword reverse direction by raising the right arm and pointing it skyward, eyes following the tip of the blade. Left hand sword-mudra and arm remain elevated.

(50b) Continue unwinding to the left on the heel of the left foot. Bring the sword into an overhead downward arc (see arrow).

(50c) As the body turns south, the sword begins to cross underneath the left arm. The eyes never disconnect from the blade's tip.

(50d) Finish unwinding into a left forward bow-stance (weight is 70% front, 30% back). Face south but continue turning the waist to the left, until both arms are wrapped snugly around the body. The left hand sword-mudra points skyward and rests on the outer right shoulder; the sword's handle is tucked under the left arm pit, angled upward at 45 degrees behind the left shoulder. The palm faces the torso; eyes and head look at the tip of the blade over the left shoulder.

(50e) Exhale and release the torque of the waist to the right and unwrap both arms from the body. Step the right foot forward to the south.

(50f) Step the left foot forward into a transitional left empty stance (weight is 90% back, 10% front). Spreading both arms up and out like wings—take a transitional pause before following the path as indicated by the arrows. Palms face forward. Circle both sword and sword-mudra down and in (see arrows).

(50g) Let both palms face each other. The sword blade and left hand sword-mudra are horizontal and point south.

(50h) Inhale and raise the sword, palm facing the earth and the blade's edge cutting skyward directly over the right shoulder. Lift the left hand sword-mudra, palm up, and extend it out in front of the middle elixir area. Raise the left foot to rest inside the right knee in a one legged stance, left knee facing south. The three are rising as one.

(51a) Hop the left foot forward and to the left at a 45-degree angle. Slice the sword across the front of the torso from right to left, palm up. Let the left hand flip over, palm open.

(51b) Step the right foot quickly in front of the left into a right transitional empty stance (weight is 90% back, 10% front) facing south. The left open palm catches the traversing sword handle, establishing a two-hand grip (the start of a figure eight pattern). Hold the sword high and horizontally, the tip of the blade pointed south just ahead of the left shoulder; the waist is torqued to the left.

(51c) Turn the wrists over to the left, directing the sword back and along the left side of the body, making a circle using the blade's sharp edge (see arrow).

(51d) Wield the sword forward and across the front of the torso in a figure-8 formation. Hop the right foot forward and to the right at a 45-degree angle.

(51e) Set the right foot down while wielding the sword to the left shoulder.

(51f) Step the left foot ahead of the right into a left transitional empty stance (weight is 90% back, 10% front). Hold the sword held high and horizontally, the tip of the blade pointing south ahead of the right shoulder; the waist is torqued to the right. Turn the wrists over to the right, directing the sword back and along the right side of the body, making a circle (see arrow).

(51g) Wield the sword forward and across the front of the torso to the left to complete the first figure-8. Hop the left foot forward and to the left at a 45-degree angle, wielding the sword up toward the left shoulder: begin a second figure-8. Hold the sword held high and horizontally, the tip of the blade pointing south ahead of the left shoulder; the waist is torqued to the left.

(51h) Step the right foot in front of the left into a right transitional empty stance. Turn the wrists to the left, directing the sword back and along the left side of the body, making a circle (see arrow).

(51i) Wield the sword forward and across the front of the torso in the second figure-8, hop the right foot forward and to the right at a 45-degree angle. Hold the sword high and horizontally, the tip of the blade pointed south ahead of the right shoulder. The waist is torqued to the right.

(51j) Step the left foot in front of the right into a left empty stance facing south. Turn the wrists over to the right, turning the palms over so that the flat portion of the blade is face up and the tip is raised at a 45-degree angle.

(51k) With a quick snap of the wrist slice with the blade's sharp edge from right to left until the handle is level with the middle elixir area. Keep the eyes fixed on the tip of the blade. Maintain a two hand grip. Weight is 90% back, 10% front.

(52a) Inhale and draw the sword pommel into the pelvic region. Bend the right leg to deepen the stance so that the torso leans forward 45 degrees, matching the angle of the sword.

(52b) Slowly exhale and straighten the body, lifting the sword and projecting it into the sky, eyes facing heaven just above the tip of the blade.

(52c) Inhale and draw the sword pommel into the pelvic region. Bend the right leg to deepen the stance so that the torso leans forward 45 degrees, matching the angle of the sword.

(52d) Step back left foot behind the right toward the north. Exhale and arch the spine back, thrusting arms and sword overhead in the same direction.

(52e) When spine and sword reach their natural limit, turn the waist to the left and pivot on both feet.

(52f) Turn 180 degrees to the north into a left forward bow-stance. Execute an overhead downward cut, using the blade's sharp edge. Weight is 70% front, 30% back.

(53a) Step the right foot forward in transition and lift the sword into a vertical position by bending both wrists upward.

(53b) Set the heel of the right foot down and shift forward into a right forward bow-stance, dropping the blade's edge back onto a horizontal plane.

(53c) Pivot left on the heel of the right foot so that the toes are pointing west. Inhale and shift your weight into the right leg. Bring the sword and left hand sword-mudra up to form an X in front of the throat: sword-mudra on the inside, palm facing out; the sword on the outside, palm facing the body.

(53d) Step the left foot north, behind and to the right of the right foot, landing on the ball. Exhale slowly and spread your arms. The sword follows the left foot to the north along the right hip; the left hand sword-mudra uses the blade as a guide, moving upward and toward the south.

(53e) Set the heel of the left foot down in what a right transitional elongated twist stance with feet perpendicular. Fully extend the left arm and sword-mudra upward and to the south at a 45-degree angle, palm facing away from the body. The right arm extends to the north at a 45-degree downward angle; eyes fixed on the tip of the blade that stops next to the inner heel of the left foot.

(53f) Inhale and unwind from the twist stance, turning the body to the left as the sword follows on the horizontal plane, palm up.

(53g) Lower the left hand sword-mudra, palm up, and cross it above the right arm to form a flat X

(53h) Let the body settle into a left empty stance, facing north. Weight is 90% back, 10% front.

(53i) Raise the sword, palm facing the earth and the blade's edge cutting skyward, so that it is directly over the right shoulder. Extend the left hand sword-mudra, palm up, in front of the middle elixir area. Draw the toes of the left foot toward the right foot into a cat stance. The three move together as one. Weight is 95% back, 5% front.

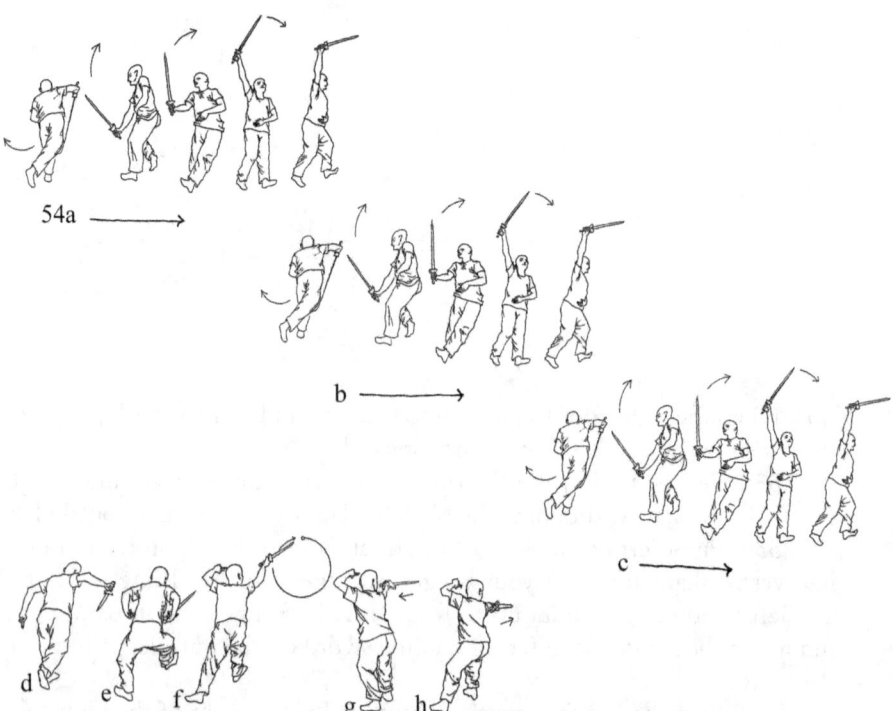

(54a) 1. Lift the left foot slightly and again place the left heel down on the ground while opening the instep to the left. Simultaneously direct the sword to dive down in front of the body on the vertical plane and in a circular fashion (see arrow), using the motion of a revolving dragon. The body naturally rotates left to face west; the right palm which holds the sword faces the torso. At the same time, the left hand sword-mudra releases and covers the lower elixir field and navel with an open palm. 2. The right foot follows the sword by stepping ahead of the left on an imaginary straight line that leads from south to north; the sword ascends with the eyes fixed on the blade. 3. Continue turning the body to the left without pause by stepping behind. 4. Step the left foot ahead of the right foot on the same line, transitioning the body to face east and ascending the sword to an apex above the head, palm facing away from the body. 5. Move forward to the north as the sword begins to descend into the second cycle, the left palm still covering the lower elixir field and navel. (Note: Both feet are walking and stepping perpendicular to this line while the sword rolls along the same line like a cartwheel. Although the body is following the sword, the footwork is the generating power source of the swords motion. The briskly taken steps are circular on a horizontal plane and remain close to the ground, pivoting on the feet.)

(54b) 1. Direct the sword to dive down in front of the body on a vertical plane and in a circular fashion, using the motion of a revolving dragon (see arrow). The body naturally rotates left to face west; the right palm with the sword faces the torso. 2. The right foot follows the sword by stepping ahead of the left on an imaginary straight line that leads from south to north; the sword ascends with eyes fixed on the blade. 3. Continue turning the body to the left without pause by stepping behind. 4. Step the left foot ahead of the right onto the same line, transitioning to face east and ascending the sword to an apex above the head, palm facing away from the body. 5. Move forward to the north as the sword begins to descend into the third and final cycle.

(54c) Direct the sword to dive down in front of the body on a vertical plane and in a circular fashion, using the motion of a revolving dragon (see arrow). The body naturally rotates left to face west; the right palm with the sword faces the torso. 2. The right foot follows the sword by stepping ahead of the left foot on an imaginary straight line that leads from south to north as the sword ascends with the eyes fixed on the blade. 3. Continue turning the body to the left without pause by stepping behind. 4. Step the left foot ahead of the right onto the same line, transitioning to face east and ascending the sword to an apex above the head, palm facing away from the body. 5. Move forward to the north as the sword begins to descend.

(54d) Thrust the sword ahead of the body toward the north while reforming the left hand sword-mudra.

(54e) Riding the momentum of the third cycle, step the right foot forward to the north and turn the right wrist to the right, palm up, near the ribcage.

(54f) Settle into a right forward bow-stance (weight is 70% front, 30% back) while thrusting the sword inward and forward from the shoulder with the speed of a bullet. Simultaneously, rotate the left hand sword-mudra to the position opposite the left temple (ca. 8-12 inches from the head), palm facing away from the body. Pause and inhale. Draw a circular talisman with the tip of the blade by rotating clockwise from the right shoulder. The sword blade is flat and the palm faces down. The circle covers the entire torso and completes the talisman at the third eye.

(54g) Rotate the right wrist to the right until the palm faces up and the sword blade is flat while bending the right elbow to pull the sword a few inches closer to the body. Align the pommel of the sword with the nose while drawing the right foot toward the left foot into a right empty stance (weight is 90% back, 10% front). Coil energy in this posture. Exhale and explode north, lunging into a right forward bow-stance (step-drag). Thrust and rotate the sword inward and slightly angled down from the middle elixir area. The left hand sword-mudra remains in position opposite the left temple.

(55a) Inhale and remain in the right forward bow-stance, lifting the right arm and sword as if raising a drawbridge directly above the right shoulder, the blade's sharp edge in line with the body. Lower the left hand sword-mudra to cross over to the mid-to-right ribcage, palm down. Lightly touch the right side of the torso with the index finger.

(55b) Step behind the left foot the right foot to the north in a transitional modified right twist stance.

(55c) Pivot to the left; hand positions remain fixed.

(55d) Continue unwinding to face north into a left forward bow-stance (weight is 70% front, 30% back).

(55e) Exhale and lower the sword and arm, cutting down with the sharp edge of the blade until it is horizontal and parallel to the ground. The left hand sword-mudra remains fixed in position at the mid right ribcage. (Note: The left foot is angled in 45 degrees so that the toes point northeast.)

(56a) Turn the waist to the right, so the body faces northeast. Bring the right foot forward, next to the left. Move the left hand sword-mudra from the right ribcage to mirror the right arm and sword out in front of the middle elixir area, palms facing one another. The right arm does not need adjusting, since it has moved with the torso.

(56b) Inhale and rotate upward from the shoulders.

(56c) Draw two large circles to the right and left sides of the body with sword and sword-mudra (see arrows).

(56d) Completing the lower half of the circles, draw them in toward each other.

(56e) Form a two-hand grip around the handle, elbows bent; the sword is set horizontally. Lift the right knee until the thigh is parallel to the ground. The blade's sharp edge is skyward.

(56f) Exhale and extend the right leg forward in a right heel-kick, while mildly thrusting the arms and sword straight out from the middle elixir area.

(57a) Retract the right leg by bending the right knee and stepping on to the right heel, pivoting to the left until the toes of the right foot are pointing northwest.

(57b) Draw the left foot next to the right and turn the waist to the left so that the body faces northwest. The arms and sword remain extended straight out from the middle elixir area and maintain a two-hand grip of the sword handle.

(57c) Inhale and rotate upward to begin to draw two large circles to the right and left sides of the body with sword and sword-mudra.

(57d) Let the arms and sword complete the lower half of the circles and draw inward toward each other.

(57e) Form a two-hand grip around the handle, elbows bent and the sword horizontally set. Lift the right knee until the thigh is parallel to the ground. The blade's sharp edge is skyward. Exhale and extend the left leg forward in a left heel kick while mildly thrusting arms and sword straight out from the middle elixir area.

(58a) Retract the left leg by bending the left knee and stepping into a left twist stance with feet perpendicular.

(58b) Step the right foot around and next to left.

(58c) Adjust and pivot on both feet, so that that the body turns left to face south. The arms are still fully extended from the middle elixir area; the blade's sharp edge points skyward.

(58d) Bending only at the wrist, lift the sword into a vertical position.

(58e) Lower the blade, letting it fall lightly until it is again parallel with the ground.

(58f) Inhale and rotate upward from the shoulders, drawing two large circles to the right and left sides of the body with sword and sword-mudra.

(58g) Step the left foot forward toward the south.

(58h) With the foot grounded, complete the lower half of the circles and draw inward toward each other. Form a two-hand grip, with elbows bent and blade flat. Step the right foot forward beyond and next to the left, keeping it approximately ten inches off the ground.

(58i) Move slowly, then exhale and pound the earth, placing with the right foot next to the left. Thrust the arms and sword, blade flat, straight out from the middle elixir area. Start a long slow inhale.

(59a) Step back with the right foot at a 45-degree angle into a left empty stance while lifting the fully extended right arm and sword up and back as if doing the back stroke in a swimming pool. The right arm and leg move in unison as if connected. Reform the left hand sword-mudra and keep your arm fully extended from the middle elixir area.

(59b) As the right arm reaches behind the body, counterbalance the motion by lifting the left arm and sword-mudra up and back, now rotating both arms continuously from the shoulders like a windmill. Slide the left foot in toward the instep of the right and step it behind at a 45-degree angle (drawing a half X).

(59c) Settle into a right empty stance.

(59d) As the left arm reaches behind the body, counterbalance the motion by lifting the right arm and sword up and back, stepping in and back with the right foot (drawing a half X) into a left empty stance.

(59e) As the right arm reaches behind the body, counterbalance the motion by lifting the left arm and sword-mudra up and back, stepping in and back with the left foot (drawing a half X).

(59f) Step into a right empty stance.

(59g) As the left arm reaches behind the body, counterbalance the motion by lifting the right arm and sword-mudra up and back, stepping in and back with the right foot (drawing a half X) into a left empty stance.

(59h) As the right arm reaches behind the body, counterbalance the motion by lifting the left arm and sword-mudra up and back, stepping the left foot back to the north into a transitional right twist stance. As if connected by a string, the left foot leads the sword in the same direction.

(59i) Move it in an overhead arc, palm facing away from the body.

(59j) Continue pivoting left, unwinding into a transitional horse stance with feet parallel. Guide the sword down and next to the waist (see arrow) with the right palm facing the body and the left hand sword-mudra leading north.

(59k) Exhale and continue pivoting left, moving into a left forward bow-stance facing north. Thrust the sword horizontally ahead of the body, the blade's sharp edge skyward. Rotate the left hand sword-mudra into the position opposite the left temple (ca. 8-12 inches from the head), palm facing away from the body. Weight is 70% front, 30% back.

(60a) Inhale and shift your weight into the right leg (back) while reversing the direction of the sword by pulling the handle past the right side of the waist, palm facing the body.

(60b) Flip the sword up in an overhead arc (see arrow), palm facing away from the body. Step the left foot to the south behind the right into a right transitional twist stance. As if connected by a string, the left foot leads the sword in the same direction.

(60c) Continue pivoting left, unwinding into a transitional horse stance with feet parallel.

(60d) Guide the sword down and next to the waist, right palm facing the body and the left hand sword-mudra leading the way south.

(60e) Exhale and turn the palm skyward, so the blade is flat as the momentum of the sword pulls the right leg forward.

(60f) Shift into a right forward bow-stance (weight is 70% front, 30% back), facing south with the blade still flat and extended from the shoulder. The left hand sword-mudra rotates into the position opposite the left temple (ca. 8-12 inches from the head), palm facing away from the body.

(60g) Pivot right on the right heel at a 45-degree angle. Raise the sword directly over the right shoulder, palm facing the earth and the blade's sharp edge cutting skyward. Lower the left hand sword-mudra near the middle elixir area.

(60h) Step the left foot forward into a left forward bow-stance (weight is 70% front, 30% back) facing south.

(60i) Gently thrust the sword horizontally ahead of the body, the left hand sword-mudra extended out in front of the middle elixir area, palm facing the body's centerline.

(61a) Lower the right arm and lift the right wrist so that the sword becomes vertical. The handle is even with the shoulder. Maintaining the vertical posture of the sword, inhale and slowly pull back the sword handle as if drawing a bow. This is called "removing the clouds so that the sun can shine in."

Draw back beyond the right shoulder as far as you can, the sword vertical, as you push the right wrist to curl in to the forearm.

(61b) Point the sword behind the body by unfurling the wrist and turning the palm down.

(61c) Step the left foot back half a step behind the right to the north, while transitioning the sword under and forward along the lower right side of the waist. The sword is horizontal and the blade's sharp edge skyward, palm facing the body. Lower the left hand sword-mudra, forming a right angle, to rest upon the upper right forearm, stopping the end of the pommel from going past the right hip.

(61d) Unwind 180 degrees to the left, pivoting on both feet and arcing the sword overhead (see arrow) without losing contact between the sword-mudra and the right forearm.

(61e) Continue pivoting to the left, unwinding into a transitional walking stance facing north (left foot ahead of right). Guide the sword down in front of the torso.

(61f) Point the sword behind the body toward the south, parking along the left waistline with the sword horizontal and the blade's sharp edge skyward, palm facing the body. With the head turned and eyes looking over the left shoulder, the left hand sword-mudra maintains contact with the forearm, left wrist bent and left elbow resting on the right wrist. Pause for a brief second.

(61g) Exhale and step the left foot to the south into a left forward bow-stance.

(61h) Walk the sword ahead of the body, held horizontally with the blade's sharp edge skyward. The left hand sword-mudra hovers above the blade, palm down, and extends ahead from the middle elixir area. This is called "snake flicking its tongue." Weight is 70% front, 30% back.

(62a) Inhale and slowly lower the sword and left hand sword-mudra to the right, traversing near the body like a pendulum. Point to the earth with palms facing the torso. Pivot the body toward the north.

(62b) Let the sword reach the position directly above the right shoulder with palm facing away and position the left hand sword-mudra near the middle elixir area, palm facing the body's centerline.

(62c) Exhale and step the left foot north into a left forward bow-stance (weight is 70% front, 30% back). Gently thrust the horizontally held sword ahead of the body along with the left hand sword-mudra which extends out in front of the middle elixir area.

(62d) Inhale and step the right foot forward to the north.

(62e) Hook it around and ahead of the left foot, while guiding the sword down in front of the torso.

(62f) Pivot left on both feet and let the left arm cross inside of the right.

(62g) Settle into a tight left twist stance with feet perpendicular and flat on the ground, facing south, arms and swords crossed and forming an X, palms facing the body.

(63a) Maintain the X-formation of the arms and lower the sword's cutting edge down, contouring (as if shaving) as close as possible to the left side of the body. Contour the right side of the body with the left hand sword-mudra's cutting edge, simultaneously forming two rings on the sides.

(63b) Let the arms come full circle and uncross them in front of the body with palms down, moving both sword and sword-mudra out and around to combine into a third ring (see arrows).

(63c) Step the right foot forward into a right empty stance.

(63d) Let the index and middle finger of the left hand sword-mudra make contact with the right inner forearm. Push the flat blade of the horizontally held sword forward from the neck, right palm up. Inhale slowly and briefly pause in this posture. Coil the energies in the body in preparation to strike. Weight is 90% back, 10% front.

Instructions / 213

(64a) Exhale and roll your weight forward into the right leg. Step the left foot forward and ahead of the right, keeping sword and sword-mudra in place.

(64b) Trot toward the south.

(64c) Quickly step the right foot forward into a right forward bow-stance, while executing a straight thrust with the blade's sharp edge skyward and rotating the left hand sword-mudra to the position opposite the left temple (ca. 8-12 inches from the head), palm facing away from the body. The left foot is slightly dragged behind and the right foot is angled in to protect the vital areas. Weight is 70% front, 30% back.

(64d) Inhale and step the left foot around the right toward the south into a right transitional twist stance. As if connected by a string, the left foot leads the sword in the same direction, moving in an overhead circle, palm facing away from the body. The left hand sword-mudra also follows the left foot transition.

(64e) Continue pivoting to the left foot, unwinding into a transitional horse stance with feet parallel. Let the sword complete the lower half of the circle in front of the waist, the right palm facing the body and the left hand sword-mudra leading the way south.

(64f) Continue rotating to the left, into a left leg horse stance with feet parallel and the torso turning at the waist to face south.

214 / Practice

(64g) Exhale and execute a straight sword thrust with the blade's sharp edge skyward. Roll the left forearm up, covering the front of the torso in an upward block that finishes overhead, palm up. Weight is 60% front, 40% back.

(65a) Inhale and slowly lower the sword and left hand sword-mudra to the right, traversing close to the body like a pendulum. The sword points to the earth, the palms face the torso, and both arms pass in front of the legs. The body pivots back toward the north.

(65b) Pivot 180 degrees on the right heel and swing the left foot around until it becomes parallel and even with the right. The feet are shoulder-width apart in a natural stance, facing east and weight evenly balanced. Fully extend and arc the sword and sword-mudra, going from left to right, side by side across the sky like the hands of a clock. Both palms face away from the body.

(65c) As the arms get close to the overhead apex, lift the right knee until the thigh is parallel to the ground and begin exhaling.

(65d) Let the sword fall, cutting down along the right side of the body until it is horizontal and parallel to the ground. Make sure it arrives just as the right foot lowers and stomps the ground next to the left. Let the left hand sword-mudra fall into position opposite the left temple (ca. 8-12 inches from the head), palm facing away from the body and pointing in the same direction as the sword. Turn the head to look over the right shoulder, eyes gazing south and fixed on the sword.

(65e) Lift the right wrist until the sword is vertical.

Instructions / 215

(65f) Raise the sword overhead and catch the upper portion of the blade between the left thumb and the open left palm. Open all fingers of both hands and point them skyward. The feet are still together, both arms fully extended above the shoulders.

(66a) Lift the left foot slightly and place the heel back on the ground, while opening the instep of the left foot to the north.

(66b) Direct the sword to dive down and to the left of the body on a vertical plane and in a circular fashion, the arms still extended, while bending slightly forward at the waist. The right foot follows the sword by stepping ahead of the left (see arrow) on an imaginary straight line that leads from south to north.

(66c) Continue turning the body to the left without pause by stepping the left foot behind and then ahead of the right foot.

(66d) Place the foot on to the same south-north line to face east. Ascend the sword fully above the head with arms extended. Pause briefly with the feet shoulder-width apart in a natural stance (weight evenly distributed).

(66e) Direct the sword to dive down and to the left of the body on a vertical plane and in a circular fashion with the arms still extended while bending slightly forward at the waist. The right foot follows the sword by stepping ahead of the left (see arrow) on the imaginary straight line that leads from south to north.

(66f) Continue turning the body to the left by stepping the left foot behind and then ahead of the right foot

(66g) Transitioning to face east, ascending the sword to the apex above the head with the arms extended. Pause briefly facing east with the feet shoulder width apart in a natural stance (weight evenly balanced).

(66h) Inhale and point the sword skyward in a vertical position and reform the left hand sword-mudra to point skyward. Lift the right knee until the thigh is parallel to the ground and begin exhaling.

(66i) Let the sword free fall, cutting down to the right side of the body until it is horizontal and parallel to the ground. Make sure it arrives just when the right foot lowers and stomps the ground next to the left. Let the left hand sword-mudra fall into position opposite the left temple (ca. 8-12 inches from the head), palm facing away from the body and pointing in the same direction as the sword. Turn the head to look over the right shoulder, eyes gazing south and fixed on the blade. (Note: Both feet walk, stepping perpendicular to this line while the sword rolls along the same line like a cartwheel. Although the body is following the sword, the footwork generates the power of the sword's motion. Steps are brisk and are circular on the horizontal plane; they remain close to the ground, pivoting on the feet.)

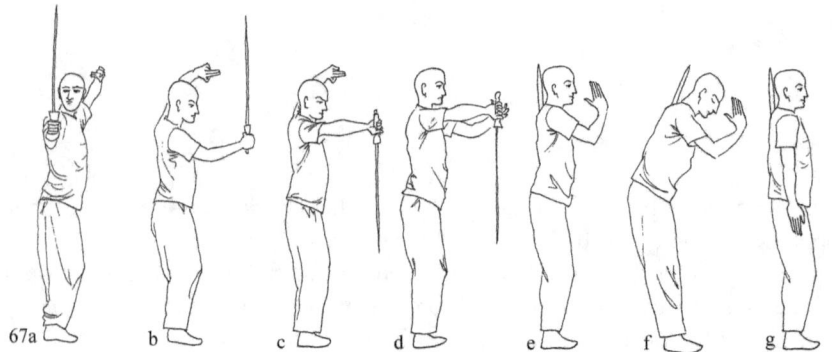

(67a) Lift the right wrist upward making the sword vertical.

(67b) Roll the right arm and sword inward, followed by the head and eyes, keeping the arm rounded until the right palm faces the middle elixir area, approximately 12-15 inches away from the body. The flat side of the blade faces the torso and the spine of the sword is aligned with the centerline of the body. After the head has rotated back to face east, the left hand sword-mudra does not adjust to the place opposite the left temple but instead remains pointing south across the forehead.

(67c) Keeping the arm rounded, guide the sword from the vertical position to free fall counterclockwise to the left forcing the right wrist to turn as if checking a watch for the time. The right palm faces away from the body;

the sword not only points to the earth but the flat side of the blade has flipped over: this is going from yang to yin.

(67d) Again grasp the sword handle with the left hand. Use an inverted grip, index finger and thumb closest to the pommel.

(67e) Lower left hand and sword along the left side of the body, while raising the edge of the blade and firmly press it between the left shoulder blade and the deltoid muscle against the Jianzhen point. The left inner elbow supports the flat side of the blade. The back is straight and the waist relaxed, tailbone gently tucked. The knees are slightly bent and the chin is one loose fist from the clavicle. Hold this posture until the mind becomes quiet. Breathe naturally. Raise the right hand into a one hand prayer posture with the tip of the middle finger no higher than the tip of the nose.

(67f) Bow with your eyes closed.

(67g) Return to an upright position and lower the right hand to rest on the right leg, the middle finger lightly touching the Fengshi point along the outside of the thigh. You have completed the practice.

About the Authors

Dr. Baolin Wu is a senior master of Daoist sword practice. From an early age he studied with Master Du Xinling, abbot of the White Cloud Monastery, training in the *Book of Changes*, Chinese herbal medicine, martial arts, swordplay, Bagua zhang, Taiji quan, Xingyi quan, and more. Especially in the *Book of Changes* and in sword skill, Master Wu reached the highest pinnacle, making accurate predictions and excelling in martial practice.

After working as a physician at Guang'anmen Hospital in Beijing for many years, he emigrated to the U.S. in 1990. Since then, Master Wu has served as a teacher of Daoist exercise and TCM practitioner in Santa Monica, Calif. He has two earlier books: *"Lighting the Eye of the Dragon: Inner Secrets of Taoist Feng Shui"* (St. Martin's Press, 2000) and *"Qi Gong for Total Wellness: Increase your Energy, Vitality and Longevity with the Ancient 9 Palaces System from the White Cloud Monastery"* (2006). Websites: www.drbaolinwu.com; www.whitecloud-qigong.com.

Michael McBride is a native of Los Angeles. For the past 15 years, has studied Daoism under the guidance of Master Baolin Wu. He trained in qigong, taiji quan, Daoist swordplay, and Chinese medical massage. He has traveled extensively in and around China for more than a decade. Please visit www.drbaolinwu.com

Vincent Wu, Master Wu's son, was born in the U.S. He currently attends high school in, Cerritos, Calif. He follows in his father's footsteps and learns Chinese martial arts from him. See www.whitecloud-qigong.com

Other Titles from Three Pines Press

Sex in the Yellow Emperor's Basic Questions, **by Jessieca Leo (2011)**
A description and analysis of sexual terms, practices, and cosmology in the ancient medical classic, a forerunner of Daoist ideas and techniques of later years: $29.95

The Way of Poetry, **by John Leonard (2010)**
First volume in the new "Dao Today" series; poetic musings on Daoist dimensions of modern poetry and the role of Daoism in the contemporary world: $13.95

Sitting in Oblivion: The Heart of Daoist Meditation, **by Livia Kohn (2010)**
New and expanded version of *Seven Steps to the Tao*, with in-depth analysis and history of *zuowang*, including revised and new translations: $29.95

Daoist Dietetics: Food for Immortality, **by Livia Kohn (2010)**
Discussion of Daoist dietary methods in relation to Chinese medicated diet and longevity techniques. Various translations: $29.95

Experimental essays on Zhuangzi, **edited by Victor Mair (2010)**
Reprint of Univ. of Hawaii classic (1983), with four new contributions: $29.95

Internal Alchemy: Self, Society, and the Quest for Immortality, **edited by Livia Kohn and Robin R. Wang (2009)**
Systematic explanation, historical grounding, and contemporary practices of this key form of Daoist meditation: $29.95

Meditation Works: In the Hindu, Buddhist, and Daoist Traditions, **by Livia Kohn (2008)**
Explication and analysis of six distinct types of meditation, discussing their physiology, worldview, and traditional practice as well as its modern medical adaptations and organizational settings: $24.95

The Way of Highest Clarity: Nature, Vision, and Revelation in Medieval Daoism, **by James Miller (2008)**
Analytical presentation of the teachings of Shangqing Daoism, with translations of three key scriptures: $29.95.

Myth and Meaning in Early Daoism: The Theme of Chaos (Hundun), **by Norman Girardot (2008)**
Reprint of Univ. of California book (1983) that still is the main resource for understanding the mythology and mystical vision of ancient Daoism: $29.95

Divine Traces of the Daoist Sisterhood, **by Suzanne Cahill**
A translation of Du Guangting's biographies of Daoist women and in-depth exploration of the role and identity of women in medieval religion: $24.95

Daoist Body Cultivation: Traditional Models and Contemporary Practices, **edited by Livia Kohn (2006)**
A comprehensive volume by a group of dedicated scholars and practitioners that covers key practices of medical healing, breathing techniques, diets and fasting, healing exercises, sexual practices, qigong, and taiji quan: $24.95

Health and Long Life: The Chinese Way, **by Livia Kohn with Stephen Jackowicz (2005)**
Overview of the theory and methods of Chinese medicine in comparison to Western systems and Daoist self-cultivation: $24.95

Cosmos and Community: The Ethical Dimension of Daoism,
by Livia Kohn (2004)
Examination of Daoist rules in lay organizations, monastic institutions, and among the millenarian or utopian groups; lots of translations: $29.95

Women in Daoism, **by Catherine Despeux and Livia Kohn**
Discussion of different kinds of women: goddesses, immortals, priestesses, and their pracitices, especially of internal alchemy: $24.95

Title Index to Daoist Collections, **by Louis Komjathy (2002)**
A combined and standardized index for all collections of Daoist texts: $45.00

Daoism and Chinese Culture, **by Livia Kohn (2001)**
A proven textbook for use in introductory classes and good general overview in chronological order: $19.95

Journal of Daoist Studies
Vol. 1 (2008) – Vol. 4 (2011)
Scholary Articles, Forum on Contemporary Practice, News of the Field

All our titles are also available as e-books in pdf format.

WWW.THREEPINESPRESS.COM

www.ingramcontent.com/pod-product-compliance
Lightning Source LLC
Chambersburg PA
CBHW051116230426

43667CB00014B/2604